WHO RESCUED WHO

WHO RESCUED WHO

VICTORIA SCHADE

THORNDIKE PRESS
A part of Gale, a Cengage Company

GALE
A Cengage Company

LIBRARY OF CONGRESS CIP DATA ON FILE.
CATALOGUING IN PUBLICATION FOR THIS BOOK
IS AVAILABLE FROM THE LIBRARY OF CONGRESS

ISBN-13: 978-1-4328-8029-3 (hardcover alk. paper)

Published in 2021 by arrangement with Berkley, an imprint of Penguin Publishing Group, a division of Penguin Random House, LLC

Printed in Mexico
Print Number: 01   Print Year: 2021

Dedicated to the generous volunteers and fosters around the world who open their hearts and homes to dogs in need

CHAPTER ONE

"Permanent hiatus?"

Elizabeth Barnes repeated the words back as if she were fumbling with a new language.

The human resources manager at Duchess Games pressed her perfect matte lips together in a tight smile and nodded. "That joke you made during the interview at Mobile Expo is still impacting our metrics. You've seen what they're saying about you on Twitter, right? 'Duchess CMO and the social network sex show.' " Gwen paused. "There's no way we can spin it to make it fit our narrative. This is our only choice."

Elizabeth coughed but her throat felt like it was lined with fleece. She glanced at her friend, mentor, and boss Cecelia Wright, who was inspecting a strand of her blond hair for split ends. Cecelia wouldn't meet her eyes, so focused on her grooming that she couldn't offer her most devoted employee a comforting smile as she fitted the noose.

The cuffs of Elizabeth's blouse suddenly felt too tight. Were her wrists *sweating*? How was that even possible? She wanted to roll up her sleeves, but that might suggest that she was ready to efficiently hash out next steps. And she was anything but ready to face the fact that her entire world was imploding.

"I'm disappointed it came to this," Cecelia finally said, still not looking up from her hair. "Some of your contributions were impactful."

Some?

The comment landed like a dropkick. Everyone in the company knew that Elizabeth's work had helped propel Duchess Games from plucky start-up to an innovator in the mobile gaming world. She'd started in coding and worked her way up to chief marketing officer thanks to her annual vision boards and a work ethic that had made her hair fall out every time they released a new game.

Elizabeth finally spoke up. "I don't know how many more times I can say I'm sorry, but I'll try it again: I'm *so* sorry. I was exhausted. The reporter wouldn't stop asking about Entomon and I was trying to change his focus. I got flustered and said the wrong thing. I thought it would be funny and he'd change the subject." She put her elbows on the table and cupped her forehead. The second after she'd made the joke she'd envisioned the Cecelia rage-storm to come, but she'd never imagined she'd end up in front of a literal firing squad.

"Your job isn't to be funny, it's to shut down rumors before they get out of hand," Cecelia replied. "You didn't even preempt with our talking points."

Elizabeth stopped herself from mentioning that there were no talking points because according to Cecelia, Entomon didn't exist. "But . . . what he said . . . it was pretty compelling. He had documentation about Entomon and I wasn't sure how to respond."

"*Stop* saying the E-word," Cecelia hissed, suddenly locked on Elizabeth. "I don't want to hear that word in my office again, okay? Or anywhere else. Don't get any ideas, Elizabeth. We're lawyered up and ready. Don't make me use them."

So now she was threatening.

Elizabeth met Cecelia's furious gaze and barely recognized the woman she'd spent so many late nights with. Cecelia's face was under the influence of a variety of fillers, so she couldn't make a truly angry expression, but the way her nostrils flared telegraphed rage. And something else.

Fear.

The three women sat in silence until a familiar, rhythmic wheezing filled the vacuum.

"Win, baby, are you okay?" Cecelia looked over her shoulder at the beloved Duchess mascot, Winston the English bulldog, her tone so maternal that it was hard to believe that she'd been spitting venom just a few seconds before. Winston snorted and licked his nose, then settled back to a snoring slumber.

Gwen cleared her throat and continued carefully. "We're reclaiming your options, of course."

The nausea hit so fast and hard that Elizabeth slapped her hand over her mouth to keep from spewing her feelings all over the artisanal, hand-distressed, reclaimed-wood conference table. Every middle-of-the-night text, endless road show, and stolen idea had been in service of the options she accrued every year. She loved the work, but the security that came with the options was her happily-ever-after.

"Wait, but how . . ." Elizabeth trailed off, unable to put her shock into words.

" 'Unexercised options forfeit upon termination with cause,' " Gwen read from the employee handbook. "And if you refer to page four of the handbook, your initials next to the behavioral agreement and your recent performance very clearly indicate that we have cause for termination."

The "company reputation" provision. The one that seemed like a punch line, until it wasn't.

"Cecelia, do you have anything you'd like to add?" Gwen asked.

Cecelia had moved on to studying her manicure, ten tiny red daggers that no one had the courage to tell her didn't mesh with her crystals-and-daily-affirmations personal brand. She shook her head.

"We've got an exit package for you . . ." Gwen rifled through the stack of papers in front of her. "We need a signature and then Frank will escort you out."

Not only was she getting fired, she was being forced to do a perp walk in front of her colleagues. Or, her *former* colleagues.

Elizabeth blinked hard when her vision started to swim. She gnawed on the inside of her cheek to derail the tears. "This is insane, Cecelia. And there's no way I'm going to sign anything now. I need someone to read through it all. You're taking away my options, that can't be legal."

"Trust me, it's legal." Cecelia glared at her.

"We need you to sign the termination letter today," Gwen said, quickly de-escalating the situation. "It outlines the conditions of our separation. You can have your attorney review the rest and get them back to us by the end of the week."

Elizabeth nodded and stared at the pile of papers on the table, worried that if she looked at Cecelia or Gwen she'd burst into tears. And there was no way she was going to break in front of them.

"Frank?" Cecelia called out when the silence got awkward. "We're ready."

The head of building security peeked into the room, evaluating Elizabeth with a head-to-toe sweep that made it clear he was assessing her threat level. She was now a potential criminal in their midst, capable of stealing anything from staplers to corporate secrets.

"I hope you manifest a better fit in your next position," Cecelia said. Winston barked at Elizabeth as she walked by, cementing the fact that she was now the most hated person at Duchess.

Cecelia's Zen-inspired open-plan office meant that all of her colleagues could see her walk of shame. She was now a cautionary tale, so of course people would steal glances at her as she left. She straightened her back, happy that she'd worn the wrist-strangling Theory blouse with epaulets on the shoulders, the one that made her look like she was part of an all-girl army. At least she was on-brand.

"I'll wait out here, okay? You've got about five minutes," Frank said softly, gesturing to the area right outside her office door. He was a buff former Navy SEAL who took his post in Duchess as seriously as his military service. They'd always had a polite head-nodding relationship, and Elizabeth could tell he was trying to be kind despite Cecelia's directive to get her off the premises ASAP. He handed her an empty box.

She fought through the fog of shame so she could focus on the work of cleaning out her office. She threw everything on her desk into the box: the stress balls from various vendors that she actually used, a hunk of expensive rose quartz from Cecelia, her diffuser, and the hundreds of packets of wellness dusts she poured in her daily kale smoothies. She sifted through her drawers and paused when she found what looked like a collection of flower petals in a back corner. When was the last time someone had sent her flowers?

She looked closer. It was a Pepto-Bismol wrapper.

Frank cleared his throat to signal that her time was almost up.

"I'm ready," she called out to him.

Elizabeth met Frank at the door with just her purse slung over her shoulder.

"But where's your stuff?"

"I don't need any of it. Let's go."

Elizabeth Barnes knew that she was only the second person to be escorted out of Duchess, and she wasn't going to make the scene any more attention-grabbing than it needed to be. Instead of carting out a box of junk like a homeless person, she pretended she was on a runway in Paris as her heels clacked through the building, shoulders back and head high. Anyone watching might think she was doing a site survey with Frank. She radiated serenity and acceptance, keeping her eyes fixed on a distant point in front of her.

Elizabeth focused on how she was going to frame what had happened on her social media accounts as she paraded through the building, past hundreds of wide eyes. Perhaps an inspirational quote about the future in a vintage typewriter font, overlaid on an image of a wave? Or a single word, like *beginning,* next to a flower bud? She had nothing but time to figure it out.

None of her devoted followers or former colleagues would have a clue that the second the Duchess campus vanished from her rearview mirror, she pulled over on the side of the highway and cried until her perfectly lined eyes left black tracks on the palms of her hands.

CHAPTER TWO

"Exhale stress, inhale serenity," Elizabeth chanted as she waited for Whitney to pick up. The mantra did nothing to calm her, but she repeated it to keep from thinking too much about what she was doing. She crossed and uncrossed her legs and tried to find a comfortable position on the couch before her friend answered. Whitney Brinkman was the closest thing she had to a bestie, even though their time together was confined to office hours and the rare networking cocktail party.

No one at Duchess used their phone to call unless it was a servers-are-down emergency. Elizabeth tried to imagine what Whitney was thinking as her name flashed on her screen. She straightened her posture and took another not-calming breath.

"*Elizabeth*? What's wrong?"

"Whit, hey, nothing's wrong." She forced cheer into her voice. "I was just thinking about you and I thought I'd call. I, uh, I miss you."

"Oh, how cute. That's adorable! I miss you too, girl." Whitney's voice was a roller coaster of inflection and added syllables, so that the word *girl* almost sounded like *gorilla.*"

"How are . . . things? I mean, can you talk?"

"Actually, I can't. You know how it is, *ugh,* annoying." Elizabeth could almost hear the eye roll. "So, what's up?"

"I was actually hoping we could hang soon. I could use a friendly face, you know? I'm feeling sort of bleak these days." She sniffled. "I'm going to Black's tomorrow and I thought maybe you could meet me for a quick coffee?" Her voice trembled like she was a fifth-grader talking to a crush. "Just to catch up, I promise we won't talk about Duchess."

"Aw, fun!"

Elizabeth waited for an actual *yes* or *no* during an awkward silence.

"Do, uh, do you think you can? I'm flexible, I can be there any time." She squeezed her eyes shut as she realized how desperate she sounded. "I've got something in the morning but any time after ten works for me."

Whitney paused. "Hey, can I call you right back? In like two minutes?"

"Sure, I'm around."

"Cool, byeeeeee." Whitney was still saying the word when the call disconnected.

Elizabeth threw her phone on the couch and imagined sitting across from Whitney at Black's Coffee. It didn't matter that Whitney was a monologist who forgot that Elizabeth also had a life. She just wanted a hug and a single comforting word. In the three weeks since her sacking she'd come to understand why shunning was a weapon.

Her new phone's unfamiliar ring tone jolted Elizabeth out of her trance. Maybe Whitney would also want to have dinner with her over the weekend? She was excited to firm up their coffee date, but when she flipped her phone over there was a strange number instead of Whitney's smiling profile photo. She'd trained herself to pick up all calls, hoping that a headhunter with an unlisted number might remember that she was a star with just one black mark on her record. One giant, career-ending black mark.

"Have I reached Elizabeth Barnes?" The British-accented voice didn't sound like yet another reporter or blogger trying to get a sound bite out of her.

"Yes, speaking."

"Finally, it's you." The man exhaled and sounded relieved. "I've been trying to reach you for quite some time. I've sent several emails as well. Have you received them?"

"I'm sorry, I'm not sure who I'm speaking with." She smiled as she spoke, hoping she sounded welcoming in case the man was calling about a job. Would a headhunter have that much trouble finding her? Did she need to revisit her LinkedIn page? "May I ask who's calling?"

"My apologies, I'm getting ahead of myself. There's so much to say. This is going to come as some surprise, I'm sure." The man paused for so long that she thought the call had dropped. "Elizabeth, I'm your father's brother, Rowan Barnes. I'm your uncle."

It was as if he'd told her he was the tooth fairy. "Oh, I think you've got the wrong person; my father didn't have a brother. You must have me confused with someone else." She flipped her phone away from her face to see if Whitney had texted while she was talking with the stranger.

"Of course, he didn't tell you about me." The man sounded like he was talking to himself. "Well, we'll get to that eventually."

Elizabeth's internal alarm pinged. She'd

19

heard about post-funeral scams, where "missing" relatives came forward to claim their part of the deceased's inheritance. Most people probably fell for the accent, but having grown up with British-accented parents, she was immune to it. Her father's estate was a modest one, and there was barely anything for her let alone any long-lost family members. And six months was a long time to wait to come forward.

"I don't think I'm who you're looking for. I know my father was an only child."

"Did he tell you that?"

"Yes."

"Oh, Elizabeth, there is so much to say," the man said with a sigh. "First, let me begin by telling you how sorry I am for your loss, and how deeply I regret waiting this long to get in touch with you. I have been trying, but technology is beyond my reach, I'm afraid. I've only just tracked down your mobile. But let me get to the reason for my call, and then we can determine what to do next. Clive, I mean, your *father,* was in line to inherit a parcel of land, even after he'd left. He chose not to respond when it came time to claim it, so it passed to me. But I've always known in my heart that the land by the river is not mine. My wife, Trudy, and I agree that it was always meant for your father. And now that he's gone, this bit of Fargrove is yours, Elizabeth."

Fargrove.

He'd gotten the town correct. And the way he spoke sounded so familiar.

"You can do with it what you like," the man said when Elizabeth didn't respond. "We just can't keep it in good conscience."

For a moment it felt like she'd just won the lottery. But it was a scam, it had to be a scam. There was no brother and there was no land. She scolded herself for almost falling for the sweet-sounding senior citizen.

The man continued to fill the silence. "Now, I know the news of who I am has caught you off guard. I still have the original documentation about the land that I'd like to send as proof, and then we can discuss what to do next."

Proof? Elizabeth would need a notarized deed to even begin to believe what she was hearing, but if she agreed to it she'd be able to end the call and wait for Whitney to get back to her.

"This is a lot to process," Elizabeth finally responded. "I'm not sure I understand, but I'll take a look at what you send." She gave him the address for her junk mail account. "I really do think you have the wrong person, though."

"Oh, but I'm confident that we've finally found you, Elizabeth Afton Barnes."

He knew her middle name too?

"Before we hang up, I feel I must . . ." He paused. "I feel I must invite you to visit. You simply have to see the land. And . . ." He seemed to struggle to say the words. "And we would love to meet you, your aunt Trudy and I. But there's time to arrange it, so look for our message and please respond. Yes?"

He sounded so sweet and hopeful that she played along.

"Of course, I'll get back to you, I promise."

She hung up and realized that her life had become an alternate reality where nothing made sense. Perhaps the quaint-sounding scammer knew she'd been fired and guessed that she'd be an easy target. She'd just ignore the email and then block his address.

Twenty minutes had passed since she'd hung up with Whitney. No call, no text. She was probably busy dealing with the usual Duchess drama. Elizabeth closed her eyes and imagined what was going on there and felt an ache in her chest. Had someone moved into her office yet, or were they keeping the door shut like it was contaminated?

Elizabeth had tried to keep busy since the

disaster at Duchess, mining for contacts that might be able to see past the wreckage of the CNET interview. She'd only heard back from one person, who promised they'd meet for drinks "soon." She'd stalked the rest of them on social media as she awaited their replies, and sure enough they weren't off somewhere hiking a remote mountain or meeting with a guru in a land with no cell service. They were as active and witty as ever, and they were ignoring her.

She was poison. Contagious. But it wasn't her first time being untouchable. She'd lived through it before, and she'd fight her way through it again.

She stared out at the premium San Francisco skyline and tried to ignore the fact that her overpriced Restoration Hardware couch was as comfortable as a bus station bench. She'd seen other much more spectacular face-plants in her industry. It *was* possible to recover. She had no choice but to recover, really. Duchess had paid her embarrassingly well, but her lifestyle didn't allow for long-term planning, particularly without her options. Her rent alone in trendy SoMa swallowed much of it each month. Her fat savings account would be a memory unless she could come up with a plan.

She looked at her phone again. Still no word back from Whitney.

Her former colleagues, the people she used to consider friends, were still living their beautiful, carefully curated, fully employed lives in their social media streams. Elizabeth knew that they were watching her too, as no one had unfollowed her, including Cecelia. They were probably hoping for a spectacular flame-out, but no matter how low she felt she wasn't going to let it happen. She had over fourteen thousand devoted and engaged followers — she called herself a micro-influencer — and even though she felt like the world's biggest loser, she continued to fill her feeds with positivity and beautiful photos so they could see that she was *still* living her best life.

No one had to know she was a liar.

Elizabeth scrolled through her feed and stopped on a recent selfie. Her father had pointed out that one eye was higher than the other in her graduation photo and she'd never forgotten it, so she always tilted her head so that it was harder to see the defect. She hated the way she photographed, but she forced herself to include a selfie every few weeks, so people could identify with her brand better. She knew how to camouflage her flaws with the right angles and filters. In some of the photos she almost looked as pretty as the other influencers she followed.

She knew she wasn't stereotypically beautiful thanks to her cheekbone-free face and muddy-colored hair, so she worked hard to improve upon nature's shortcomings with the help of a glam squad that sculpted her body, steamrolled her naturally wavy hair, and lasered her face to erase the freckles that kept popping up. Without her crew of health and beauty experts she was just average.

Elizabeth gently touched the puffiness beneath her eyes. The stress of the firing registered all over her face, from the dark bags to the patch of pimples above her neglected eyebrows. Elizabeth Barnes had never lost at anything, and the crush of failure was so foreign to her that if she didn't know better she'd have thought she was coming down with something. Wanting to stay in bed all day, getting clammy and light-headed every time she stood up, no appetite — the symptoms were all there.

But she had no one to smooth back the damp hair from her forehead like her mother used to do when she was a girl. She thought back to the times when she was little, before her mom got sick, when she would wake up with a tickle in her throat.

Her mom would make her stay home from school, ignoring her dad's disapproval, and tuck her in on the couch under an ocean of blankets. She doted on Elizabeth, bringing her soup and ice cream and comforting hugs as they sat together watching daytime TV. After her mom passed, the theme song to *The Price is Right* made Elizabeth well up every time she heard it.

She was *so* alone.

Elizabeth had never had the bandwidth for a boyfriend. Sure, she'd had extended flings with fiscally appropriate guys, but nothing that qualified as a real romance. Just decent-but-not-great sex and a heart that never veered into pitter-pat territory. She was thirty-two and she'd never said the L-word to anyone but her parents. Now, though, she wished for a warm body beside her, to reassure her that everything was going to turn out okay. A rom-com boyfriend who told her she was beautiful and kissed her until her knees went weak.

With every day that passed without contact from a living, breathing person, she felt a little more removed from humanity. The likes and hearts from strangers were her only connection to the world outside her apartment, which was enough for her until she realized that she was one slip away from dying and becoming a pile of liquefied goo on her bathroom floor. No one would notice she was missing for weeks.

Because there was no one *real* who gave a shit about her.

She'd learned to be self-sufficient when she was twelve, right after her mom died. Her little girlfriends began avoiding her on the playground as her mom got sicker, treating her like cancer was contagious, as if their own mothers might disappear if they spent too much time with Elizabeth. Her father told her that friendship was overrated, so she turned into the industrious girl, the one who studied so hard that she didn't have time to play freeze tag. It didn't matter that they had sleepovers without her; she was too busy achieving and hoping that each award might be the one that made her father proud. The memory of little girls with sleeping bags under their arms loading into minivans gave her a familiar hollowed-out sensation in her gut.

For a second it sounded like the Priority Mail shipping box sitting on the edge of the table by her front door whispered her name, which meant that she was spending *way* too much time alone. Were hallucinations next?

The box hadn't moved in months, and she was past accidentally mistaking it for a package from Net-a-Porter or Neiman's. Sometimes when she was ripping through her latest deliveries, she picked the box up and put a knife to the seam, only to realize in horror how close she'd come to slicing it open and seeing what was inside. She knew if she put the box in a closet she'd forget about it forever, so she kept it on the table, a final silent reprimand. Since everything in her life was upside-down, maybe it was possible that she did have an unknown uncle. Maybe, if it turned out to be real, which of course it wasn't, maybe then she could finally be done with the box.

CHAPTER THREE

There was no text or return call, but there was a chance Whitney was still going to show. Elizabeth had sent her a few messages, letting her know that she was going to be at Black's as discussed. It wasn't a surprise she hadn't heard back. Whitney was gorgeous and flighty, which helped everyone forgive her for her inability to be polite.

Elizabeth checked her phone for the millionth time as she waited in line. If Whitney was going to stand her up, she wasn't sure why she'd even left her apartment. It felt like every real human surrounding her was silently judging her and determining that she was, in fact, a loser. But online, her life was still perfect, and she needed fresh content to post. She took her latte to a table in the back, arranged it just so on the rugged wood table, and snapped an off-centered photo. She wanted to look busy when Whitney showed up. If Whitney showed up.

She smoothed the front of her black wrap tank and noticed a trail of deodorant dotted along the side seam. Elizabeth grabbed a napkin and attacked the stain, hoping she could get rid of it before Whitney noticed it. Whitney's ability to laughingly point out shortcomings, like a poorly camouflaged pimple, was rarely funny to the person on the receiving end.

The cloud-based photo-editing app Elizabeth used to manufacture her posts kept suggesting a greenish filter for the photo of her coffee cup, so she attempted to reset the app by reversing out of it until she came to the main page. She'd linked the app to her various social media accounts, and it cycled through random images from her accounts with suggested edits, like evening her skin to Barbie doll perfection and brightening her teeth until they looked blue-white. This time the photo the app suggested made her index finger tremble above the image.

It was Cecelia's smug face.

Elizabeth thought that she'd erased all evidence of Duchess from her phone, but somehow there it was, like a final *fuck you* from the cloud. She zoomed in on it, trying to remember the context for the shot. Cecelia was sitting at her desk with Winston in her arms with just her laptop and a small stack of papers marring the vast white expanse. Elizabeth zoomed in more, trying to make out the words on Cecelia's computer screen. She enlarged the image and realized that it was code.

Entomon code.

The backslashes, brackets, and random words wouldn't make sense to anyone without a programming background, but Elizabeth could read enough code to know that she'd stumbled onto something huge. She changed the app filter a few times, hoping that a different contrast would make the characters on Cecelia's screen stand out more. Elizabeth applied the Clarity filter and it was like shining a flashlight on it. Every last semicolon was visible.

Elizabeth smiled her first genuine smile in weeks.

She had proof.

Proof that not only was Entomon real, but Cecelia was in on it the whole time. Releasing the photo would prove that Elizabeth had taken the fall for something that Duchess was trying very hard to hide. There was no way Elizabeth could release the photo herself, but there were other options. Geeky insider websites that could verify that the photo wasn't altered, decipher the code, and then release it to news sites so that she could clear her name. And more importantly, so that she could take Cecelia down. The public would scream for Cecelia's head when they discovered Entomon was real and downloaded invasive facial recognition software with their new games.

Elizabeth had heard the rumors about the Entomon spyware but always filtered them out. Duchess didn't need to cheat to stay on top. But when the reporter presented compelling evidence about Entomon during her infamous CNET interview, Elizabeth felt cornered. She sputtered nervously for a few minutes, then pivoted to accusing Duchess competitors of monitoring their clients. Her joke about other app companies surveilling their clients' sexual habits was meant to be funny — she still regretted using the phrase *gettin' busy* — but it turned out to be anything but.

Her palms sweated as she screenshotted the image a half-dozen times and saved the original on three different platforms under a code name. Elizabeth hadn't felt this positive in weeks. She finally had a plan. Or at least half of a plan. She shimmied her shoulders and danced in her chair to vent the adrenaline coursing through her, but stopped when she realized that people might think she'd been snorting something.

If Whitney walked in the door now, Elizabeth would have a hard time keeping the secret from her. She scanned the room, looking for Whitney's can't-miss combination of supermodel height and striking features, but there was no sign of her.

Elizabeth needed a moment to hit the reset button, to do something that would calm her down. She hadn't checked her junk email account since the phone call from the scammer with a familiar accent. Had "Uncle Rowan" followed through? Her father had been a man of few words despite making his living teaching people to find the beauty in them, and though he rarely talked about his life in Britain, she at least knew of the town where he was raised and her grandparents' names. He certainly would have mentioned a brother.

She logged in, searched for his name, and was surprised to discover a genuine email address with the subject line *Fargrove Property.*

She'd expected a slick overview of the land, written like a brochure for a high-end cruise, but the email merely listed the property's borders and included a line with the dimensions of a stone structure on it.

Please review the attached, it said, followed by *Yours very truly, Uncle Rowan.*

Opening an attachment from an unknown source was a mistake that could shut down a network. Even the temps that passed through Duchess knew to delete messages with potentially unsafe attachments. Opening it was too stupid to even consider.

Elizabeth hovered her mouse over the X to click out of it, but her fingers started moving like they were on a Ouija board, controlled by a ghost that was determined to digitally murder her. She clicked the first attachment and held her breath as a Word document loaded. The document had a series of photos, probably the only way they knew how to send them. The first was of a vast undulating field, dotted with sheep and capped by a sky so blue and perfectly cloud-dappled that it looked like Maxfield Parrish had painted it. The second was of a heavily wooded area with a small stone structure in the distance. Inserted in the middle of the photos was a scan of an ancient-looking document filled with property law legalese that she couldn't translate.

She kept scrolling down and stopped in shock at an image of a cheerful-looking older couple with their arms around each other.

Elizabeth pulled her fingers away as if they'd been scorched by the keyboard. The man, smiling at her from beneath a tweed cap, had her father's eyes. Granted, they were squinting in the bright sun, but there was no mistaking the shape and glint of green. His nose was a match too, and Elizabeth unconsciously touched the turned-up tip of the nose she'd inherited. Clearly her father's bloodlines were stronger than her mother's, as evidenced by the genetic patterns she was witnessing for the first time.

Her suspicious streak was inexplicably dormant. Perhaps her instincts were dulled by the trauma of her very public firing. Perhaps she wanted to believe that she had an additional inheritance from her father now that she had no income, and that the land was a peace offering from him from beyond the grave.

Or perhaps it was impossible to ignore the fact that the couple she was looking at, he of the jolly smile and kind eyes and she of the soft sweater and long white braid, weren't hucksters looking to cheat her but long-lost family members who were very likely telling the truth.

CHAPTER FOUR

"Did you have a good flight?" the old man asked for the third time.

"It was good, yes, thank you," Elizabeth answered as brightly as she could manage given that she was exhausted and her phone wasn't working properly. After over twelve hours of spotty connectivity she felt disconnected from the world.

She'd sent out a few vague emails to underground tech websites about possibly publishing the incriminating photo of Cecelia, without mentioning specifics, and was eager to check for responses. Plus she had three photos from the trip that she needed to post — one with a moody filter of her looking out the window at a plane on the tarmac with an angle that camouflaged her double chin, a close-up of a glass of Prosecco (#bubblelife), and one of her Vuitton luggage near a Heathrow sign to prove that she was doing something amazing.

The decision to go to Fargrove had been a sudden one. She thought she could wrap up the property details in a day or so, take care of the box issue quickly as well, then use her remaining time in the UK to do a little touring. The trip would be a palate-cleansing sorbet between the end of Duchess and the beginning of the next phase of her career, whatever that was. The fact that her Airbnb'ed apartment more than covered the cost of her flight and hotels made her feel less guilty about traveling while unemployed, and the prospect of selling off her father's property made the trip seem like a business transaction.

"You've arrived just in time for an absolutely lovely week of spring weather."

"Is that so?" Elizabeth hoped the old man would do the heavy conversational lifting during the drive to Fargrove, since she had no idea what to say to him. Rowan and Trudy couldn't pick her up from the airport because of a meeting they said was impossible to rearrange, so they sent a thousand apologies and the chatty elderly man with a plaid flat cap and fuzzy gray eyebrows who kept peering at her in the rearview mirror instead. Rowan had first called him their gardener when he explained that he would be picking her up, then referred to him as their friend. Elizabeth guessed William Burke was both. He'd politely insisted she sit in the back seat, said it was more comfortable, and she instinctively liked him even if she was at a loss for what to talk to him about.

Elizabeth had hoped for some sort of magical response to being in her parents' home country — a wave of psychic recognition, or a sense of belonging — but all she felt was overtired and nervous. As she sped toward Fargrove it dawned on her that she had chosen her vacation poorly. Why wasn't she on a tropical beach with a drink in her hand?

"These clouds are going to clear up. Just a few more moments, then it'll be sun evermore."

Elizabeth looked up at the muddy sky and sure enough a few rays began to pierce the darkness. The sun made short work of the remaining clouds, as if heeding his words.

"Brilliant," the man said quietly with a nod. He looked at Elizabeth in the rearview mirror for the millionth time. "Are you hungry? Trudy and Rowan will be waiting for you with a feast. They were disappointed to miss you at the airport, but Rowan is a busy man these days."

"I hope they didn't go out of their way,

I'm not a big eater." Her stomach rumbled as she said the words, but she was unwilling to gain an ounce during her ten days away. "I'll have a cup of tea, but then I need to get to my hotel."

Elizabeth's itinerary was planned to the hour. She'd briefly visit with Rowan and Trudy over dinner, then spend her first night at the Coach and Horses in the nearby village, get up the next day to discuss the property, which could take all day if lawyers were to be involved, spend a final night in Fargrove, then depart the following morning for her actual vacation.

"Hotel?" The old man chuckled. "This is Fargrove, dear, not London. It's an inn. Comfortable, clean, a fine place to lay your head. But why won't you stay with your aunt and uncle?"

It still jarred her to hear the words. She'd grown so used to the idea that her family consisted only of her parents that she still couldn't come to terms with the fact that there were other Barneses in the world. She had always assumed that there were distant second cousins littered across England, but her parents' lack of interest in connecting with home-country relatives was enough to keep Elizabeth from asking about them.

Rowan had seemed to sense her unease

when they spoke again after his initial call, and had Trudy email an old photo of himself with her father, gently proving that he was who he said he was. The young man standing knee-deep in a stream next to her father was rakishly handsome, with thick dark hair, a model's jawline, and a smile that made him look like he'd just cracked a dirty joke. Her father looked vibrant and happy, so much so that she had difficulty squaring the dispassionate man she knew with the joyful man in the photo. The brothers had their arms wrapped around each other in the photo, and the intimacy of the pose confused Elizabeth. Their smiles were broad and genuine. Why hadn't her father told her about this brother he was once so close to?

"I didn't want to put them out by staying with them. It's easier to stay at the inn."

"Put them out, you say? You're about to get an education in hospitality. Just wait." He nodded again. "Just wait."

The landscape shifted as they drove on, and the desolate view was replaced by rolling green fields bordered by tidy rock walls. The sun saturated the colors, and the impossibly bright emerald of the fields perfectly complemented the bluebonnet sky. Soon the scene outside her window started to resemble the photo Trudy had sent, sheep included, and she relaxed for the first time since she touched down.

It was real. Elizabeth closed her eyes and fell asleep.

She awoke to the sound of the wheels coming to a stop on crushed rock. Through her sleepy haze she saw a jumble of well-tended flowers, a fairy-tale house beyond the curved driveway, and a black-and-white dog eyeing the car in a predatory crouch. She had barely taken in her surroundings when William Burke jumped out of the car and opened her door with surprising agility. Elizabeth tried to compose herself, raking her fingers through her hair and smoothing her gray cashmere wrap as she got out of the car. Her heart thudded when she spotted Rowan and Trudy Barnes standing a few steps away.

Rowan took two steps toward her and his eyes filled with tears. He was tall and thin, with posture so straight that it took years off him. His close-cropped white hair was tidy, as if he had gotten a fresh haircut just in time for her visit. In his face she saw her father, if her father had been capable of wide, genuine smiles and the crinkly eyes that go with them. The combination of familiar and foreign caught her off guard.

"Elizabeth Afton Barnes." He paused and

smiled at her despite the tears welling. "Welcome home."

This stranger was her family, there was no denying it. Everything from the way he looked to the way he moved seemed familiar, and it knocked Elizabeth off balance. Having never met relatives, she wasn't sure how to act, so she deferred to her go-to greeting, the one that worked with everyone from janitor to investor.

"It's such a pleasure to see you!" Elizabeth quickly wiped off her sweaty palm beneath her wrap and offered it to Rowan as he strode to her. He swatted her hand away and pulled her close, enveloping her in a hug that lifted her onto her toes. She couldn't remember the last hug she'd received, but she knew that it probably only included the edge of a shoulder blade and spaghetti arms. Getting hugged by Rowan Barnes felt like she was being schooled in the art by a human teddy bear.

The black-and-white dog ran circles around them, barking insistently as they embraced. Elizabeth wasn't sure what to think about the barky editorial given that her primary exposure to dogs was Cecelia's dog Winston, who was more wheezing, mole-covered lump than canine. The barking sounded serious, like the dog was seconds away from attacking her, but no one else seemed to care about the spiraling canine threat level.

Rowan beamed at her, ignoring the noise. "Look at you. You are the best of your father, with a little of your beautiful mum Felicity thrown in to sweeten it up. And there's the Barnes nose!" He touched his own nose and winked at her. "Trudy, isn't she lovely?"

Trudy stood at his elbow, dwarfed by him. Her close-set brown eyes sparkled as she took Elizabeth in. She was pillowy, not overweight exactly, but not as fit-looking as Rowan. She wore a long-sleeve pink sweater with a wide, messy knit, perfect for the cool air as the sun started to set. Her white hair was in a braid that fell on her shoulder, tied off with a collection of multi-colored yarn. She took Elizabeth's hands in hers and squeezed them, as if she could sense that another hug might overwhelm her. "We are thrilled to have you here, and Major is as well despite the commentary." She turned to the dog dervishing around them and gave a long low whistle. He stopped barking and plopped down as if someone had swept his legs from under him.

Trudy looked at Elizabeth like she was searching for something in her face. "You must be famished and exhausted. We have supper prepared. William, will you be joining us?"

The old man stood knee-deep in a climbing rosebush near a stone wall, rooting through it with a keen eye and a small pair of pruning shears. "What? Oh, no, I'm afraid I can't join this evening." He was distracted by the work. "I've missed some canes. I'll finish here, then be on my way."

"Right. Keep at it, then. Thank you!" Trudy waved, but he was too engrossed in the work to notice.

She laced her arm through Elizabeth's and began to walk her to the house, with Rowan trailing behind them with her luggage and Major once again complaining about her presence. Elizabeth was finally able to take it all in as they approached the large white house. They followed a tidy crushed-stone path that branched off in various directions, all edged by a razor-cut hedge and an artist's palette of lush flowers. The house had mullioned windows and an oversized arched doorway in the center. The undulating shingled roof sat low on the structure like a too-big hat and had three dormer windows and a chimney at either end. Elizabeth could see a collection of stone buildings farther down the drive. The property looked like it had sprung from Middle-earth, and she could already envision how she was going to frame it in a post. She might even include the dog, if it ever stopped barking at her.

"We'll take you to your father's spot after we eat. You look like you could use a good meal, and tonight we're having salmon en croute."

"I hope you didn't go to any trouble, I don't have much of an appetite," she lied.

"That's what you say, but wait until you have a taste of Trudy's puff pastry," Rowan replied.

"I still need to check in at the Coach and Horses Inn. Is it far from here? And what time is it now? I don't want to lose my reservation." Elizabeth was nervous and felt herself babbling about details, trying to gain some control of this unfamiliar situation. She cringed inwardly, though. Did she seem rude?

"It's just a hop down the road, don't you worry. I'll drive you there after we eat," Rowan said comfortingly.

Elizabeth glanced over her shoulder at him as they walked to the house and noticed that Rowan was holding her oversized leather carry-on to his chest with one hand while pulling her suitcase with the other. She thought of the box she'd put in the bag as she was walking out the door, almost as an afterthought, even though it was half the reason she was where she was.

The brothers were finally reunited.

CHAPTER FIVE

Elizabeth awoke in a panic. She sat up quickly and looked around the dark room, trying to get her bearings. There were embers glowing in a massive fireplace a few feet away from her. A low beamed ceiling above her. A large rustic table in front of her. An exposed stone wall across the way. A nubby moss-colored wool blanket across her body. She was in a beautiful kitchen, on a cushioned window seat beneath a bay window.

Still at Rowan and Trudy's. But why?

She heard a low rumble by the fireplace and squinted toward the sound. It was Major, lying in a plaid dog bed, making strange rumbly-whiny lip-smacking sounds at her. He was staring at her, and his body looked as if he was ready to pounce if she moved too quickly. Elizabeth started to get up, and the noises intensified. She pulled her feet back up on the window seat and eyed the doorway, wondering if she should make a break for the bathroom. Could her two legs beat his four? Major's eyes remained fixed on her and his tail thumped the side of the bed, filling the room with his impatient rhythm. The dog had made it clear that he didn't like her during their meal, to the point where Trudy had to put him outside with apologies for what she called his chatty behavior.

She craned her neck to try to find her purse in the dark room and was happy to see it at the far end of the bench. She pulled out her phone — slowly, so as not to incite Major again — and tapped through her various accounts. Still nothing. Elizabeth already had a dozen brand-enhancing images to post, even a few of Major from a distance since dogs were good for social media engagement. She'd walked around the driveway while Trudy set the table for supper, trying to find a spot that might allow her to connect, but the Fargrove Barneses were in the deadest dead zone.

She thought back to the evening before, trying to make sense of why she was still there instead of at the inn. She remembered eating a full portion of pastry-wrapped salmon along with asparagus and a shocking helping of crispy oven-roasted potatoes.

And the drinks. First, a glass of champagne to celebrate her safe arrival, then two glasses of white wine with dinner poured by Rowan's heavy hand, topped off with a larger-than-normal glass of port for dessert. The last thing she remembered was thinking that she'd just close her eyes on the comfortable bench for a second, while Trudy and Rowan busied themselves at the sink with the dishes.

The drinks had helped to calm her nerves and allowed her to chat like a brand ambassador at a product launch. They'd kept the subject matter light at first, talking about Major's unusual behavior, her flight, the weather, and if she'd packed appropriate clothes for the trip, until the wine began to take hold.

She briefly told them about the firing, spinning it so that it sounded like a mutual parting that would allow her to focus on an exciting new direction. Their interest was unwavering, like she was a celebrity and they were fawning co-anchors on a morning news show. It felt strange to be the subject of their undivided attention, without a cell phone to interrupt at just the right moment and break the tension. With hers essentially a thousand-dollar paperweight in her purse, she had no easy out.

When the conversation veered toward her father's passing, Elizabeth shut it down with the same practiced responses she always gave: it was a beautiful service, well attended, his colleagues and students will miss him. She almost took the opportunity to ask them why her father had never mentioned them, but the weighty question didn't feel natural, and she didn't want to make their interaction any more awkward than it already felt for her. She had twenty-four hours to uncover the truth; there was no need to push.

Elizabeth heard the ancient floorboards creaking as someone headed toward the kitchen. Major stepped out of his bed, stretched into an exaggerated downward dog, and trotted over to where she was sitting. She froze, not sure what he was capable of. Hopefully whoever was coming could call him off before he sank his teeth into her flesh.

"Please don't bite me. I swear I'm not delicious. I taste like detox tea and kale," Elizabeth begged the dog, leaning away from him to minimize his potential strike zone.

Major took a step closer, then placed his head on the bench next to her thigh, his mouth inches from what she imagined was a perfect latching-on spot. He looked up at her and made a little noise as Trudy burst into the room.

"Making friends, are you? Just look at that waggy tail, Major loves you already!" She grabbed the teapot and began her morning rituals, and Major finally walked to his mistress for attention. "How did you sleep on that wicked old window seat? Was my throw warm enough? I weave those, dear, and I have dozens strewn about. I'm quite the wool *artiste,* if I may say so. I'll show you my studio later, let you pick out a few things. I'll just put the kettle on and off we go. You need to meet the ladies. What size boots do you wear? Your lovely shoes will be destroyed by the muck. I'm sure I have wellies to fit you, Lord knows Rowan has a closet full for guests. And wait until you see Major at work. He'll dazzle you with his prowess, I'm sure." Trudy took a breath and realized that Elizabeth was staring at her from the edge of the bench, overwhelmed by her early-morning energy.

"I don't think Major wants anything to do with me. He was growling right before you came in."

"Growling? Oh, that wasn't a *growl!* He's been whingeing, because he wants you to pet him. He's chatty, I told you that, and if he feels like he's not getting the attention he deserves, he complains. Just give him some love and he'll be your best mate for life. Same with the ladies."

"Who are the ladies?"

"You have to meet them in person, they defy explanation. Come." She waved her hand to coax Elizabeth off the bench. "We have a lovely dotty print that should fit."

Trudy disappeared around the corner and returned with a pristine pair of rubber boots printed with cabbage roses and hot pink and red polka dots. Elizabeth hadn't worn anything so colorful since she was a child. "Let's be going, the kettle will be ready by the time we get back."

Elizabeth slipped her cell phone in her back pocket, pulled on the boots, and tried to figure out how she could gracefully demand to leave. She felt like she was being held hostage by a friendly pigeon.

"Don't worry, Rowan will get you sorted at the Coach right after breakfast." It was as if she'd read her mind. "Let's hurry, dear, they're waiting for us."

Trudy continued chattering as they walked toward the collection of stone buildings down the driveway, naming the flowers and trees they passed, taking note of the haze on the fields in the distance, and commenting on how the weather would shape up later in the day. The property was expansive, and the different hues of the pastures stretched patchwork-quilt-style up the hill and into the distance. Elizabeth wondered which nature-inspired hashtags would get the most likes.

"You stand here for now, so you can see them in their glory, and then I'll bring you in to meet them." Trudy positioned Elizabeth by the edge of a metal fence door and walked into a stone building. Elizabeth heard shuffling and Trudy speaking in comforting tones, and then two brownish-white sheep ambled into the muddy field.

"Elizabeth, meet your cousins, Blossom and Rosie. Blossom is the graceful one who thinks she's the Kate Middleton of the sheep world." Trudy leaned over and put her face close to one of them, and the sheep snuffled her hair. She straightened and scratched behind the other sheep's ear, and it leaned into the petting like a dog. "This is Rosie, who has the soul of a troubadour and the kind eyes of a nursemaid."

They looked identical. The sheep stood in the field, observing Elizabeth from a distance. She had never seen live sheep and had no clue how to react to them. Should she say *Good girls!* as if she were talking to a dog she was pretending to like, or coo over them like a human baby? Trudy hadn't mentioned children, so Elizabeth wondered if the sheep were her replacements.

"Well, look at them! So . . . fuzzy." Despite making her living finding the perfect thing to say in any circumstance — except when ambushed at a tech conference — she couldn't summon another word.

"They are indeed fuzzy. Shearing day is almost upon us, and then my ladies will be free of their fleece. Why don't you come in and meet them? They're very friendly. I brought ginger biscuits; if you give them a few they'll follow you for life."

The sheep were milling around Trudy, nibbling at her pockets.

"Um, that's okay. I can see them just fine from here." They looked nothing like the pristine white sheep she'd always seen in photos, and they probably smelled like poop and mud up close. Elizabeth mentally framed images of them from her safe vantage point at the gate, hoping the zoom on her phone would make it look like she was close to them. Even though she was petrified of the massive creatures, she had to fake that she adored them. She added *researching sheep hashtags* to her to-do list.

Just then Major slipped in through a small

gap in the fence and inched toward Trudy and the sheep in an exaggerated, belly-dragging crouch. Trudy spotted him and gave a low whistle, and he collapsed into a down.

"Now then, let's show Elizabeth what you can do."

Trudy walked to the far end of the field and opened the gate while Blossom and Rosie picked at the grass where she'd left them. She did a series of impressive whistles, which triggered Major to leap up and dash around the sheep, moving them from left to right and finally through the gate and into the larger field. Despite Major's dedication to the cause, it looked like the sheep were unimpressed by his passionate wind sprints. They took their time making their way, as if they were on a Sunday stroll, occasionally stopping to watch him as he dashed and stalked. At one point it looked like one of them was about to head-butt Major when he got close.

"That'll do, Maj." He trotted back to Trudy with his tongue hanging out. She looked back at Elizabeth and said in a stage whisper, "He believes he's really helping me, but those girls know exactly what to do every day. They let him *think* he rules the flock. Sweet of them, really."

Elizabeth nodded and fished her phone from her pocket, eager to try to connect from the new location while Trudy fussed over her dog. She navigated the useless thing while swatting away the flies that kept landing on her hands, nearly sending it tumbling into the mud.

Rowan ambled up beside her. "Good morning, Bess!"

She looked at him quizzically. No one called her Bess, but she didn't have the heart to correct him. He seemed so happy to see her.

"Ladies, I have some interesting news," he said, raising his voice so Trudy could hear him. "Sam over at the Coach rang this morning to ask what happened to our American guest, since she never checked in last night. It seems the Clermont wedding had unexpected additions, and one of his employees gave your room to them. And they're now fully committed."

"Wait, I don't have a room for tonight?"

"Well, not at the Coach, but we have plenty of room for you here. Much nicer than that bench in the kitchen, I promise you. Lovely rooms, far too many rooms for two doddering old knock-abouts, in fact. How long are you staying? I've forgotten what you told me."

Elizabeth had never intended to stay *with* them, despite what had happened the prior night. There was no need to put them out by staying longer.

"Oh, I have a car picking me up early tomorrow morning at the inn, and then I'm heading to Bath. I wish I could stay but I have a pretty tight itinerary for the rest of my trip, so I'm hoping that we can work out the details of my father's property today. Oh, and I have another, uh, issue to take care of before I leave."

Trudy joined them at the fence. "Is it something we can help you with?"

"Actually, yes." Elizabeth had been dreading this moment, with the weighty potential of the two of them shedding more tears and asking questions that she couldn't answer. "My father requested that his ashes be scattered in the River Dorcalon. I looked it up and it's a long river. Can you help me find . . . the right place?"

"He wants to be here?" Rowan looked at Trudy.

Trudy placed her hand on his shoulder. "You see?" Something passed between them that Elizabeth couldn't understand. Trudy's bottom lip trembled, and they embraced each other awkwardly over the stone wall. Elizabeth felt unnecessary, as if she were spying on a private moment of bereavement even though the man they were mourning was her father.

Rowan collected himself and turned to Elizabeth. "Yes, we'll bring you there. The river runs along the edge of the property. It was a very important place for your father. We would be honored to be a part of spreading his ashes, if you feel it's appropriate."

"Of course." Elizabeth wasn't sure what her father would have preferred. She'd managed to push the dispersement instructions from her mind the moment after the attorney finished reading the letter with her father's final wishes. It didn't feel like a real request until the box with Priority Mail labels arrived and parked itself on her front hall table. How could a six-pound box take up so much space?

She couldn't understand why her father wanted to "go home" when he had barely spoken of the place. And he had to have known that forcing her to disperse his ashes in Fargrove meant that she'd discover Rowan and Trudy. It was yet another mystery from the man she had given up trying to decode.

"Are there any other hotels or inns nearby?"

"We won't hear of it. You're with us

tonight. In fact, we were hoping to convince you to stay a tad longer; we have something monumental coming up on Saturday night," Trudy said. They drifted down the lane as they talked, trailed by a skulking Major, who opted to walk directly behind Elizabeth. She steeled herself for the inevitable nip to her bum, like she was a naughty sheep that needed a reprimand.

An extra day in Fargrove? Impossible, but she tried to break it to them gently. "My plans are fairly solid. I really can't back out —"

Trudy interrupted her so that she didn't have to formally decline. "We understand. It's fine. We would love to have you stay for the retrospective party, but we understand if you can't."

"Retrospective?"

They'd ended up in front of the largest building down the lane from the house, an ancient white barn made of irregularly shaped rocks and bricks with a high peaked roof. Rowan pulled the handle on the door and slid it along a track, emitting an ear-piercing shriek as it moved.

"Yes, we're celebrating Rowan's fifty years."

It didn't make sense. Rowan was well over fifty.

"Come see," he said, beckoning her into the building. He spread his hands and gestured around the room. "Welcome to the Operculum."

Elizabeth followed him in and waited for her eyes to adjust to the change in light. She was greeted by a familiar aroma that she couldn't quite place. Three slit windows high on the roof threw blinding slivers on the far wall, and Elizabeth could make out a huge window facing out to a perfect puffy-cloud-dotted blue sky over a field. But she couldn't match the scene to what she had just walked past on the driveway. She was sure there were trees beyond the building, but the window looked out on an open meadow. She noticed windows of various sizes around the room, each with a vastly different view and each as crisp as a high-definition photograph.

Then it hit her; she was looking at paintings. Paintings hanging from floor to ceiling, stacked six deep against each other in corners, leaning against every wall and piled on every flat surface. Gorgeous, photorealistic, widely sought-after, museum-worthy paintings.

Her mouth dropped open and she turned to him. "Oh, my God. You're Rowan Barnes."

CHAPTER SIX

Elizabeth sputtered and blushed as Rowan roared with laughter.

"You didn't know?" he brayed, slapping his leg and gasping for breath. "My friends at the gallery were sure that you were an opportunist coming to beg for a landscape or two before you sold off your father's plot and disappeared back to the States."

"Rowan!" Trudy said sharply. She looked at Elizabeth with an apologetic expression. "I knew it wasn't at all like that."

Rowan Barnes had paintings hanging in the National Gallery, had been commissioned by the queen to paint her favorite vista at Balmoral, and had been the subject of a documentary that chronicled his prickly relationship with Her Majesty as he worked on her landscape. Elizabeth had merely noted his last name when she saw the documentary mentioned on Huffington Post, chalking it up to an interesting coincidence and nothing more. She'd watched a few minutes of the preview, which showed his hands at work on a painting in extreme close-up while he described his process. Surely her father would've mentioned the relationship when the documentary hit the news?

Once again she was speechless. She looked at Rowan with wide eyes, then looked around the barn at the collection of work.

"These aren't included in the retrospective at the museum, though they should be," Trudy said, throwing another angry look at Rowan. "He paints like a madman, locked in here for days at a time, and then they never see the light of day. He hoards most of them, and selects a few per year to show and sell. Someone needs to organize this mess."

Elizabeth looked around the room and quickly tried to count the paintings. She had no idea what they sold for, but even at a few thousand a piece she was standing amid a fortune. And there wasn't even a lock on the door, or protection over the windows. And what if the old roof sprang a leak?

"Why aren't these at a gallery or museum?" she asked.

"They will be, someday, when I'm dead

and gone. For now, they keep me company."

"His gallery doesn't even know how many are here. He won't let anyone in. He set up a pretend studio in a different barn when they filmed that documentary. Do you know what *operculum* means, Elizabeth?" Trudy asked.

She shook her head.

"It's that little trapdoor that a snail uses to close itself off from the world. That's what Rowan does in here, closes the door and disappears. I'm shocked he let you in. You're among an honored few."

"Family is different," he said with finality. "Now, Bess, you must know that I'm mortified by this museum retrospective. My gallery forced me to do it, but the good news is that we're having a raucous party here on the property to kick it off. We've got a group of marvelous people coming, all ages, not just fuddy-duddies like us, and there will be plenty of good food and drink. It won't be all drab art talk, I assure you. Would you reconsider staying?"

Trudy tutted at him for forcing the issue, then looked at Elizabeth with a hopeful expression.

The change in circumstances intrigued her. She was no art-mooching schemer, but she knew a business opportunity when she saw it. The party was bound to attract the top tier of British society, probably all the way up to the monarchy given Rowan's history. The potential social media opportunities alone were mouthwatering. She could envision Cecelia and Whitney scrolling through the party pictures, jamming their fingers on images of Elizabeth next to people hashtagged with #duke and #royalfamily.

Plus she was shocked to realize that she wasn't quite ready to say good-bye to her newfound relatives.

"What's the dress code?"

"It's ridiculous. The gallery insisted on 'creative landscape cocktail,' whatever that means," Trudy said. "I'm sure I'll be wildly inappropriate, and the society pages will have a good laugh at my expense."

"Will there be hats?"

Rowan looked at her with a twinkle in his eyes. "Will there be hats? *Everyone* will be in hats, from Major to the sheep-ladies to yours truly. Our milliner has been on high alert. Just wait until you see what she's dreamed up for the Barnes clan." The more he talked about it, the more animated he became. "Now, the invitation said 'creative,' and this crowd is creative to the core. That means the average dress from your suitcase won't —"

"Rowan, please." Trudy interrupted. "You'll scare her away." She turned to Elizabeth. "You don't have to give us an answer now, Bess. Think it over and let us know, yes?"

"Thank you for the invitation, I definitely will."

Elizabeth crossed her arms and smiled at Rowan and Trudy, touched by the hope that radiated from them. They barely knew her and yet they wanted her to stay.

So this was family.

CHAPTER SEVEN

Elizabeth followed Rowan to her room after a healthy breakfast, featuring muesli, Ryvita crispbreads with lemon curd, endless bowls of blueberries, and many cups of tea. To her surprise she enjoyed it immensely, but she silently lamented the lack of coffee. She was in full-on withdrawal mode.

Rowan was right, the room was beautiful and probably much more luxurious than what she would have had at the ancient inn. Though the décor was too fussy for her taste, she could appreciate how the blue stripes, florals, and chevrons came together. One of Rowan's smaller landscapes hung unceremoniously in a space that was nearly obscured by a lampshade.

After a hot shower, a pathetic attempt at straightening her own hair, and a long-overdue change of clothing, it was time to see the property. Her property. They planned to disperse her father's ashes in the river at the same time, so she dressed appropriately for the occasion in what resembled mourning attire even though she wore shades of black and gray nearly every day. She thought she should at least look the part even though she had no tears left to cry for him. Elizabeth buried the box in the bottom of her bag so that it wouldn't feel like they were at a second funeral until the very last moment.

Trudy and Rowan had also dressed the part in sedate, dark clothing. "Well, Bess," Rowan said, clapping his hands together when she came downstairs, defiantly sticking with the nickname. "Off we go, shall we?"

Major began twirling around in anticipation of a walk, but Trudy shook her head at him, which was enough to make him understand that it was a humans-only event. He shot an accusatory look at Elizabeth as he slunk past her, his ears plastered against his head. Major hated her, there was no denying it.

"Oh, dear," Trudy said, looking at Elizabeth's feet. "Are those high boots comfortable enough? We'll be doing some walking. Would you like the wellies instead?"

The thought of dispersing her father's ashes while wearing rubber clown boots almost made Elizabeth laugh. "No, I'll be fine. Promise."

Trudy once again kept up a steady stream of one-sided conversation as they made their way past Rowan's studio and farther down the lane to where the gravel driveway disappeared into the tall, wild grass. Rowan seemed well versed in nodding along as Trudy talked, half tuned in to her and half tuned inward. Trudy and Rowan both managed to ignore the small black flies dive-bombing them, while Elizabeth furiously swatted and ducked from the assault.

They walked farther than she thought they would, until the open pastures began to merge with long rows of trees planted like soldiers in formation. The only sound other than Trudy's running commentary came from occasional birdsong and the babbling river that roped along beside them.

"Aren't these poplars majestic?" Trudy asked. "Your father's parcel is just beyond this section, where the land turns primitive. It's a magical spot." She talked about the land like a museum docent.

Trudy's love for the property made Elizabeth feel like an interloper, imposing on the two strangers. How could she claim the property in good conscience, even if it had been earmarked for her father a million years ago? He'd chosen to remove himself from these people and this life, and whatever the reason was, it was enough to keep them apart until death. Why would they welcome her and hand over what was obviously an expensive piece of real estate when they could've kept it without anyone the wiser? Elizabeth argued both sides in her mind and tried not to focus on the blisters that were forming on the backs of her heels, or the fact that the six-pound box in her bag was getting heavier with each step.

Rowan helped Trudy over a fallen moss-coated tree and then offered his hand to Elizabeth as she attempted to scale it. She grasped it and was surprised that his hand nearly enveloped hers completely.

"Just down there," he said quietly, still holding on to her hand as he looked off into the distance. She untangled herself from his hand gently, hoping that he wouldn't notice. Rowan turned to Elizabeth. "I don't want to ruin this important moment with talk of business, but I fear that's why you're here, after all," Rowan said. "We would love for you to keep this land, but if you ever decide to sell it, Trudy and I would like you to sell it to us. We feel very strongly that it should stay in the family. Well, what remains of our family."

She started talking before she even knew what was coming out of her mouth. "I think it makes the most sense for you to just have it. I'm not even sure if I have an actual claim to it. Let's just keep everything how it is, no handover, no paperwork. This land isn't mine, it's yours."

"Nonsense," Rowan replied. "I was never the rightful owner of this piece, and it's been a weight on me for all these years. You are the rightful heir, no arguments. The papers are already being drawn up."

It still didn't feel right.

They walked on, wading through knee-high ferns, dodging dead limbs hanging from trees, and avoiding camouflaged slippery rocks. Elizabeth considered how best to frame and filter a photo of the woods. Nature wasn't part of her brand, and she debated if she should even bother to try to capture it. Would posting a close-up of a moss-covered rock make her lose followers? Or what about a timer photo shot from a distance, to show off how tiny she was compared to the giant trees? Maybe, if she could get just the right angle, she could post a filtered profile selfie looking off into the distance, and overlay an inspirational quote in a pretty script just below her chin?

"Bess?" Trudy called. "Did you hear me?"

"Sorry," Elizabeth said. "What did you say?"

"I asked if you liked the ruins." She pointed down the hill to a stone structure nearly hidden in the overgrowth. The vines had grown across the open roof so perfectly that it could've been a part of an Anthropologie window display.

"Was that a house?" Elizabeth asked.

"A mill. It started off as a grist mill — you can see the millstones half buried near the edge of it — and then they wisely converted it to a textile mill given the woolly neighbors. Hydro-powered, quite a marvel of technology for the times, really," Rowan answered.

"How old is it?"

"We're not exactly sure, but we think it dates back to the 1700s. Your father loved the antiquity of it. He used to come here and work on his poems."

"You mean he wrote his *own* poems?"

Rowan said it casually, but Elizabeth processed the news like it was part of her DNA report. She wondered if that was what her poetry professor father had been doing every time he closed his office door on her. Imagining him obeying his muse made his choice to lock her out hurt a little less.

71

"Did he ever let you read them?" she asked.

"Maybe. I can't recall. It was such a long time ago," Rowan answered as he walked away from her, down toward the ruins before she could ask him more questions.

Elizabeth wanted to learn more about the poet her father used to be when he lived in Fargrove, but it was clear Rowan wasn't ready to talk about it. And given they were about to leave him in his final resting place, she didn't think it was appropriate to bring up a time in their lives that had resulted in estrangement. But she wanted to hear everything about him, to find out if he'd ever been happy.

"Come down to the river," Trudy called to Elizabeth, already at the water's edge just beyond the mill. Elizabeth gingerly made her way down the hill, her inappropriate footwear making her far less agile than her septuagenarian relatives. Trudy and Rowan were talking quietly as Elizabeth approached them.

"What were your father's specific instructions?" Trudy asked.

"The will only said dispersement on the River Dorcalon. I guess that means *in* the river?"

"Indeed," Trudy said.

72

" 'What was he doing, the great god Pan, down in the reeds by the river?' " Rowan said, staring at the water.

Elizabeth recognized the quote immediately. It was from the poem "A Musical Instrument" by Elizabeth Barrett Browning, the poet she was named for. It was her father's favorite.

She leaned against a tree clutching the box in front of her. She was about to say a final good-bye to her father in a place that would swallow him up forever. Did she want to keep a bit of him, a final act of parental defiance, before he was released into the wild? Something to go back with her to San Francisco, poured into a small decorative vial and stuffed in the back of a drawer? Elizabeth looked around and realized that even if she wanted to keep a spoonful, she didn't have anything to put him in. She felt a wadded-up tissue in her pocket. Could she siphon out a bit of Clive Barnes and tie him in a Kleenex until she could find a more suitable vessel? She shook her head. He wanted to be here, in Fargrove, in the river, for reasons she didn't understand yet. It didn't seem right to deny him that, though she didn't feel that she owed him any favors.

"Are you ready, dear?" Trudy asked.

Elizabeth nodded, and they walked to the edge of the river, where the current ran strong.

"I don't know what to do . . ." Elizabeth said, trailing off.

"Say your good-bye, then bend low and pour slowly," Trudy replied softly.

Elizabeth did as she was told but avoided looking at the contents of the box, choosing to focus on Rowan and Trudy instead. Rowan blinked back tears, and Trudy leaned into him and sniffled quietly against his chest. Watching them mourn her father shifted something inside her. She tried to imagine the man they had known and that they still loved, despite the years apart. For an instant she saw him, a ghost standing in the river laughing with Rowan, filled with joy, hope, and poetry.

The wave of grief caught her off guard, making her knees buckle.

"Bess, dear, are you okay?" Trudy asked.

Elizabeth rearranged her face so that she wouldn't have to talk about what she was feeling. "I'm okay."

Rowan walked over to her and took her hands in his. They were as soft as rising dough, and though his raw emotions made her uncomfortable, she allowed it. He needed it more than she did. "Bess, I know you have questions about . . . what happened. Why he never discussed us. We'll have a cuppa tonight and tell you everything."

"I'd appreciate that. I'm sure it won't be easy, but I want to know," Elizabeth answered.

CHAPTER EIGHT

She'd said it before she could question herself, during the long walk back to the house. Elizabeth refused to be moved by what they'd just done in the river, but something rumbling inside her felt sad-adjacent, and she wasn't ready to leave the only two people in the world who understood what she was going through. If she decided she needed to be comforted, which she definitely didn't, Rowan and Trudy would be there for her.

"I'll stay. For the party, I mean. I would love to stay for it."

"Oh, splendid, splendid," Trudy trilled, clapping her hands. "How wonderful!"

"Our friend Harriet has a vintage shop in town, and I'm sure she'll have something clever for you to wear," Rowan added while he beamed at her.

He offered to drive her into Fargrove so she could stop by their friend's vintage shop, but when she discovered it was just a ten-minute walk she opted to make the trip on her own. Her true destination wasn't the vintage shop at all, but a place where she could sit quietly and reconnect to the real world on her phone, even if it meant walking on a poorly paved street and following directions that used crooked trees, stone walls, and herds of cows as landmarks.

Elizabeth repeatedly touched her back pocket as she walked to make sure her phone was still there. The lack of connectivity was painful, like a toothache that she kept worrying with her tongue. If she made a wrong turn at the second cow on the left there was no Google Maps to save her.

The sun was warmer than she'd anticipated, and she soon had to roll her sleeves up over her elbows and unbutton her blouse to just above her bra. Even though the blisters on the backs of her heels were now open wounds, she'd kept the boots on for the walk because they completed the outfit. She had a pair of workout-only sneakers that made her feet look huge buried in the bottom of her suitcase, but there was zero chance they'd see the light of day for anything other than burning calories.

Just as she was starting to get worried that she'd made a wrong turn, she spotted the low bridge Trudy had mentioned as the final landmark before town. The road evened out, and the quaint stone houses merged toward each other until they touched shoulders, and it became obvious that she was on the edge of the bustling metropolis known as Fargrove. She snapped a photo, convinced that she'd have an opportunity to post it at some point.

Elizabeth walked as if she knew where she was going, passing a butcher, chemist, hardware store, greengrocer, and church without any sign of a place where she could sit down and connect to Wi-Fi. The narrow lane opened up to a tidy town center surrounded by businesses under colorful awnings, where people bustled through their daily lives as if walking on cobblestone streets while surrounded by twee stone buildings were the most natural thing in the world. The Disney preciousness of it all made her long for the shiny new buildings that kept popping up in her neighborhood.

Elizabeth narrowed her eyes to try to read the store names from a distance. A pub called the Three Tups with a fat black dog sleeping in front of the open door, a bookstore called only *Book Shop* on the navy awning, a children's shop called Frog Hollow. She walked toward an alcove, where the shop's sign was obscured by a large tree. There were yellow tables and café chairs out front, where people sat working on laptops, chatting with friends, and reading. They all had mugs in front of them. Her heart quickened — it had to be. As she got closer she could make out the first word on the sign — *HiveMind* — and then as she passed the tree she saw the words she'd been hoping for.

Coffee Co.

Finally, finally, caffeine and a connection to her life, as it was a part of the universal coffee shop code of ethics to provide customers and loiterers alike with free Wi-Fi. Even quaint Fargrove had to understand that the real world was connected and earning and innovating beyond the ancient village limits.

Elizabeth strode between the tables like a junkie on her way to a fix, not noticing a man gathering his things. He stood up abruptly and they collided, which made the table in front of him wobble from side to side. The clumsy redheaded man tried to grab both his coffee mug and phone as they pinballed across the top of the table, and his awkward lurch pushed Elizabeth off balance. He slapped his hand on top of his phone, which caused the table to tip even more, sending his mug crashing to the ground. Coffee and mug shards splattered on Elizabeth's boots as she struggled to stay upright, and everyone turned to see what was happening.

"Fantastic," she muttered as she surveyed the damage to her expensive boots.

"My apologies, the table must have jumped out and tripped you. Are your *boots* okay, madame?" the man asked as he knelt to pick up the mug remnants. He was the reddest redhead Elizabeth had ever seen. His hair, the eyebrow slashes above his bright blue eyes, and his coppery stubble made him a giant, unmissable ginger beacon. Even the bit of chest hair that peeked out from his V-neck screamed for attention.

"Doubtful, given you basically spilled an entire cup on them," she replied. She walked past him with her eyes on her boots, eager to get away from him, and wrenched open the coffee shop's door. She found a stack of napkins and tried to salvage the leather.

The familiar toasted-nut smell immediately made her mouth water. Rowan and Trudy were generous hosts, but they'd forgotten that not everyone appreciates tea. She didn't dare ask for coffee because she didn't want to come across as demanding.

80

The inside of the shop was surprisingly modern given their quaint surroundings, with matte-black walls, a floor made of wide scuffed planks, and a dozen Edison bulbs hanging from black cords at various lengths behind the bar. It wouldn't look out of place back home in San Fran. The chalkboard menu behind the bar listed the Wi-Fi password, *BeeGood,* and dozens of options. Elizabeth had finally found a home in Fargrove.

There wasn't a soul inside the shop. The beautiful day had everyone basking in the spring sunshine, and while Elizabeth knew where the patrons were, she couldn't figure out where the proprietors were hiding. She cleared her throat a few times as she scanned the menu, and set her bag on the counter with an intentional thud. Still no one.

Elizabeth settled on an espresso blend called the Swarm and finally called out, "Excuse me? Can someone take my order?" She pulled out her phone and worked on logging in as she waited.

The door opened and the angry ginger man stormed in with the shards from his mug in one hand and his phone in the other. He walked behind the counter. "Ready?" he asked gruffly. His temperament seemed true to his red hair. He was tall with a blue-collar thickness to his build that looked like the result of farmwork rather than CrossFit.

"I am. I've been waiting." She didn't look up from her phone. She was just seconds away from connectivity and there was no time to bicker with a grumpy coffee jockey.

"Another patient American." He nodded to himself and threw the pieces of the mug in the trash behind the counter with an exaggerated slam. "I was cleaning up from a spill, you might recall it? Now, how may I serve you, madame?"

"The Swarm, please. To go." In an instant the coffee shop had flipped from a taste of home to a battleground.

She paid and he turned away to begin making her drink, so she stepped outside to check her phone. Finally, a link to the real world. Her phone chirped as a text message downloaded from her Airbnb guests looking for various household items. She checked her social media analytics and was dismayed to discover that her feeds were holding strong but still not growing. Was life moving on without her already? She quickly uploaded the luggage photo, hoping that no one would call her on the lag time since her flight the day before, and plotted how and where to post the other pictures she'd taken without looking desperate.

Two news outlets had emailed responses about her Entomon photo: TechGeek, an insider website with a Twitter feed that regularly toppled giants, and GossipBot, a blog that made the tech world sound as glamorous as Hollywood. She'd reached out to them from a fake email address and had only alluded to the photo bombshell, but both were eager for more information. She continued her cagey courtship dance with them, waiting for just the right timing to take Cecelia down in the most public and damaging way possible.

Elizabeth leaned against the brick wall and turned her face up to the sun. The warmth on her skin felt so good that she hardly worried that she'd forgotten sunscreen. She wanted to park herself in a yellow chair and continue plotting her comeback, but the redhead made her feel unwelcome.

She surveyed the people sitting in the courtyard. A tired-looking mother placated her cheerful toddler with a wooden cow toy while she drank her coffee and stared into space. Two gray-haired women leaned toward each other across the table, so in sync with one another that they almost looked like twins. A couple speaking another language studied brochures spread on the table in front of them. An elderly woman sat with her flat-faced brown dog perched on her lap as she picked at a sandwich, offering the dog tiny bites. Elizabeth nearly missed the man sitting alone at a table on the very edge of the courtyard, glued to his laptop.

Once she spotted him she couldn't look away. Why was no one else staring at him? Even at a distance she could tell he was the kind of handsome that made people stupid. He seemed oblivious to the world around him, so Elizabeth continued studying him. He had stickers plastered on the back of his laptop, but she couldn't make out any of the logos to uncover his tribe. His dark wavy-curly hair was on the right side of bed-head. She squinted to make out the details of his face. Stubble. Thick, dark eyebrows. She was focused on the strong contours of his nose when he suddenly looked up and directly at her.

For a moment his light green eyes held hers. The shock of being caught staring made her look away immediately, but not before something electric flicked through her. He was even more stunning head-on. She looked down and pretended to check her phone, then peered up at him again when enough time had passed to justify a second look.

What she was feeling was clearly only something that *she* was feeling. The handsome stranger was immediately reengaged with his computer, typing so intently that Elizabeth could swear she heard the keystrokes from across the courtyard. She stole glances at him, hoping that he might tear himself away from whatever was so fascinating on his screen to observe her back, so that their eyes might meet again.

Nothing.

Perhaps he was on a deadline or had a quota to meet. The way he was focused meant he was probably doing actual work; Elizabeth could tell by the little furrow in his brow. He was clocked in, and she respected his dedication to whatever it was, even if it made her invisible.

Elizabeth walked back to the door when her staring started to verge on stalking. She willed him to watch her, pausing to look at her phone when she was perfectly positioned within his sightlines. She posed prettily with one hand on her hip and tossed her hair, like a bird doing a mating dance. She envisioned channeling the moves Insta-models used, hoping that she looked less stupid than she felt. She snuck another look in his direction.

Still, nothing.

She glanced over her shoulder at him one last time as she walked back into the coffee shop to claim her drink, then refocused in case she was heading into another confrontation with the grumpy ginger. He was nowhere to be seen, and the lone to-go cup on the counter said *Yankee* on it, so she grabbed it and walked out in a huff. It didn't look cute enough to post. She took a sip and it felt like she'd just mainlined caffeine. The hit made her want to close her eyes in ecstasy, but she kept her face neutral in case the ginger was watching her. He had every right to be cocky; the guy knew how to brew.

"You're welcome," she heard a voice call after her as the door shut.

Elizabeth knew Rowan would ask about her trip to his friend's shop, so she had no choice but to stop in. She found it a few doors in on a side street, just off the main square: *The Siren, the Stitch and the Wardrobe,* which reminded her of reading the book with her mom. The logo on the carved wooden sign depicted a mariner-style mermaid wearing a dress, her tail peeking out from underneath. The window display was tasteful enough, with an Audrey

Hepburn–esque shift on a headless dress form, surrounded by faux climbing roses.

Elizabeth walked in and was once again surprised by the shop's aesthetic; it seemed well organized and minimalistic, with dresses and coats neatly arranged on bars that seemed to levitate in midair. Amy Winehouse pumped through hidden speakers.

A voice called out. "You are Bess! So nice to meet you, welcome to the Siren!"

Rowan's nickname, again. She had to gently ask him to stop, especially before the party. Elizabeth turned to the sound of the voice and was shocked by the source. Harriet Welbeck was no contemporary to Rowan and Trudy; she was young enough to be their granddaughter. She stood behind the counter with a giant smile on her face, as if she were about to blow out the candles on a birthday cake. She looked out of place in the elegant space, with a messy ombre ponytail on the top of her head, dark burgundy '90s lipstick, and a black ribbon choker around her neck.

"I guess you were expecting me," Elizabeth said. It seemed the only secrets in Fargrove resided within the Barnes clan.

"Your uncle told me to be on high frock-and-chapeau alert, so I already have a few things pulled for you. Trudy guessed your size, correctly by the looks of it." Harriet walked out from behind the counter and Elizabeth couldn't miss her swollen belly, perfectly outlined in a tight green plaid dress. "They're chuffed you're staying for the party. And I am too. We can sit in the corner and gossip about all the society ladies. You can drink my share of champagne, too." She rubbed her stomach.

The thought of being anchored to a stranger throughout the party made Elizabeth queasy. At first glance it seemed like they had absolutely nothing in common. Harriet was way cooler than Elizabeth could ever hope to be, starting at her dark purple Doc Martens. Elizabeth had always wanted a pair of black ones — she knew she didn't have the style to carry off any other color — but even basic black seemed like too much for her. She peeked at Harriet's finger, and the diamond-and-sapphire ring proved that she was happily coupled. The belly was the final divide that she knew she couldn't cross. Elizabeth had no idea how to talk about formula or onesies. She ached to see if the Siren had a feed to see if they shared interests other than industrial-style boots, but it didn't feel right to check while Harriet stood a few feet away grinning at her.

Elizabeth felt something brush against her

legs and jumped. An asymmetrical mass of black and orange splotches on top of white fur purred loudly and seemed to grin at her as it rolled its head up and down her leg. She took a half step away from it but remembered to reach for her phone. Cats meant clicks, and no one had to know that a single sneeze triggered by a nearby cat at age ten had convinced her that she was allergic. She wiggled her nose to check if any dander had found a way in.

"Sorry for the fright. That's Barnabas the shop monster, the most doglike cat you'll ever meet. A *male* calico, so he's a posh moggy. Do you have pets?"

Elizabeth shook her head as she framed the shot. Barnabas played the part, rolling on his back and draping a paw over one eye.

"Kids?"

She shook her head again, and Harriet looked at her quizzically.

"I work," Elizabeth said by way of explanation. "My job is intense. Or *was* intense. I'm on a bit of a sabbatical. It's a long story," she said with a tight smile, praying that the overly friendly woman wouldn't ask for details. It was easier for Elizabeth to not think about it unless she had to.

"Sabbaticals are healthy now and again, good for you. Before we get to it, may I ask you to leave your cup on the counter? We've had a few accidental spills over the years and now I'm extra careful with my one-of-a-kinds. Did Reid make your drink?"

Elizabeth put the cup on the counter. "I don't know who he was, but I'm pretty sure he hated me."

"Giant fellow with red hair?"

She nodded.

"That's Reid. He's usually a love, but if he heard your accent it explains the attitude. He's a tad snobby about Americans, and he doesn't hide it well."

"No, he doesn't. I wish that weren't the case, because he makes an amazing espresso."

"He'll be at the party as well, so maybe you can change his mind about your kind?"

"I'll keep my distance, thanks." Elizabeth considered asking about the dark-haired stranger in the courtyard. *That* was who she wanted to see again.

"Right, let's get on with it. I have six dresses picked for you, all lovely and perfect for the party." Harriet led her to the back of the shop and Barnabas followed, throwing come-hither glances over his shoulder at Elizabeth.

Harriet pulled out each dress and described its history and why it worked with the party's theme. All Elizabeth could see was color, color, color. She gently said no to a pink, a red, a purple and black, a bright blue, and a yellow.

"Well, that leaves us just one." She pulled out a sleeveless gray silk 1950s fit-and-flare dress with layers of black, gray, and white tulle over the skirt that gave it a Gothic ballerina flair. "I was thinking you could go as Rowan's *Morning Mist* series. I have the perfect hat too." She handed Elizabeth the dress and disappeared in back.

Elizabeth held the dress up in front of herself and looked in the mirror. She swished the skirt back and forth, making the tulle float around her, and considered doing a twirl to get the full princess effect. She stopped when she heard Harriet stomping back.

"Put this on," Harriet said, handing her a confection of feathers and netting.

Elizabeth placed the hat on the top of her head.

"Nope, not quite right." Harriet laughed good-naturedly at her. She adjusted the hat so that the coiled black feather base rested just above Elizabeth's left ear. The frothy netting swirled around the top of her head and dipped over one eye. Tiny crystals embedded in the netting glistened like morning dew on grass. She looked like a film noir starlet.

Harriet clapped her hands. "It's perfect! With the dress you *are* the mist! And I must tell you about the hat's origins. It belonged to Georgina Hargrave, the loveliest lass in Fargrove, as they once called her. That's her," she said, pointing to a painting on the wall near the back of the shop.

It was of an arresting woman with blond hair and perfectly arched eyebrows. She was wearing a simple white off-the-shoulder gown that looked a little like a wedding dress, along with a chin tilt and smug expression suggesting that she knew exactly how stunning she looked. Not movie-star pretty, but handsome. Strong.

"She had her pick of the men in town and beyond, she was that dazzling, but she never married," Harriet continued. "She died in her massive old house, alone except for her dozen cats. Now she's remembered as the crazy cat lady of Fargrove, but I, as the purveyor of her beautiful relics, prefer her former title." Harriet looked at Elizabeth in the mirror. "The hat could use a party, wouldn't you say?"

Elizabeth turned her head from side to side, admiring herself in the timeless hat. "I'll wear it, I just hope it's not haunted."

"This is from her jolly youth, so it's curse-free, I promise," Harriet said, grinning at Elizabeth's reflection.

CHAPTER NINE

Elizabeth didn't care what Trudy had told her, Major was out for blood. The dog leapt at her when she returned from her trip to Fargrove, throwing his head back and making high-pitched noises while clawing at her with his front paws. Elizabeth could see every one of his teeth as he chattered and gnashed.

"Help? Is anyone around? Rowan? Trudy?" she called as she tried to sidestep Major, hoping that they couldn't hear the terror in her voice.

Trudy met her in front of the house looking far more casual than appropriate given that Elizabeth was fighting for her life.

"Maj, leave her be," Trudy scolded. The dog immediately stopped his assault but continued making rumbly sounds, turning in sharklike figure eights in front of Elizabeth. "That's no way to treat your cousin. But you're going to have to give in to him at some point, Bess. He'll be relentless until you agree that he's the most handsome dog you've ever seen."

Elizabeth wondered if Trudy was right. Was a simple pat on the head enough to secure a truce? She reached toward Major tentatively, and he went for her hand like her fingers were sausages. She jumped away before he could make contact.

"Oh, dear. You're nervous." Trudy was watching Elizabeth intently, frowning. "Bess, Major isn't vicious. Naughty, yes, but he's just trying to be your friend."

"I don't think he likes me at all. The barking, the jumping . . ."

"You don't know dogs, do you? I'm so sorry I didn't notice sooner," Trudy said as she gave Elizabeth's arm a comforting pat. "I'll make him mind his manners and take care that he doesn't frighten you from now on."

The childhood memory flooded back. The dog was black and shaggy, and even though it had probably weighed no more than thirty pounds and was still a puppy, she recalled it as a drooling, snarling beast that towered over her. It had run from the neighboring yard into theirs and tackled her, pinning her down beneath dirty paws and licking her face with a glee that she misinterpreted as

95

menace. She screamed for help, and her father came out of the house and scolded her for being afraid. "It's just a puppy," he'd said. "You're bigger and smarter. Push it off you." He'd stood beside her as she struggled to throw the wiggling dog away, not offering any help as she wrestled with it. Once she was finally free he'd grabbed the dog by the collar. "Never be afraid of something you have the power to control," he'd said over his shoulder as he led it back across the yard.

She was seven.

Elizabeth hated feeling like the helpless little girl in need of protection. "No, it's okay. I'm not scared," she protested weakly.

"Never you mind. Now come inside, the tea is ready." Trudy whistled quietly and Major fell in step beside her without a backward glance at Elizabeth.

Rowan was sitting at the cozy kitchen table with three robin's-egg-blue teacups in front of him. They looked perfect on the rustic table and Elizabeth wondered if it would be rude to snap a quick photo of them. Artfully photographed hot beverages were always on-brand.

"Well!" he said brightly. "And how was Harriet? Looks like you found something for our little party." He gestured at her bag from the Siren.

"She knows her merchandise," Elizabeth replied. "The dress isn't my usual style, but it should work. It's —"

"Don't tell us!" Trudy interrupted, waving her hands at Elizabeth. "We'll have an unveiling the night of the party." She sat down across from Rowan and arranged her burnt-orange shawl a little tighter around her shoulders.

"Sit," Rowan said, pulling out a chair for her. "It's time for us to have the chat."

Elizabeth felt a mix of curiosity and dread over what they were about to reveal. Who was to blame for the Barnes civil war? It had to be her father. She was sure he'd said or done something to cause the lifelong rift. She wrapped her hands around the warm teacup and waited for Rowan to begin.

He took his time, stirring and blowing on his tea. His mannerisms were just like her father's: triple-tapping the spoon on the edge of the cup, the first tentative sip that bordered on a slurp. Elizabeth wondered if the rituals went back a generation, picked up from their father. He was her blood, and even though she barely knew Rowan, there was a familiarity that made it easy for her to feel comfortable around him.

"Bess, this isn't easy for me to talk about,

because it paints me in a rather unflattering light." He ran his thumb along his cup's handle and paused, as if summoning the courage to begin. He cleared his throat and the words came out quickly.

"Your father and I loved one another, but we also hated one another, as brothers do. Clive and I competed at everything. Sport, school, friends — no matter what it was, we were vying with one another, each trying to best the other. Even when it came to family. Every child likes to think that he's his parents' favorite, yes?" Rowan took off his glasses and rubbed his hand across his forehead. He continued in a soft voice. "This pains me to say, Bess. I *know* our parents favored me. We all knew it. Clive called me 'Golden Boy,' and he didn't mean it as a compliment. He tried so hard to prove his worth to them, but it was clear that no matter what he did, he'd always come in second place."

"It happens with boys close in age," Trudy added. "But your father wasn't outwardly bitter about it. He accepted it and continued to try to best Rowan at every turn."

"And now for the part of the story that reflects the ugly core of me, the part I'm embarrassed to admit." Rowan's voice dropped to a whisper, and he kept his eyes downcast. "I enjoyed the competition. I liked seeing him lose. I *wanted* to be better than him, and for him to know it. I'm not proud of that side of me. Do you think I'm a terrible person, Bess?"

She shook her head. How could petty boyhood squabbles change her impression of him? So far he'd been nothing but kind. Plus she knew firsthand how cold and distant her father could be.

Rowan paused and looked off into the distance for so long that Elizabeth thought the story was over. The only sound in the room was the grandfather clock ticking off every uncomfortable minute. Trudy gave his arm a gentle squeeze, which broke through his trance.

"Then your father fell in love." Rowan looked at Elizabeth with a sad smile on his face. "Back then, your father was a poet, given to a poet's temperament. It's not an insult to say that love came easily to him. His heart was enormous. He loved everyone in his orbit *fiercely*, even me, despite my shortcomings."

Rowan had to be talking about someone else. The father Elizabeth knew loved sensibly, in modest doses at appropriate times. She could only recall three occasions when he'd actually said he loved her out loud:

when she'd fallen off her bike at age nine and broken her arm, moments after her mother died, and when she'd graduated from high school with honors. The tearful bedside admission after her mother had passed was particularly vivid, because he'd embraced her as he'd said it, which made it seem like he meant it. In that moment she'd hoped that the dam between them had finally broken open, only to discover that losing her mother, Felicity, their common thread, had bricked it up tighter.

The heavy conversation roused Major from his bed, as if he were a therapy dog clocking in. He stretched his old bones, wandered over to Rowan, and settled down beside him with his head across the top of Rowan's feet. Rowan leaned down to scratch him absent-mindedly. It was like Major was a different dog, monitoring the vibe in the room and adjusting his behavior appropriately. For a moment Elizabeth questioned what she thought she knew about him.

"Clive had fallen head over heels for a beautiful young lady, and for a time it seemed as though he was winning. He was a teaching assistant at a small school in Headsford, getting ready for his professional skills tests to become a teacher. He had his true love. He was happy." Rowan paused and took a deep breath. "I, on the other hand, was not. Our father thought my painting was aimless. He didn't approve of it, so he pushed me to start a real career, and I tried to find a fit. But I was miserable. I coveted Clive's happiness, and I reacted to it in the way that I always had any time I thought he was close to beating me." Rowan looked down at his hands. "I set out to topple him. And what did I set my sights on? His true love. I didn't intend to do more than make her realize that she had fallen for the lesser of the Barnes boys, then move on to the next girl. That alone is reason to hate me, Bess."

"No, of course not. It was a long time ago," Elizabeth answered. She refrained from saying more, hungry for more details about the stranger Rowan was describing.

"What I didn't expect when I set out to win her was that my thoughtless little conquest would lead me to the great love of *my* life."

Rowan reached for Trudy's hand and brought it to his lips.

"That's sweet. How did you two meet?" Elizabeth asked.

Neither one said a word for a few moments, and the silence felt strange given that they were telling a part of the ancient story that had a happy ending. Trudy finally spoke. "Bess . . . *I* was your father's first love."

It took Elizabeth a minute to process everything. "Rowan, you . . . stole my father's girlfriend . . . and it was *you,* Trudy?"

Trudy adjusted her shawl and leaned toward Elizabeth. "Now, this is why I wanted to be a part of this conversation. You need to hear my side of the story, so that you understand exactly what happened."

Trudy sat silently for a moment, as if steeling herself for what she needed to say.

"Your father and I *weren't* a couple. I loved your father, so very much, but my love for him was based in friendship. I never had romantic feelings for him, and I never led him to believe that I did. But your father could find sunshine in a puddle. He *believed* that our love was equal, and that made it so for him. No matter how hard I tried, I couldn't make him understand that we were nothing more than dear friends. I knew that his feelings for me surpassed mine for him, but I didn't have the heart to tell him that I didn't love him that way. So we continued to see one another, me keeping my distance and your father always striving to cross it."

She stared off and smiled, as if watching something play out in front of her. "We went to a dance once. The Harvest Dance. I wanted to enjoy it with my girlfriends but I could feel that the night was important to him, that he had something to prove to everyone. So I danced with him." She paused and looked at Rowan. "And then I danced with Rowan, and the moment he took me in his arms, I knew that I never wanted to dance with anyone else."

"That night . . ." Rowan trailed off.

"That night" — Trudy made an angry face at him — "Rowan spent half his time pretending I was the most interesting woman he'd ever met, and the other half flirting with every other girl there."

"All part of the plan. I couldn't seem too interested, after all. As far as my brother was concerned you were spoken for."

"It worked," Trudy said. "By our second dance I wanted his full attention for the rest of the night, but he was still charming his way around the room, making eyes at all the other girls. But I could tell he liked *me,* and the other girls were just for show. He never stopped watching me. So I did something terrible. I stomped over to your father and pulled him back out on the dance floor. I waited until I *knew* Rowan was watching, and I kissed your father, right in front of everyone. It was a quick kiss, as if he were a brother, but it was enough."

"I wanted to rush out and punch Clive in the jaw when I saw it," Rowan said.

"I never should have done it, knowing the depth of your father's feelings for me. I used him to get to Rowan. And it worked. Rowan never left my side after that." She sighed and shook her head. "We were so young and thoughtless then."

It was hard for Elizabeth to visualize the ancient people sitting before her embroiled in passion plays, particularly with her stoic father at the center of it all.

"We hid our relationship for as long as we could, sneaking off whenever possible," Trudy said. "We knew we wanted to be married, but we didn't know how to break it to your father. I think he recognized that I was pulling away from him even more, but he never gave up on me."

"You mean, he never stopped loving you," Rowan corrected.

"No, he didn't." Trudy stared at Elizabeth, searching her face for judgment.

Elizabeth tried to process the old hurts presented to her, and the man her father had once been.

"So that's why my father left?" she asked.

"He found out about you and ran away?"

"No, not exactly," Rowan replied. "He had an opportunity with a small school in Boston, which he'd been debating, but when he found out about us I think he felt as if he had no other choice, so he left. Even our parents supported my relationship with Trudy."

The scope of what her father had dealt with as a young man started to dawn on Elizabeth. To be the black sheep of the family no matter what he did, to feel as if no one was on his side, and then to discover that he'd been betrayed by the two people he'd loved the most. Who could survive it unscathed? But it didn't seem like enough to cut off contact for life. Wouldn't all have healed eventually, especially when he fell in love with her mother?

"Do you have any questions?" Rowan asked. He and Trudy were still holding hands.

"He never came back? Ever?"

Rowan shook his head.

"Did you ever visit him in the States?"

"We tried, trust me, we tried," Rowan answered. "We sent letters and invited ourselves countless times." He shrugged.

"How did you find out about . . . me?" She hated to turn the conversation to herself, but she wanted to know.

Rowan smiled. "Your mum, sweet Felicity. Her loyalty was to your father, of course, but she mailed a birth announcement that I'm sure she didn't tell Clive about. There was a tiny photo of you in it. We were thrilled to get it."

Trudy dabbed at the corner of her eye with her sleeve, then cleared her throat. "I knitted a beautiful blanket for you. The softest cotton in a delicious oatmeal color with four different kinds of cables shot through it. The most challenging cables I'd ever made. I wonder if they gave it to you . . ."

Elizabeth thought of the many boxes she'd helped her father pack after her mother died. There was one filled with old bedspreads and blankets. Could her baby blanket have been among them?

"It's a shame that his stubbornness prevented me from meeting the rest of my family. I mean, I could've known my grandparents, right?"

"No, your grandfather died a year after your father left," Rowan said quickly. "And your grandmother a year after that, so no."

"But I could've gotten to know the two of you sooner," Elizabeth said quietly.

Rowan's eyes filled with tears. "We did miss so much, and I regret it every day. We blame ourselves. It's our fault. But you're finally here, and we can begin to make up for it."

Elizabeth felt something move within her. Sympathy for the people sitting across from her, and unbelievably, for her father. He was a product of the ancient hurts he didn't have the strength to get past. It didn't excuse the way he'd treated her, but it helped to explain some of it.

But she didn't want to dwell on it, so like every conflict she faced, Elizabeth put the story away. Better to move on than focus on an unhappy past she couldn't change.

CHAPTER TEN

Elizabeth spent the day before the party shadowing Trudy as she herded and bossed everyone from the chair delivery people to the event planner herself. There were moments when Elizabeth doubted the team would finish, but by seven o'clock the next day the Barnes property was completely transformed. The already picturesque grounds became a magazine-spread-worthy dream of twinkly firefly lights, lush flower globes hung from fat pink silk ribbons, and acres of pale yellow linen-draped tables and chairs ripe for witty repartee. Elizabeth peeked out her window and spied chefs in white toques bickering at a grill hidden behind a wall of climbing roses. The aroma of something mouthwatering wafted through the open window, causing her stomach to growl in anticipation. She spotted well-dressed photographers snapping away as waiters straightened silverware and polished crystal.

She hated being early to any event, but as a houseguest of the host she had no choice. Elizabeth looked at herself in the mirror a final time and was pleased with her last-minute outfit. Harriet was right, the combination of the gray swirling skirt and frothy fascinator did approximate what mist might look like, if it could be captured and worn.

She snapped a half-dozen photographs of herself in the mirror and mulled over what hashtags to use. Rowan's art world connections would open her up to an entirely new community of followers. And Cecelia would see her living her best life, surrounded by beautiful, exciting people. Perfect. Or it would be, once she could walk back to Fargrove and steal Wi-Fi from the coffee shop owned by the world's grumpiest redhead.

Elizabeth opened her bedroom door and jumped when she saw Major waiting outside her room, not sure why he had opted to stand guard at the post. He sat leaning against the wall, looking dapper in a tiny wool top hat and bow tie. Elizabeth pulled her phone from the decorative belt at her waist and took a photo of Major. It turned out blurry and off-center, and she cursed her nervous hands for blowing what would've been an adorable shot, dog lover or not.

"Hi there, Major. Hello there," Elizabeth said in what she hoped was a soothing voice. She had no idea what his sentry post outside her door meant. Was he ramping up his campaign of terror now that Trudy was busy with the party? Would she be able to fight him off before his claws ripped through the delicate tulle on her skirt? Major walked toward her as if reading her thoughts, and she braced herself against the wall for impact. She wasn't going to call for help this time.

He turned in a tight circle in front of her, so close that his shoulder brushed her calf, then sat down next to her and stared up at her face, his tail thumping the ground. He scooted closer to her, so that his body rested against her leg.

"Okay, okaaaay," Elizabeth said, more to calm herself than Major. "I just need to get by you. Everything is fine, just stay *right* there."

She stepped away slowly, but Major put his paw on top of her foot and she froze. He snorted, then sneezed, which made the top hat he was wearing fall over his eyes. He swung his head from side to side trying to dislodge it.

"Someone should fix that for you," Elizabeth said, wishing that Trudy would appear and right the hat. The narrow hallway was empty, but a thrum echoed up from the first floor. Major pawed at his face but couldn't get the hat off.

"I guess I have to do it." Major stopped flailing as if he could understand what she'd said, and Elizabeth reached down to him tentatively, realizing that she was about to touch the dog for the first time since she'd arrived. Her hands shook as she fixed the hat, unsure if her touch might trigger him in some way. It was a delicate maneuver, forcing her to pull at the elastic under his chin, just centimeters from his tooth-filled mouth, and slowly move the hat from over his eyes to the top of his head. Major sat still, even when she accidentally pulled the soft fur beneath his chin. Once the hat was perched on his head again, Major slapped his paw on top of her hand, then drew it toward his chest.

"You want me to pet you? Okay, I think I can do that." She placed her fingertips in the fur on his chest and moved them rhythmically for a few seconds. Major leaned into the petting, which made her realize that she was doing it right.

"Are we good?" she asked as she moved

her hand away from him. "Truce?"

Major dipped his shoulders down so that his elbows touched the ground and yipped at her, then danced in a circle and disappeared down the hall. It felt like an invitation to follow, so she did.

The ground floor was buzzing with staff. Elizabeth wandered among them, feeling overdressed and silly amid the uniformed waiters, until a woman with a severe updo in a headset asked what she needed.

"Rowan? Trudy? Have you seen them?"

"He said something about the studio?" The woman tapped her waist and held her other hand up to the earpiece. "Copy that, I'm on my way." She disappeared into the swirl of activity.

Elizabeth wandered down the lane toward the Operculum. She felt eyes on her back, and she half turned to find a photographer snapping photos of her. She knew she cut a lovely figure in the dress, and the lights from the setting sun and torches along the lane cast a no-filter-needed glow on her as she strolled. She pretended she didn't see him and drifted over to the fence by the ladies' barn, trying to look graceful even though the uneven pebbly lane made her wobble in her heels. The juxtaposition of her in her elegant dress interacting with the sheep

112

deserved a stand-alone photo on whatever social media account he represented, so she pretended to have something in her pocket and called the sheep to her. He was far enough away that she didn't have to stress about her makeup or hair, but close enough that she could repost the photo and her followers would know it was her.

Rosie and Blossom eyed her from the center of the field. As promised, they were both wearing tiny flower crowns, but they seemed more interested in removing them from each other's heads than chatting with Elizabeth. One of them let out a burp-like bleat. Still, she leaned over the fence prettily and stood on her tiptoes so that her leg muscles popped, hoping that the photographer was framing the moment in the way she was envisioning. She wanted to run her phone over to him and make him snap a few that she could post, but she knew it would ruin the fake spontaneity of the moment. She stepped up on the edge of the fence, lifting one leg straight back like a ballerina. She leaned farther over the fence for maximum drama. Farther, a little farther still until the top railing started to bite into her thigh. Rosie took a step in her direction and Elizabeth made an encouraging noise, so focused on realizing her picture-perfect moment that she couldn't sense the ancient wood groaning against her weight. The railing shifted suddenly, and the smooth bottom of the pump on her supporting foot skidded her forward. She windmilled her arms dramatically, trying to maintain her balance and nearly sending her over the top of the fence and into the muck. She grabbed on to the top railing right as her heel finally gave way, breaking off with a loud snap. She caught herself before her foot slipped all the way through the fence and stood still, trying to collect herself.

She couldn't bear to look in the photographer's direction.

A splinter on the beam had drawn a thick editor's pen of blood along the side of her leg. The scrape was painful enough to make her want to punch something in retaliation. She surveyed her shoe. The heel was attached with just a sliver of muddy black satin, like a piece of connective tissue on a severed limb. The back of her foot was filthy with mud and whatever parasites lived in sheep habitat. She couldn't decide if she should tiptoe to Rowan's studio while still wearing the broken heel or take them off and surrender completely.

She finally peeked up the lane and saw the photographer retreating to the house.

Of course he'd seen the entire thing, and the photos would be posted so she'd end up a punch line in the UK as well. She'd seen enough copies of the *Daily Mail* to envision the half-true headline: *Barnes babe's pert posterior on display as she falls headfirst into the muck.*

Elizabeth sat on the edge of a large stone by the barn and removed what was left of her shoes in a huff. She had no other footwear that would work. Her boots would look ridiculous, plus she still had angry blisters from the dispersement. Flats or sneakers weren't even a consideration. She was furious with herself. How could she possibly pose with Britain's top tier while barefoot and bleeding? She'd look dumpy. All of the styled photos she'd imagined were ruined without shoes. She stormed over to Rowan's studio and banged on the door.

"Enter."

The track shrieked as she pulled it open. She stood in the doorway, shoes dangling from her hand and shoulders sloped. Rowan sat at his easel with a paintbrush clenched between his teeth, looking delighted with whatever he was working on. The smell of the barn, of ancient sun-warmed wood mixed with the familiar aroma of paint and pungent solvents, made her want to skip the party and hide in a corner.

"Why hello, lovely. What happened to your shoes? And you're muddy and bleeding! What's this?"

In that instant, the throbbing pain in her leg coupled with the humiliation of her fall and the intensity of everything she'd been through since she arrived overwhelmed her. Her bottom lip trembled and her eyes filled with tears, but she bit the inside of her cheek to stop the tears.

"Oh, Bess, oh, dear. Come, now." Rowan jogged to her side and put his arm around her.

She turned into his embrace and couldn't hold back any longer. She didn't have the strength to keep from crying this time. The feelings of being out of place, unmoored, and alone washed over her. She was angry about her father's final puzzle, forcing her into a situation far outside her comfort zone. She couldn't envision what her new normal at home would be. And she was embarrassed by her tears and need for comfort. Rowan hugged her closely, stroking her back and murmuring until Elizabeth realized how pathetic she was and stepped away from him.

"I'm sorry. It's just a shoe." She held it up and sniffled.

"It's not just the shoe. You've been through so much since arriving. At this point you have to surrender a little."

Elizabeth sniffled and changed the subject. "You look fantastic."

"Why, thank you." He pointed to his shirt. "Monet, an early inspiration of mine."

Elizabeth looked closer and realized that the muted colorful pattern on the shirt under his fitted green velvet-trimmed blazer was actually one of Monet's *Water Lilies* paintings. A silk lily pad and pink lily dangled from the breast pocket. His green driving moccasins picked up the colors in the shirt perfectly.

"And may I say you look like a vision. Harriet took good care of you. Now if I had to guess I'd say you were . . ."

"Mist. Fog." She shrugged. "From your *Morning Mist* series. It's a stretch."

"No, it's wonderful! I see it. And that makes your bare feet even more appropriate, since mist is stealthy and fleet-footed, not hobbled by heels."

"I feel ridiculous without shoes."

"My dear, just wait until you see what shows up tonight. This is an eccentric crowd, so there's bound to be partial nudity, if not full by the end of the night. Your bare feet won't even register. Now, are you feeling well enough to face the masses, or do you need a few minutes to freshen up? And how about a plaster for your scrape?" He gestured to the blood that had dripped down to her ankle.

"I'd like to slip upstairs to fix myself up a bit," she replied, trying to keep her voice steady.

He nodded. "Of course. Take your time and come find me or Trudy when you're ready." He placed a black bowler on his head, festooned with another lily pad and flower, and they walked into the twilight together.

CHAPTER ELEVEN

"There you are, you marvelous misty creature! Let me have a look." Harriet gave Elizabeth a smothering hug, almost spilling her glass of champagne, and stepped back to take her in. "Perfection. The bare feet are a wonderful touch. Nice pedi."

Elizabeth was reminded of the once-over Whitney gave her every day when she arrived at work. No matter how put together Elizabeth felt, Whitney always pointed something out in a way that sounded like a compliment but wasn't, like admiring her blouse and mentioning that she'd seen it in the clearance section. Elizabeth's bare feet would've been an easy target.

"Can you tell what I am?" Harriet asked as she twirled with her arms out.

Harriet was wearing a fitted brown dress with tie-dyed patches of white across her chest and on the top of her bulging belly, paired with a diaphanous white fascinator on her head.

"I can't make it out. What are you?"

"I'm an Albert Bierstadt mountain range! Get it? These are the peaks." She pointed to her stomach and breasts, then to her head. "Clouds!"

"I see it now, very clever. You look great."

"My feet are fuming at me already for wearing these things," she said, showing Elizabeth black lace-up boots. "Shall we sit?"

"Oh, I'd love to but I really need to find our hosts . . ." Elizabeth was ready to start clocking boldfaced names.

Harriet stared over Elizabeth's shoulder as if she weren't listening to her. "Finally, there they are. You must meet my husband and daughter." She waved and grinned.

Elizabeth checked behind her and saw a man who looked like an ebony-skinned runway model walking toward them, carrying an equally beautiful curly-haired toddler in a flower crown. He reminded Elizabeth of a fitness coach she followed, the one with an eight-pack and cheekbones that cast shadows on his face. The man kissed Harriet and handed the little girl to her at the same time.

"Really, Des? You said you were getting me a drink. Do I have to cause a scene? The

120

fat lady needs a nonalcoholic drink, now please!"

He ignored her and held out his hand to Elizabeth. "I'm Desmond, but everyone calls me Des. Or you can call me *Starry Night over the Rhone.*" He gestured toward his bright blue blazer, dotted with splotches of paint to represent Van Gogh's signature yellow stars and squiggles. "And this is our daughter, Poppy, dressed as one of Van Gogh's poppies, of course." The little girl wore a bright red smocked sundress with an elaborate crown of poppies on her head.

"I'm Elizabeth," she replied, putting emphasis on her name so that it would imprint before the nickname could take hold.

"Of course, I recognized your Hargrave hat. Harriet has always loved that one. Can I bring you something to drink, since I'm clearly on my way back to the bar?"

"I'm set for now, thank you." She held up her glass.

Des gave Harriet another kiss on the cheek and headed into the crowd.

"It's almost time for bed, little one," Harriet said to the child at her side. "Enjoy it while you can. Poppy, can you say hello to Miss Bess, Mummy's new friend? Isn't Miss Bess pretty?"

The little girl stared up at Elizabeth through a waterfall of golden brown curls.

"*You* are very pretty," Elizabeth said to her, then instantly regretted it, remembering how the Duchess moms talked about teaching their daughters to be intelligent instead of pretty. "I bet you're smart too. Are you smart?"

Poppy buried her face in her mother's leg.

"Shy, this one. Takes after me!" Harriet snorted and shot Elizabeth a look.

"I've got to find Rowan and Trudy, but I'll catch up with you later," Elizabeth said, hoping that she could figure out a way to chat with a crowd of strangers without an assist from a working phone.

Everyone had gone all out to celebrate the guest of honor and find their own ways to stick to the theme, so Elizabeth found herself ducking around human trees complete with towering branch-hats, shiny blue dresses that shimmered like flowing water, rainbow fascinators, and a dapper gentleman wearing a suit and top hat made entirely of AstroTurf. She finally found Rowan talking to a couple dressed like cherry trees.

"Ah, there she is!" He crowed when he saw Elizabeth. "My sakura friends, allow me to introduce you to my niece, Bess."

From that point on Rowan led her around the party like a show pony, glowing with familial pride. Elizabeth was reminded of the lone holiday faculty party she'd attended with her father, shortly after her mother died. She was the only child at a party that was clearly meant for adults, without a Santa or brightly wrapped present in sight. He'd spent the hours talking quietly with his colleagues as if Elizabeth weren't even there with him. She sat by herself in a corner, twisting the tassels on her Christmas sweater until they started to unravel.

Rowan, on the other hand, introduced her to everyone within striking distance, always as Bess. Her attempts at correcting him were drowned in polite questions and party chatter. She met an earl, a baroness, curators, collectors, restorers, gallery owners, and too many "the thirds" to count. On Rowan's arm she was the celebrity, not him. He absorbed his guests' congratulations, then deftly deflected all attention to her, beaming next to her as she charmed his friends in her bare feet and swirly dress.

Elizabeth spotted Trudy talking with the party planner underneath a rustic wooden arch covered in a flowering purple plant. She had Rosie and Blossom on colorful ribbon leashes, wearing their half-eaten flower crowns. The sheep acted like well-trained dogs, nibbling on the greenery and accepting goodies from passersby. Major, his top hat still in place, watched them from a few feet away in a focused crouch, looking up at Trudy and waiting to boss them into submission.

Trudy was hard to miss in a brilliant yellow dress that faded to pinks, reds, and blues at the bottom, topped off with a textured navy shawl shot through with glints of silver that she had no doubt woven herself. On her head, a crown of silver stars. It was the first costume Elizabeth could immediately identify; her aunt was dressed as dusk, the magic hour when sun, stars, and moon share the sky at the same time. It was a loving tribute to Rowan's most famous painting, *Sunset over Blenheim.*

Elizabeth watched Trudy while pretending to listen to a performance artist in a sheer silver blouse and lightning-bolt hat talk about her latest site-specific installation. Trudy looked agitated, as if the party planner wasn't following what she was saying. She pointed to the sky over and over. William Burke, the gardener, joined them under the arch, looking exactly as he had the night he picked Elizabeth up from the airport except for orange and yellow leaves peeking from his pockets and tucked in his cap. He, too, seemed concerned about something.

Rowan tapped her on the shoulder. "Bess, dear, may I introduce you to our dear friend Reid Burgess, owner of HiveMind Coffee and the finest beekeeper in Fargrove. Reid, this is my niece, who changed her vacation plans to be with us tonight."

"We've already met." Reid held his pint glass up to her in a halfhearted toast. "What are you supposed to be?"

"Mist."

"Missed what?"

Rowan jumped in as if sensing the tension between them. "She's *the mist,* an homage to my *Morning Mist* series, of course. And you are from Seurat's *A Sunday Afternoon on the Island of La Grande Jatte,* yes? The gentleman in the front?"

Elizabeth had recognized the outfit immediately, but she would never have given him the satisfaction of admitting it. His black baseball cap and sleeveless red shirt were standard issue, but coupled with his coppery five o'clock shadow and long prop pipe, he was the embodiment of the boatman in the foreground of the painting. His broad shoulders and sculpted arms caught her off guard. In San Fran a physique like his came courtesy of a trainer, but Elizabeth guessed that his muscles were actually the product of physical labor.

"*Oui, oui,* I am the boatman," Reid replied.

Rowan looked off in the distance with a concerned expression. "Will you excuse me? Trudy is beckoning me." He slipped away, leaving Elizabeth and Reid alone.

"Breaking any mugs tonight?"

"Funny. Making any lattes tonight?"

"Ha. I'm off duty. I'll be back to serving the caffeine addicts tomorrow."

Elizabeth sensed an opportunity. "You had quite a crowd when I was there. Do you know all of your customers? Are they regulars?"

"Most."

"The lady with the little dog? So cute." She kept her voice neutral.

"Mrs. Redvers and Lark the pug."

"And there was a mom and child, and what looked like some old friends chatting, and, oh yeah, that dark-haired guy on his computer." She tried to play it off, like she was just interested in learning about the locals.

"Kelly Malthus and her son Ben; Patricia and Judith Balfour, they're sisters, not friends; and James Holworthy."

She felt a ripple of victory at discovering his name so stealthily. "That James guy, he looked very busy. Do you know what he does? I mean, he was the only one working; everyone else seemed to be taking it easy."

Reid turned to look directly at her and studied her before he answered. "Why don't you ask him yourself?" He pointed across the yard to a crowd of women tittering around someone. One of the women doubled over with laughter and Elizabeth spotted him, holding court in front of the rapt group. He was wearing a single-breasted black blazer buttoned high with a white silk scarf knotted at his neck. The wild wavy hair was tamed, and he had elaborate sideburns drawn on his cheeks. She wasn't sure how his costume fit with the theme, but it didn't matter. He looked like he'd stepped out of a Regency romance.

James Holworthy was magnificent, and he looked even better laughing. He was gesturing with his pint glass, and the women watched him with eager expressions, ready to laugh again when the time was right. They looked like they wanted to eat him, and she didn't blame them one bit. He was more delicious than she remembered. How had she missed those cheekbones?

Elizabeth refocused on the grumpy ginger

and realized that she had to make him an ally so that she could secure an introduction. It wasn't going to be easy given the twin strikes of her Americanness and recent mug murder.

"So you're a beekeeper," she said, hoping that talking about a hobby might open him up. "Are you helping to save the world from hive collapse?"

"I'm doing my part. Half a dozen hives on top of the shop. Are you an artist as well? Does it run in the family?" Reid scanned the crowd as if trying to find someone else to talk to while keeping the volley of questions going between them.

"Not anymore. I'm in tech. Gaming, some web design, a little programming." It wasn't exactly true at the moment, but it would be soon enough, once she toppled Cecelia with the photo. Everyone would connect the dots and realize that Elizabeth was fired to create a smokescreen for something much worse than a stupid joke.

Reid stopped scanning everyone else and took a step closer to her. He looked at her in awe, like she'd just told him she was a fighter pilot.

"Really? I'm in need of an app developer. Can you suggest someone?" It was as if a switch had flipped. Suddenly Elizabeth was irresistible and worthy of his full attention.

"Depends on what you want. I actually have a development background, so I can do the basics." Elizabeth suggested it before she could think twice about working with him. Without the cushion of a steady paycheck, it made sense to pursue any and all work that came her way.

"I think all I need would be the basics," he replied, locked in on her. "It's a very straightforward app for the Hive. But we don't have to talk about it now, not while we have cocktails in hand. Would it be possible to set up a time to meet before you shove off? I'd much rather work with someone I've met in the flesh, and developers are hard to come by in Fargrove. If you decide it's something you can take on, I'll pay you, of course." The change in his reaction to her was comical.

"Sure, I'm heading out tomorrow afternoon, but even if we can't make it happen before I go, we can Skype or something." She still needed to work out the details of the land with Rowan and Trudy.

"Excellent. I'm at the Hive all day tomorrow, so if you can squeeze in a quick drop-by, there's a coffee and warm pie awaiting you."

Elizabeth nodded and tried to think of a

way to gracefully request an introduction to James Holworthy before they drifted apart. There was no way she could force herself into James's conversation with the impenetrable wall of estrogen around him, so she needed an in. And it was almost like Reid owed her, now that she was going to help with his app. But maybe it was rude to ask Reid to introduce her? It felt like Reid was checking her out, and she didn't want to do anything that might derail their pending work together. She could shut him down gently once the project was complete, tell him that she never mixed business with pleasure. It wouldn't be the first time she'd had to juggle inappropriate interest with work.

She was just about to ask if anyone else in town needed programming help and steer the conversation to James, even though she had no idea what he did for a living, when Des, Harriet, and Poppy walked over.

"You two have made peace, I see," Harriet said, recalling the first meeting that Elizabeth was trying to scrub from Reid's memory.

"I'll make an exception for this American," Reid said. "She's going to help me with the new Hive app."

Harriet draped her arm on Elizabeth's

shoulder and gave her an approving nod. "Partners, how lovely. I had a feeling you'd get along. I'm an excellent judge of people." She beamed at the group like a proud matchmaker.

Elizabeth shivered at the word. She didn't want them thinking that she needed anything more from Reid than a paycheck. She took the opportunity to excuse herself to look for Rowan and Trudy before Harriet or Des coupled them off. She found them consulting with the planner again, so she stood behind them and eavesdropped.

"I assure you, Mrs. Barnes, the weather is going to hold. And if not, the large tent can accommodate everyone. Please, I'm *begging* you, trust that I have it all under control." The woman's voice was strained, but she was smiling. Elizabeth recognized the face of a woman trained to please.

"I'm worried," Trudy replied. "There are three things I know better than most: plants, animals, and weather. This sky says rain, heavy rain, and I think it's going to be much more than that flimsy tent can take."

"Trudy, please . . ." Rowan interjected. "Let's enjoy ourselves now and worry about rain when we feel the first drops." He started swaying to the music. "Do you hear that? They're playing our song."

She paused to listen to the band. "That's not our song, Rowan. I've never even heard that song."

" 'But I'm distracting you, distracting you, come dance with me, my Trud-a-loo,' " he sang as he took her hand and moved her toward the dance floor.

She tutted at him but gave in, and they joined the other couples moving on the floor. The crowd parted and made a fuss for the man of the hour, clapping as he twirled Trudy. It was obvious they were adored.

Elizabeth downed her champagne and watched James Holworthy from a distance. He was never without a smile, a full pint glass, or a crowd of admirers. She pulled out her phone to look for his socials only to remember that she was in the Barnes dead zone, which made her feel like she was about to be tested on material she couldn't study. How could she casually strike up a conversation with him if she couldn't stalk him first? To compete with the pack of hair models already gathered around him, she'd need to use her secret weapon, the one that made people think she was a brilliant conversationalist even though she typically sweated through her wrap dresses at events: on-brand questions. No one could resist answering questions that played into their preferences, but without her phone she had no way of knowing what his were. She grabbed another drink from a passing waiter so that if the opportunity presented itself and she said something stupid or embarrassing to him she could blame the alcohol.

The party raged on with such force that the first raindrop felt like a mistake, and no one took the weather seriously until the wind whipped a few tablecloths off empty tables, sending dinnerware crashing to the ground.

Elizabeth started to follow the throng to the largest tent when a gust yanked the Hargrave hat from her head. She turned to run after it and collided with a gorgeous Regency-romance chest. James Holworthy steadied her with his free hand, then jogged a few steps after the hat as it cartwheeled away.

"Stay there, I'll get it," he said to Elizabeth over his shoulder. He set his pint down on a stone wall and took two giant steps after the hat, and when it danced out of his reach he dove for it like he was stealing home. He ended up on one knee and stretched to grab the hat, snagging it by the delicate tulle. He stood up and held the hat over his head in triumph as the rain pelted him, exposing a sliver of his stomach beneath his white shirt.

Wet Regency romance James Holworthy looked positively pornographic.

James picked up his pint on the way over and handed the hat back to her. She stared at one of his ridiculous muttonchop sideburns because she was afraid to look directly at him, like he was a solar eclipse that might blind her with his perfection.

"My hero," Elizabeth said, and instantly regretted it.

"At your service," he replied with a heel click and bow.

She plopped the ruined hat on her head in a trance, not caring that it looked like a dishrag. "You're . . . uh." She realized that if she said his name he'd know she'd been stalking him.

"John Constable." He offered his hand to her.

She tilted her head. The name was familiar, but he was James Holworthy, not John Constable. Then it hit her. "The landscape artist. I see it now. Nice to meet you, I'm Elizabeth Barnes, aka *Morning Mist.*" She reached out and shook his hand. The shock of his warmth in the cool rain felt like foreplay.

"You're the American Barnes. Yes, Reid

mentioned you, of course. Nice to meet you."

The accent sounded different coming out of James Holworthy's mouth. Deeper. More mysterious. It was the first time she understood what people meant when they talked about the sexy British accent.

"I guess everyone in this town knows everything?" she asked as they followed the crowd to the tent even though the rain was letting up.

"Basically, yes. Except I don't know that much about *you*. Reid only mentioned how you met. Great first impression, by the way." He grinned at her and it looked wicked.

Elizabeth worried what else Reid might have said to James. Had he already called dibs? Would James step back if Reid brocoded that she was spoken for?

"I'm going to be working with Reid." She stressed the word *working.*

"Fantastic! Reid needs all the help he can get." It sounded more like a brotherly jab than a true insult.

They walked along in silence for a few minutes, and Elizabeth felt James staring at her feet.

"Shoe accident. Probably a good thing I'm barefoot." She shrugged and pointed up at the drizzle. "My heels couldn't handle a

Fargrove typhoon." She was convinced that he was disgusted by her muddy toes.

"No, your leg. You're bleeding." James put a gentle hand on her arm, which stopped her like a jolt of electricity, then knelt beside her. "Cripes, what happened here?"

The rain had dislodged the bandage and turned the trickle of blood from the scrape into bright red modern art on her calf.

"It looks worse than it is. It doesn't hurt," she lied. The area around the scrape was already turning black and blue.

"I don't have any plasters on me, but I do have this." He unknotted the white scarf from around his neck.

"Oh no, don't ruin your costume," Elizabeth protested as he unwound it.

"Costume? This is cut from an old shower curtain. This whole outfit is thrifted and thrown together. These are my dad's old riding boots. Pretty convincing, huh?" He held his arms out and did a half turn with the shower curtain scarf trailing from his hand.

"Yes, you look incredible," Elizabeth replied more breathlessly than she meant to. "I mean, the outfit is really impressive. Sideburns, even." She willed herself to shut up.

James knelt beside her and Elizabeth realized that he meant to bandage her himself.

"No, no, I'll do it!" she exclaimed, jumping away from him. As much as she wanted to feel James caressing her leg, she didn't want him getting up close and personal with blood and filthy feet.

He handed the scarf to her and watched as she mopped up the mess with a quick swipe, hastily triple-wrapped it around her calf, and tied it with a bow.

"That's not going to stay," James said with concern in his voice. "Are you sure you don't want me to do it?"

"It's fine." She waved her hand to dismiss the idea. Elizabeth was desperate to change the subject from blood and bandages to something more flirty. "So, what do you do?" She cringed after she said it. Since she hadn't been able to assemble a James Holworthy profile it was all she could think of, and it was such a San Fran thing to ask. In Fargrove it was probably the equivalent of asking how much he made.

They were near the tent, standing at the back edge of the throng of people trying to squeeze beneath the meager shelter.

"Me? I do this." He held a full pint up in front of him as if he'd conjured it from the air. "I'm the co-owner of Lost Dog Brewery, so I do a little of everything. Selling, promoting, and lots of drinking. Now to you." He shifted his stance. "What do you do for a living, Bess?" His take on an American accent was laughable.

She accepted his unspoken challenge and responded in perfect Fargrove-ese. "Well, when I'm not in Blighty I faff about with computers."

"Whoa," he responded with eyes wide. "You sound native. I'm impressed."

They stood shoulder to shoulder, waiting for everyone to find space under the tent. Elizabeth hoped they'd wind up at a table together in a dark corner. Based on the way his arm kept grazing hers, it seemed likely.

They were nearly under the tent when a rogue gust swept through the crowd and ripped the Hargrave hat from Elizabeth's head again. The rain picked up and the people around them surged forward so that James was propelled farther into the tent as Elizabeth fought her way through the crowd to chase the hat. She ran after it and looked to where she'd left James, throwing a "one second" finger in the air so he'd know she was coming back to him.

She fumed as she chased after the hat, the scarf-bandage slipping down her leg with each step. Was it the Georgina Hargrave curse at work, ensuring that she would also end up lonely and alone? By the time she made it back to the tent she'd not only be a swamp creature, she'd probably have to compete for James Holworthy's attention with a perfectly dry duchess or countess. Or a pack of them.

The hat finally came to a stop tangled in low branches at the edge of the field. The rain was starting to come down harder, but she refused to turn back until she'd recaptured it. She untangled the netting from the branches, swearing under her breath as she heard the delicate fabric rip.

She started to jog back to the tent with the hat clasped against her chest, her bare feet slipping on the wet grass, when a shrill noise stopped her. She couldn't place it. Was it one of the sheep? She waited a moment, standing under the meager shelter of a tree, but heard nothing. She started to move and once again heard the desperate sound. The single note was impossible for Elizabeth to ignore. She waited to hear it again and had almost convinced herself that she was imagining it when the keening sounded off closer than before. She squinted into the darkness at the base of the tree, peering into the twisted roots and gulleys that would trip the most surefooted sober person. The noise repeated, beckoning her to locate it.

Then she saw it.

Huddled in the gnarled roots was a tiny filthy puppy, soaking wet and trembling. When they locked eyes the puppy took a tentative step toward her and rolled onto its side into the mud. Elizabeth looked around, unsure of what to do, but there was no one nearby to help.

She considered running away and pretending that she hadn't seen the thing. Perhaps the mother dog was nearby and would be back soon? Based on the puppy's sorry state, it didn't seem likely.

She stood a few feet away from it. It looked helpless, head down and shuddering. It tried to make its way over to her but seemed too exhausted to move more than a few steps. Elizabeth walked to the puppy slowly. It seemed to understand what was happening and froze in place so that she could pick it up without a struggle. It was freezing and trembling uncontrollably, and she knew she had no choice but to take it back with her.

Elizabeth held it under its front legs with her arms outstretched, and it dangled from her hands like a frog. Its tiny legs swam through the air and its little body shook as she ran through the rain back toward the tent. They bounced along awkwardly until Elizabeth realized that the whole production would go more smoothly if she held the animal against her chest. She stopped under another tree, adjusted her hat so that it was tucked more securely beneath her arm, and moved the dog so that it rested against her chest, mud and all. It immediately stopped trembling, as if all it needed to be comforted was contact with another living being, and adjusted its tiny body so that its nose rested against the bare skin on her neck.

The dog let out a shuddering sigh and surrendered against her body. Elizabeth ran on, wondering what other drama the Hargrave curse had in store for her.

CHAPTER TWELVE

"It's bad luck, you know," William Burke said as he gently wiped the mud off the puppy with a thick linen napkin. "If you find a dog, it was meant to be yours. You can't just pass on what nature has gifted you, Bess."

A cooing group of a half-dozen people had gathered around them under the party tent, and a few murmured in assent. She strained to see if James Holworthy was among them, but he'd vanished, along with the scarf-bandage he'd given her. *Georgina Hargrave strikes again.*

"Maybe it belongs to someone? Maybe it ran away?" Elizabeth said.

William shook his head. "Someone considered this puppy a mistake," he said as he gently turned the loaf-sized thing over in his hands. "It's not a full border collie, you can tell by the coloring, so it was either left to die in the elements or it managed to escape before it was to be drowned in a sack. You saved its life and now it's yours."

She switched into political mode. "I'm happy I could help, but I can't keep it. I'm leaving tomorrow afternoon and I have a week of travel in front of me. Plus, to be honest, I'm not much of a dog person. They don't seem to like me." She smiled sadly, looking around the crowd for a kindred spirit amid the trees, flowers, and rivers.

William shielded the dog from her, placing a hand over its tiny ears. "What does that even mean? 'Not much of a dog person'? That's like saying you're not much of an oxygen person. Dogs and people together . . ." he sputtered, trying to find a way to express undefinable emotions. "Dogs and people together are . . . *everything.*" He gestured emphatically with his free hand and cradled the puppy in the crook of his other arm as a lone yellow leaf drifted down from the brim of his hat. The puppy's fur was matted and its stomach looked disproportionately large compared to its head, but it seemed at peace in William's care.

The dozen people standing around them "hear, hear-ed" in drunken agreement, and Elizabeth held her tongue, aware that she was outnumbered.

"Take the puppy," a voice in the crowd

said. Another joined in, until they were all chanting, "Take the puppy, take the puppy," in gleeful, drunken unison.

William looked her in the eyes and held the sleepy brown, black, and white lump out to her. Nestled in his hands, the puppy looked like a tribal offering, and with the crowd intoning around her it was clear she had no choice but to take it from him. The puppy mewled as he handed it off to her, then settled back to sleep immediately. The crowd cheered in victory. Elizabeth could almost feel the acceptance and support coursing around her.

"What will you call it, Bess?" someone asked.

She still had no plans to keep it, and she didn't want the weighty task of christening it. "I don't even know what it is." She looked at the crusty dog in her hands, then at William. "Boy or girl?"

"That's a lass. Name her well."

The sound of breaking glass and a shout at the far end of the tent interrupted them. The crowd scattered and ran toward the sound, and by the time Elizabeth got there, puppy still in hand, she had to stand on her tiptoes to peer over shoulders and see what everyone was looking at.

Trudy was on her side on the ground,

clutching at her arm and trying to hold back tears. Rowan knelt beside her, his face white, while Reid crouched in front of them. Elizabeth couldn't hear what they were saying, but she could tell that they were attempting to assess the severity of her fall. Trudy nodded her head and squeezed her eyes together. Rowan, Reid, and a few other men gently helped her stand up. Her forehead was a map of pain.

They walked her slowly out of the tent and into the rain, and Elizabeth heard a few people murmur "hospital." Should she go with them? She worked her way through the crowd, trying to get more information from people closer to where the fall had happened. "Tripped on a tent line," a moss man informed her. "Probably a broken arm."

She reached the car just as Reid finished loading them in. "Stay here. I'll let you know," he said.

Elizabeth watched Rowan as he gently dabbed at the blood on the side of Trudy's forehead with a handkerchief. Her eyes were clamped shut.

"What can I do, Rowan?" Elizabeth had the same tingly feeling she used to get when her mom had a bad spell, like she had all the energy in the world and could lift a car or insert an IV line in a hard-to-find vein in order to help. She'd always been too young to do anything more than worry, but now the ready feeling could actually be put to use.

"We'll be fine, we'll be fine," Rowan chanted softly, and rubbed Trudy's shoulder. "I'll ring you when we know more. Don't worry, dear."

The car took off down the lane. Elizabeth and a few other guests stood in the rain watching the taillights disappear in the blackness. Major chased after the car until a sharp whistle changed his direction. He ran back to William, and the pair walked off together.

Elizabeth realized that she was still holding the tiny dog. She shifted it so that it was again in the curve of her neck without a thought about the dirt getting on her dress. She was ruined, soaked through. She welcomed the puppy's warmth.

Elizabeth had once heard that a bad fall could mean the difference between a healthy old age and a rapid descent into helplessness. She hated to imagine sturdy Trudy turning frail, like her mother had as the cancer consumed her.

The little dog inched in closer, as if she could sense Elizabeth's inner turmoil. Elizabeth rested her cheek on the tiny body, shielding her from the rain as they walked back to the house.

CHAPTER THIRTEEN

Elizabeth awoke to something attacking her.

The puppy was pouncing at the lumps created by feet beneath the duvet. She watched it pause and track the movement, then belly-flop onto her feet. She shrieked when one of its needle teeth penetrated the layers of down and found a toe.

The puppy froze and looked at her. It stared at her for a second, then seemed to smile in recognition, then ran full-tilt at her face. Elizabeth pulled the blanket over her head and the puppy pulled at the strands of hair poking out, making little *rrrr-rrrr* noises and tugging hard. She shrieked and the noise seemed to encourage a greater show of canine force.

William had taken Major home for the night, leaving Elizabeth to deal with the sleeping lump of puppy on her own. He nodded solemnly toward the puppy in Elizabeth's hands before he left. "Take care of her, Bess. At this moment you are her everything. She needs you."

Elizabeth had brought the puppy to bed with her because she had no idea what else to do with it. It was barely moving and wouldn't open its eyes, so she'd placed it at the far end of the bed, hoping that it would remain comatose until someone took it off her hands. They'd both slept soundly, but now she was seeing a completely different side of the dog.

She rolled over, keeping her head under the blankets while the puppy battled her hair. She grabbed her phone off the night-stand out of habit, even though there was no hope of connectivity. It was seven forty-five. How was she going to find out what was going on? She felt adrift without Rowan and Trudy nearby.

The puppy finally backed off and sat on the pillow beside her. Elizabeth lifted the cover to see what it was doing, and it immediately darted underneath and started licking her face. She tried to push the thing away, envisioning the germs and dirt that it was spreading, but every time she put her hands near it she ended up getting nipped.

Just then she heard ringing from down the hallway. She'd seen the phone on a narrow table but assumed it was a relic, not something that Rowan and Trudy actually used. She leapt up, sending the puppy spinning tail over head across the bed. She ran to answer the call, hoping that someone was going to tell her what to do next.

"This is Elizabeth Barnes," she answered, sounding like she was clocked in at work.

"Bess, hello, it's Rowan." He sounded exhausted. "Are you well?"

"I'm fine, please tell me what's going on. How is Trudy?"

"She took quite a tumble and broke her arm, badly. They've set it, but she's under observation for a head injury. She's . . . forgetting things." His voice cracked. "She's going to have a full neurological workup and a scan later today. I'm so sorry to ask you this, but could you postpone leaving for a day? William has to take care of his grandson for the next few days and can't help us. Would you mind terribly, Bess?"

She imagined Trudy returning home, weak and confused, and was immediately brought back to images of her mother in bed in her darkened room. She could still smell the tea rose lotion her father used to rub on her mother's numb hands, asking "Does that help, Felicity?" She remembered her mother's wan smiles as Elizabeth showed off the paintings she'd made in art class. She shook her head to banish the thoughts. As much as she hated the rituals of illness, she knew there was no way she could refuse Rowan's request.

"Of course. Happy to help. It's no problem," she lied. The itinerary changes would be difficult to address, particularly without cell service, but she wasn't about to give Rowan something else to worry about.

The puppy started barking and yipping from the edge of the bed down the hall.

"Is that Major? What's wrong with him?"

"No, William has Major. That's . . . I found a puppy in the field last night, right before Trudy fell. William made me keep it and I have no idea what to do."

The barking continued, more insistently.

"So you've earned yourself a puppy. That's lovely, Bess." His words came slowly. "It probably wants breakfast. Major's food is in the closet where we keep the wellies. Oh, and could you turn the ladies out as well? And soon?"

The idea of dealing with the sheep on her own terrified her. "How do I do that? I'm not sure I can, I mean —"

Rowan muffled the phone and Elizabeth could hear him speaking with someone else. "I'm sorry, I must run but I'll ring back when I have more details about Trudy.

Thank you so much for helping." He hung up abruptly.

She held the phone, marveling at the conversation-stopping dial tone. She hadn't touched a landline in ages.

The puppy's yips turned into a full-blown meltdown, and it ran from one end of the bed to the other. Elizabeth worried that it was going to tumble off the edge. She speed-walked back to her room right as the puppy turned in two tight circles and dropped an enormous mound of poo on her duvet.

The puppy danced to the opposite side of the bed, clearly pleased with its accomplishment. The stench spread quickly, forcing Elizabeth to hold her nose to keep from gagging. She had no clue where to find cleaning supplies or what to do with the dog while she attempted to clean the mess. She placed it on the floor and began to gingerly approach the pile — *how could something so small make a mound so huge?* — only to look down and see the puppy midsquat with a stream of urine pooling behind it. The slope in the floor caused it to run directly to the expensive-looking wool throw rug. The dog, now empty and undoubtedly feeling better, sprinted around the room, barking and biting at anything that got in her way.

Elizabeth had spent her career charming morning news anchors, going toe-to-toe with the titans of her industry, and leading product launches in front of hundreds of customers. But she couldn't control the tiny crapping, peeing, biting monster that was barking wildly and running in circles around her feet.

CHAPTER FOURTEEN

Elizabeth walked to the barn with the puppy bundled sling-style in an orange wide-knit scarf she'd found in the wellie closet. Its needle teeth were dangerously close to her boobs, but the belly full of Major's food was lulling her into a morning nap. Even though Elizabeth was still freaked out by the creature, it didn't feel right leaving the tiny thing alone in the house. She couldn't find a leash and collar for it, so she defaulted to the baby-wearing technique she'd seen the new moms around Duchess using. She'd need both hands free for whatever the sheep-ladies doled out during her maiden voyage.

They stood in the corner of the barn eyeing Elizabeth and her colorful wellies warily. Their ears twitched, and one let out a deep smoker's-voice *baaa*. Elizabeth could feel sweat beading in her hairline, partly from the warm puppy body pressed against her and partly because the sheep were only a few feet away with no fence to protect her. Though they had teddy bear faces and sheepy grins, their bulk could do damage if they opted to charge her. Plus, they had to have teeth in their happy-looking mouths.

She tiptoed past them and opened the gate leading to the field, then speed-walked back to a safe spot near the door.

"Go," she said to them, waving one hand in front of her while the other supported the puppy in the sling. "Go out."

They remained motionless.

"It's a beautiful day, go to the field," she said. "Don't you want to go out and do sheepy things?"

One of the sheep turned her back to Elizabeth in an act of defiance.

"Away with thee!" she said, channeling the Fargrove accent, waving both her hands over her head.

The one that was closer to her looked toward the field, then back at Elizabeth.

She followed its gaze and realized that she'd failed to prop open the gate leading out of the barn and it had swung shut. The judgment she thought she'd been imagining was real — the ladies thought she was an idiot. She slipped by them, plastering her back against the wall, and secured the gate with an ancient hook-and-eye lock. They filed out quietly.

"Sorry," Elizabeth said. "Your people will be back soon. You won't have to deal with me again."

The ladies stood a few feet away, regarding her with mean-girl glares. Were they waiting for food? Elizabeth trotted back to the barn and looked for a big bag of lamb chow, perhaps with a photo of a happy sheep on the side. She found nothing.

She thought back to the morning she'd watched Trudy turn them out and realized that she'd failed yet again; the final gate leading to the open pasture was still closed.

"Yes, yes, I'm a stupid city girl. Stop judging me!" She walked down to the metal gate and swung it open, propping it with a rock as she'd seen Trudy do. Still, the sheep remained motionless. She was failing at everything.

What do you want?" she shouted at them. "Major isn't here! Trudy isn't here! Just go already!"

The puppy poked its head out of the sling and one of the sheep took a few steps toward Elizabeth. She looked down at the dog, then back at the sheep. "Is this what you want? You need a little canine inspiration?" She shrugged and took the puppy out of the sling, plopping it down on the ground several feet away from where the sheep stood. Maybe seeing a dog would trigger their usual routine?

The puppy stared at the sheep, then went into the same crouch she'd seen Major assume when near the ladies. Elizabeth realized that she was watching instinct at work. When the sheep glanced away the puppy crept toward them with tentative tiptoeing steps, and when they looked back at her she lowered her head and froze. Elizabeth crouched down too, getting as low as she could without touching the muddy ground. She took a quick photo of the trio, then slipped her phone in her pocket. A puppy plus sheep was bound to be social media gold — when she could get back to Fargrove to post again.

Rosie and Blossom both turned their full bulk to the encroaching pup, as if they'd had enough of her freshman attempt at herding. Instead of moving away, they ambled toward the little dog, reversing the power dynamic and slowly sending her back over the ground she'd covered.

Elizabeth's heart thudded as the sheep moved closer to the puppy. One kick and the little thing would be injured, or worse. She thought about dashing over to it and scooping it up, but she was too afraid to approach the sheep. The sheep came at the puppy as if their roles were reversed. Closer, closer, until the larger sheep stopped, took three dramatic reverse-Rockette steps backward, then put her ears back and charged right at the pup.

The puppy turned and ran back to Elizabeth, yipping like someone had cut off its tail. It stood on its back legs and leapt at her, while Elizabeth backpedaled to maintain her distance from the charging sheep. She managed to scoop up the puppy right as the sheep stopped abruptly about a foot away from them. It — Rosie — Blossom — she still couldn't tell them apart — glared at the two of them for a moment, then walked casually toward the open gate, meeting up with her partner in crime at the threshold and strolling into the pasture.

"What a bitch!" Elizabeth exclaimed, looking down at the trembling puppy in her arms. "She did it on purpose. I'm so sorry I put you through that."

The puppy scaled her body and burrowed its head in Elizabeth's hair, as if trying to hide in the now-familiar spot.

"You were brave," Elizabeth said. "You really thought you could take that fat old lady, huh? I like that."

She realized that she still didn't know

what to call the dog. She'd hoped to hand it off quickly, but she realized that it was probably hers until the end of the day at least. She walked back up the lane to a small landscaped sitting area surrounded by a low stone wall. The event planners had done a spectacular job cleaning up after the party. There were no remnants of the night before on the grounds that Elizabeth could see except for an indentation in the grass where the dance floor had been and a huge, wet turquoise feather resting on the rocks, molted from a woman dressed as a bluebird. She sat down on a bench and placed the puppy at the other end, but it toddled over to her, positioned itself so that its body rested against hers, and placed its tiny paws on her thigh.

"I suppose I should give you a name."

Elizabeth studied the dog and tried to determine if her looks held the key to her name. All of the dirt that coated the dog the night before had flaked off, more than likely on her sheets. The dog's fur was a mixture of wiry and gossamer smooth. It stood out from her body as if she had just taken off a static-charged sweater. She was mostly white, with a few black and brown dots on each leg, and what looked like a black cape draped over her back. Her tail was pure black from base to tip, as if someone had dipped the skinny appendage in ink and used it as a quill. The dark tail was book-ended by a black-and-brown mask that wrapped from the back of her head and around each eye, leaving a trail of white down the middle of her nose. The wispy light brown fur on the edges of black nacho-chip-shaped ears looked like the fringe on the edge of a fancy pillow. Her belly was fat, her legs were short, and even though Elizabeth had never met a dog she couldn't ignore, she knew the thing was adorable.

"You're very scruffy, but that's a horrible name." Elizabeth shook her head.

The puppy gazed up at her intently, as if trying to decipher what she was saying. Elizabeth slowly reached out to touch the fur on the top of the puppy's head, and the little dog met her fingers with another needle-toothed bite.

"Ouch! Okay, I get it, you don't like me. It's sort of a thing with me." The nip left a pinprick of blood on the side of her pointer finger. "I'll call you Sharkey. Or Barracuda."

The puppy rolled onto her back next to Elizabeth and gnashed at the air maniacally, squirming and making little growly noises that sounded serious and a little scary. The puppy snatched her own front paw as if it weren't attached to her body and chomped down on it.

"You are so weird." Elizabeth looked around the property, hoping for name inspiration amid the flowers and trees. She thought of the tree where she'd discovered the dog. "Willow?"

It was good, but she kept thinking, the scene playing out in her head like a movie as the idea started to take shape.

She'd found the puppy when two elements converged: wind and a hat. Without one or the other, she never would've discovered her. And without them she'd never have met James Holworthy either. The more Elizabeth thought about exactly how she'd come to discover the puppy, the more obvious the name became.

It wasn't a curse at all.

She clapped her hands in victory, startling the puppy from its paw-gnawing. "I hereby christen you Georgina Hargrave the Second."

CHAPTER FIFTEEN

Elizabeth waited by the phone in the kitchen for two and a half hours, venturing outside occasionally to let Georgina take a potty break while keeping one ear trained for a ring. She was tethered to the house in a way that felt archaic, particularly because she had technology in her back pocket that could connect calls from the middle of the ocean if necessary. Without her phone, Fargrove was as remote as the moon.

The numerous trips outside didn't prevent the puppy from peeing on the floor, twice. Georgina ranged from rabid attack mode, all teeth and growls going after Elizabeth's fingers, to dead asleep, in thirty-minute cycles. Even though she could ward the puppy off with only minor damage sustained, the intensity of Georgina's bites during her waking moments scared her. Were some dogs "born bad"? Could puppies get rabies? Was it possible the puppy was a wolf-dog hybrid, since she had been found alone outside? And was it true that dogs could get a taste for blood, and now that Georgina had sampled hers, a dormant bloodlust within her had been awakened?

Elizabeth couldn't do what she would normally do when confronted with a problem; there was no Internet to search, no expert to summon. She'd seen an ancient desktop computer in a book-filled office down the hall from her room, but assuming she could use it felt as presumptuous as borrowing someone's car without asking. Instead, she worried about worst-case scenarios and examined the tiny punctures on her hands and forearms.

The moon-faced grandfather clock in the corner of the kitchen ticked on, and it finally dawned on her that Rowan didn't actually need her at the house waiting to hear from him. Updating her was merely a courtesy, not a requirement. His next move didn't hinge on her sitting by the phone. He might have even forgotten she was there during the stress of the diagnostic process. Plus she still needed to cancel cars and rebook hotels, and the only way she could make it happen was to trek into Fargrove.

"Hey, Georgina, want to walk into town?" The puppy bounded to her and tried to latch onto her toes.

A shower and outfit change later, Elizabeth was wellie-clad and ready to reconnect with the world via Fargrove. She'd found one of Trudy's narrow scarves to use as a makeshift leash and collar for Georgina, though the three-pound terrorist fought against any efforts to be led on it. She alternated between carrying Georgina and drag-walking her.

Elizabeth repeatedly checked her phone as they got closer to town, hoping she'd find service, but the Fargrove dead zone extended well beyond Rowan and Trudy's house. She flipped the camera around to get a quick peek at her hair and realized that the sunlight behind her cast a beautiful glow around her head, like she was wearing a halo. It also put a flattering shadow on her face so that with a basic filter she'd look presentable. She hoisted Georgina a little higher on her shoulder and tilted her head from side to side, trying to find the best angle. She settled on her favorite three-quarter view of the left side of her face that hid her wonky eye and pushed Georgina's head closer against her cheek. She did an "I'm surprised we're so cute" expression, the one that always seemed to get other influencers thousands of likes, and got ready to snap the photo. Right as she pushed the button, Georgina reared back and bit Elizabeth on the ear so hard that she dropped her phone.

"*Ow!* What was that about?" she shrieked. Elizabeth massaged her ear with her free hand, still holding the puppy with her other. Thankfully, her phone was scratch-free in the grass at the side of the road. "You are the worst. The absolute worst!" Georgina panted at Elizabeth with a happy expression on her face.

She retrieved the phone and scrolled to the photo. It was hideous and amazing. Georgina looked like a wild animal, all flashing teeth and out-for-blood expression, and Elizabeth had her head tilted away with a terrified expression on her face. Her perfect brows were blurry slashes on her forehead. It looked like an ad for a horror movie. Elizabeth debated what it would mean to post the hysterical but very off-brand photo and moved Georgina to her hip, far away from any dangling body parts.

The puppy finally started squirming again once they hit the bridge into Fargrove center. Elizabeth placed her on the ground and held on to the makeshift leash as Georgina pranced beside Elizabeth like a show pony, with her little head held high.

"Trying to make me look good, huh?" Elizabeth asked Georgina.

Elizabeth scanned the courtyard outside HiveMind, hoping to see James Holworthy again. She'd dreamed of him the night before, still in his costume and on horseback. She'd been trapped in a tree in the pouring rain wearing Georgina Hargrave's elegant white gown split up to her thigh so James's bloody scarf-bandage was visible, clutching puppy Georgina and screaming for help. James had dashed up on a white horse and pulled her onto his lap with a single strong arm. In his other hand, a pint of beer.

"Guys are into dogs, right?" Elizabeth asked Georgina. "His brewery is named for a dog, so of course he is."

Elizabeth walked into HiveMind and was instantly comforted by the familiar aroma. Reid was behind the far end of the counter, laughing with a skinny older man in a flattop cap. She tucked Georgina under her arm and stifled a shriek when the puppy nipped the soft skin by her elbow. Elizabeth wasn't sure what the rules were about dogs in food establishments, so she tried to make the puppy as invisible as possible, even if it meant sacrificing more skin.

The stranger turned abruptly and nearly

ran into Elizabeth. He spotted Georgina immediately. "Oi, who's this?" he asked, reaching out to stroke the puppy's chin, and Elizabeth felt Georgina's tail whip against the side of her body.

Elizabeth stuttered. "Um, her name is Georgina, uh, is it okay if we're in here, Reid?"

"Of course, we welcome all sorts of customers, including Americans." Reid walked around the counter, wiping his hands on a towel tucked into a black ticking-stripe apron and leaned in close to scratch Georgina on the head. The little traitor licked his cheek.

Reid nodded to the skinny man. "Bess, meet Nigel, HiveMind's first and most loyal customer. Nigel, this is Trudy and Rowan's niece, Bess."

"Right, I heard they had a visitor! And by the looks of you, you could be their daughter. The Barnes nose. Your uncle has it, as did your father. Shame what happened all those years ago, innit?" He tsked and shook his head. "So how's Trudy? Quite a fall, I hear."

Elizabeth was both surprised and not that a complete stranger knew all about her ancestral nose and what had happened to Trudy a mere twelve hours before. "It was very scary. I'm still waiting for the latest news."

"Rowan called me not five minutes ago," Reid said. "He told me he rang the house but you didn't answer."

"Wait, he called *you*? You know what's going on?" Elizabeth was upset she'd missed his call after waiting for so long.

"I'm sort of the second line of defense for them, after William. Oh, William stopped by with Major a bit ago. Said he was going to drop Maj off on the way to his son's house, so he'll be waiting for you at Rowan and Trudy's when you return."

She considered how the Major-and-Georgina meeting might go without a knowledgeable dog person in the mix and shuddered. It was sure to be fangs and bloodshed from all parties, human and canine. "Tell me what's happening with Trudy. Is she okay?"

"She's doing much better. Scans and tests all came out clear; it's a mild concussion, lots of bruising, and a spiral fracture. She'll be in a cast for a bit, so no weaving or crafting. Home this evening."

Elizabeth exhaled and placed her hand on her heart. "Okay, that's great it's nothing worse. I was worried."

"You and everybody else," Nigel said.

168

"Your aunt and uncle are tops. Please give them my best, speedy recovery and tickety-boo. Nice to meet you, Georgina." He scratched the puppy behind the ears, and she refrained from biting him again. No one would believe that the puppy was out to get her.

Reid assumed his position behind the counter. "I said I'd pour you a cup if you agreed to talk apps with me. Are you able to focus on business for a bit?"

"Of course. I'll have another Swarm, please." Georgina started to squirm in her arms. The meeting was sure to be a quick one if the puppy had anything to say about it.

"A Swarm it is. Grab a table in the back. Would Georgina like something too? I've got a lovely raw marrow bone left over from yesterday's beef and onion."

Elizabeth had no idea if dogs could eat raw marrow bones, or what a marrow bone even was. She shrugged helplessly. "I know nothing about dogs. She's not even mine, I found her last night and William made me keep her." She held the wiggly puppy out to him. "You want a dog?"

"You found her? She's yours, then. No question."

Reid disappeared into the room behind

169

the counter and returned with an empty burlap coffee bean sack and something nightmarish on a plate. He folded the sack in quarters and placed it on the floor next to where Elizabeth was sitting. He took Georgina from her arms, placed her on the bag, and presented her with a blood-speckled hollow white bone. The puppy snatched it from the plate as Reid lowered it, then turned her body so that she faced the wall with her prize.

"When's the last time you fed this poor thing? She's famished!"

"I told you, I know nothing." Elizabeth felt like a wicked stepmother.

"Trudy will teach you. She knows dogs." He crouched down and looked at the puppy. "Can you make it a few more hours till your great-auntie gets back?"

It sounded like an insult, but Elizabeth chose to ignore it. She wanted to stay on Reid's good side and learn more about his app concept. She wanted to get paid.

"I just have to log in for a bit and re-arrange my schedule before we start the meeting, do you mind? Looks like I'm staying an extra day or so to help Trudy get settled."

"That's wonderful, I'm sure they appreciate it. I'll finish your cup and get your slice warmed up. Would you like sweet or savory pie?"

Normally she wouldn't touch either, but her hunger was making her light-headed and prone to bad decisions.

"Sweet, please."

Elizabeth's phone sang an angelic chorus as it connected. She browsed through the texts and emails, hoping for word back from recruiters or any of the Entomon photo feelers she'd put out. Someone had to want her.

But there was nothing in her inbox but spam.

She felt a wave of anxiety ripple through her. She was not only unemployed, she was *unemployable.* An about-to-be-broke has-been with no future. Her nose prickled painfully but she pinched the skin between her thumb and pointer finger to stop the tears. She blinked and sniffled rhythmically, trying to make it seem like she was fighting off allergies instead of overwhelming emotions.

Elizabeth's hands trembled as she checked her social feeds. Watching the likes pile up always made her feel better. She squinted when she saw the numbers. It couldn't be. Was her phone even *working*? Was the Fargrove Wi-Fi screwing with the algorithms? Based on her latest engagement metrics, she was invisible.

Everything she'd worked for was crumbling away like a sand castle in the tide. She was worthless. Elizabeth grabbed onto the sides of the table to keep the room from closing in on her and tried to harness her breathing. Did anyone even know she was alive? Did anyone *care*?

She jumped when Georgina pressed her head against her calf. Elizabeth eyed her warily, afraid that if she moved too quickly the puppy would playfully nip her leg. Instead, Georgina looked up at her with an expression that made Elizabeth well up again.

The little dog *knew*. Perhaps the molecules around Elizabeth were charged with her sadness and fear, or she was giving off some sort of distress pheromone, but there was no doubt that Georgina could sense that something was very wrong.

She held Elizabeth's gaze, then stood on her back paws so she could rest her chin on Elizabeth's leg. Georgina tipped her head to the side and swatted a paw at Elizabeth's hand.

"You want me to pet you? Do you promise not to bite?" she asked quietly, still sniffling.

Elizabeth reached out tentatively and stroked the puppy's head. It fit perfectly in the palm of her hand. Georgina remained motionless and watched her with inky eyes as Elizabeth caressed her wiry fur.

She felt her shoulders relax as she massaged the little dog. She wasn't sure how she knew it, but she could tell Georgina wasn't going to bite her. For the first time, now that she wasn't fearing for her fingers, she could understand the appeal of a furry best friend, particularly one that seemed to psychically understand her need for comfort. They were connected by something visceral and so unlike anything that Elizabeth had ever experienced that she didn't want the moment to end.

"Thank you," she whispered to the puppy with tears in her eyes. "Thank you for noticing."

Reid came stomping around the corner and placed a giant yellow mug in front of her alongside a hunk of food-blog-worthy pie, not realizing that he'd interrupted something magical. "Right, here you are. Apple raisin," he said, nodding at the slice. "And how's the little one faring with the bone?"

Georgina immediately reengaged with the bone as if their moment of telepathy hadn't happened, clutching it between her tiny front paws and gnawing with her eyes closed.

"She's doing great." Elizabeth smiled at Georgina, then switched into business mode and locked onto Reid with the look that made most men forget what they were about to say. "So tell me about your app. What's the elevator pitch?"

Reid dove into his concept, outlining how his service-speeding app would modernize his coffee shop. Elizabeth was impressed with the buzzwords he used as he described his vision, but as he explained it she realized that he wanted something far more complicated than he actually needed. Reid was so excited about his app that Elizabeth felt like she was about to tell him that Santa doesn't exist.

Elizabeth steepled her hands in front of her. "Reid, I'm going to be honest with you. I love your enthusiasm for this app, and it's obvious you've done a ton of research, but I don't think you need it."

It wasn't the response he was expecting, and he stared at her with his mouth hanging open.

She continued. "I don't want you to waste your money. Plus, I'm not sure I have the skills to make something this complicated. And that's really the heart of it, that it's complicated. You're taking something simple and overengineering it. People want *you* when they order, not some app."

"Huh."

"I'm sorry to be the bearer of bad news, I know you really wanted to do this. I can guarantee that someone will build this for you if you search for developers online, but I think you'd be wasting your money. No, I *know* you'd be wasting it."

"Well, that's shite. I've been dreaming about this app for ages. Now what?" He slumped onto the table.

"How's your website? And what about your social media presence?"

"Uhhhh . . ."

Elizabeth quickly found HiveMind's Instagram account. "You haven't posted anything in three months." She navigated to the shop's website. "This site hasn't been updated in years! That's where you need to invest, Reid. And I can help you with it. I can fix your website and coach you on social stuff. If you want to, that is."

He shrugged. "I guess."

"Trust me, this is going to be great. I already have a ton of ideas. You'll love it."

"Done." He slapped the table in front of him. "Now let's talk bees and honey."

She cocked her head at him.

"Money. Let's talk money. Is this more expensive than designing an app, or less?"

She didn't want to depress him any more by being honest about what he could expect to pay for either option. "Less. I'll give you a friends-and-family deal."

Elizabeth savored the pie and coffee as they quickly hashed out a rough plan and timeline. Reid finally perked up as he realized how much Elizabeth could do for him.

"Huh." Reid leaned back in his chair and studied her. "You're fancy on the outside but a techie on the inside. Quite the juxtaposition."

Elizabeth gestured to the polka-dotted wellies she'd been forced to wear because of the blisters on the backs of her heels. "I've hardly been fancy since arriving."

"You'd be fancy in that bean sack," he said, pointing to the bag under Georgina. "There's an air about you. Regal. Almost like you smell something unpleasant in the peasants surrounding you."

"Ouch."

"Sorry, didn't mean to offend."

Reid gave her a good-natured punch to the shoulder and left to take care of a customer. Elizabeth wondered if it was a clumsy attempt to flirt with her.

Before she dove into Reid's project, Elizabeth stole ten minutes to finally stalk James Holworthy. Perhaps he'd show up at Hive-Mind while she was there and she could use the intel she uncovered to connect with him? She found his brewery quickly, Lost Dog Brewing Company, which, according to a quick map check, was in nearby Thatchmarkle. She held her breath as she clicked the Team page. There he was, barely visible in the background of a group shot with his arm draped around one of his colleagues. She couldn't make out any details in the blurry image. She scrolled down, past his co-founder's profile, until James Holworthy's photo filled the screen.

Elizabeth caught her breath. He photographed well, standing in rugged terrain with a giant brown dog next to him. The photo looked impeccably styled, with perfect lighting, a rumpled but attractive outdoorsy outfit, and the on-brand dog. She speed-read through the gold mine of details to the right of the picture.

Co-founder of Lost Dog Brewing Company. VP of sales. Favorite beer, the Chocolate Lab Stout. Dog's name, Porter. Hobbies, drinking beer and hiking with Porter. That was it. No mention of hiking with anyone other than his dog. Elizabeth scrolled through the rest of the profiles and found mentions of girlfriends, wives, husbands, and partners, so unless he'd purposely left out his significant other, James Holworthy was single.

"Want another?" Reid startled her out of her fantasy. He pointed at her mug.

"Sure," she said too quickly. "Look, Georgina is still working on that bone." She hoped to divert his attention away from what was on her screen, but he took a step closer and peered at it.

"That's James. Why are you on the Lost Dog Brewing website?" He narrowed his eyes at her.

"It's, uh, market research. I met him last night and I just wanted to check out some other local websites. See what's popular around here, you know?" It sounded convincing enough.

"Ohhhh, okay. Research. Got it." He smiled at her like they were sharing a private joke. "Let me get you that refill."

Elizabeth quickly clicked out of the brewery website and descended into her typical state of altered consciousness as she dove into the HiveMind website. When she was finally able to disengage from the work two hours later she realized that she'd barely moved. She leaned over the back of her chair and stretched her arms out wide, the stiffness in her joints a sensory reminder of her old life. Once Elizabeth committed to working on something she never paused, to the detriment of her neck and shoulders.

Reid was in the kitchen behind the counter singing along to the radio, and Elizabeth could see Georgina exploring the low shelves next to him. She wanted to ask him for another slice of pie, but her pants felt tighter after just a few days of Fargrove food.

The bell hanging above the door rang and Elizabeth's stomach turned inside out when she realized that her stalking had summoned him.

It was James Holworthy, in the flesh. Looking no less romance-novel-perfect in a fitted navy blazer with a charcoal hoodie underneath, jeans, and gray trainers.

"Hey, mate," James called to Reid as he headed straight for the counter without glancing around.

Elizabeth pretended she hadn't seen him and quickly checked how she looked in her phone's camera. Concealer splotchy, forehead shiny, but she didn't have time to primp.

"Hey yourself. Look, our new friend is here," Reid said to James before he even reached the counter and pointed to where

Elizabeth was sitting.

"It's the American hat girl. Did you recapture your chapeau? And how's that nasty scrape?" He glanced at her calf as if she might still be wearing the scarf-bandage, then back into her eyes with genuine concern.

She swallowed the tremor in her throat and tried to act normal. "Scrape is fine, thanks, and the hat was recovered. And look what else I found." She pointed to Georgina, who bounded from behind the counter to greet her new victim. The little dog jumped and twirled in front of James.

"Aw, what a *charmer,*" James said as he reached down to pet Georgina. "Looks like you found a winner."

Elizabeth joined them at the counter and watched Georgina flirt with James. The big eyes, the kisses on his hand, the lack of flesh-tearing chomps — Georgina was giving a masterclass in wooing.

"Yeah, I just *love* dogs," Elizabeth said. She thought of the photo of Porter she'd just discovered. "Especially labs, they're my absolute favorite. Do you have a dog?"

"That's funny, I have a chocolate lab named Porter." James turned to Reid behind the counter. "Anyway, I need some caffeine, and I wanted to make sure you know about the Fizz at the Tups tonight. Harriet and Des are in."

Elizabeth crossed her arms and shuffled her feet as James chatted with Reid. Suddenly she was invisible. She reached for her phone in her back pocket so that she wouldn't look desperate and eavesdroppy, but it was still sitting on the table.

"Right, it's tonight!" Reid said, slapping his forehead. "I'll be there, but late. Bess here can probably go too." Reid nodded at her.

"So it's Bess, not Elizabeth?" James asked her.

"Her friends call her Bess, so you pick," Reid replied, answering for her.

She shrugged her shoulders. She didn't want to correct Reid and say that no one actually called her Bess in real life, she just wanted any version of her name on James's lips.

"Aren't you leaving?" James asked. "I thought this was just a quick stopover in Fargrove, then you're off to greener pastures."

"I'm staying on a bit to help with Trudy, at least through tomorrow afternoon." She shrugged again. It felt like she was waiting to be picked for the kickball team. "I'm around tonight." She wanted to sound casual but it came out desperate.

"By all means, stop by the Tups if you like. It's our friends' band. They're amazing."

It was a forced invitation, and normally she'd take the hint and opt out. But there was something about James Holworthy that made her forget the too-cool act that she faked so perfectly at home.

"Maybe I will, if Trudy and Rowan don't need me." She busied herself with Georgina, who immediately took Elizabeth's entire thumb in her mouth and bit down hard.

CHAPTER SIXTEEN

"I'm just so tired. I've barely slept," Trudy said as Rowan led her into the house later that afternoon. "All those machines beeping, and those relentless nurses checking in every five minutes. I want my bed."

Rowan looked exhausted as well. He stopped and turned to Elizabeth. "Bess, dear, would you put the kettle on so we can have a cuppa?"

"Of course," she replied before she realized what she'd gotten herself into.

The brilliant blue stove looked like nothing she'd seen in the States. There were four windowless doors on the front and two covered burners on top, without a knob in sight. The small nameplate said *Aga*, and she unconsciously reached for her phone in her back pocket to search for a how-to video, forgetting that it wasn't an option. Was she really so helpless that she couldn't even figure out how to boil water? At the very least she could fill the black checkered teapot and have it waiting for Rowan when he returned.

She placed the teapot on the counter and looked over at Major and Georgina playing in his bed by the sleeping fireplace. Her fears about their first meeting were pointless. Major had greeted Georgina with the patience of a kindergarten teacher, allowing nips on his ears, piercing barks, and every other type of youthful misbehavior that drove Elizabeth insane. Now, though, they were wrestling with each other in a way that was tipping into brawl territory. She considered trying to break them up but realized that she didn't have the confidence to get close when their teeth were snapping the air loud enough for her to hear.

She thought about Rowan helping Trudy to bed, likely exhausted himself and desperate for a proper cup of tea. She couldn't let the stove best her, so she walked back to the behemoth and stared at the covers on top of the burners. There were no knobs, nothing to twist or pull that she could see. She lifted the spiraled metal handle on the burner cover and passed her hand over the flat black burner.

Warmth!

The stove was always on, no need for

knobs. She triumphantly set the kettle on the burner and felt like she'd cooked a four-course meal.

Rowan returned to the kitchen right as the kettle started to fuss. Major lifted his head off Georgina's body and seemed to scan his person for feedback, debating whether Rowan needed his attention. Rowan pulled out a chair and slumped in it, making it clear that he was waiting for Elizabeth to pour the tea for him. Because of her parents she knew that tea prep was polarizing. She hoped that their preference for tea bag first, then hot water, steep, and then milk mirrored Rowan and Trudy's.

She handed the finished cup to Rowan.

He sip-slurped and smiled. "Lovely. Now, would you mind running one to Trudy? I just need to rest for a few moments."

She watched as Rowan leaned back in his chair and closed his eyes with one hand still on the teacup.

Trudy was propped up in bed and dozing with the lights on, looking like a doll beneath a lavish gray padded headboard. Elizabeth hovered in the doorway, unsure if she should enter or bring the tea back downstairs. The scene in the bedroom was too familiar, too painfully evocative. The bottles of pills on the nightstand next to a glass of water. The sleeping figure with a slack mouth, head lolled to the side. She tiptoed in and placed the cup on the crowded nightstand, and the almost imperceptible click of porcelain hitting wood was enough to rouse Trudy.

"Oh, hello, dear," she said groggily. The pain medication was doing its job.

"Tea," Elizabeth whispered, pointing to the cup.

"Grand, thank you." She closed her eyes, and Elizabeth turned to leave. "Bess, dear?"

Elizabeth returned to her bedside. "I'm here."

Trudy's eyes were closed as she spoke. "I wish you could've known your cousin. I wish we all could've known him. Our little bird."

Elizabeth didn't know how to respond. Cousin? She tried to formulate an appropriately vague reply, but Trudy was snoring quietly before she could find the right words.

When she returned to the kitchen, Rowan had Georgina on his lap and Major at his feet.

"She's sleeping," Elizabeth said.

Rowan nodded and continued massaging Georgina's shoulders. "You've got a lovely little pup here." When Georgina spotted

Elizabeth she leapt from his lap and ran to her.

"Oh, I can't keep her," Elizabeth said as she sidestepped the tornado of teeth and claws. "With my schedule I don't have time to take care of a puppy."

"Well, it sounds to me like your life has changed quite a bit in recent weeks," he replied.

"It has, but I'm still very busy." She bristled at the reminder of her firing. "I spent most of today working on my new project."

"Ah yes, Reid's little computery thing. Related to that subject, I'd like to ask a favor of you."

"Of course, what can I do?" She envisioned helping Rowan fix his printer or teaching him how to buy something online.

"I'd like to have a conversation with you in the Operculum tomorrow morning. Could you meet me there at nine?"

It felt like a formal invitation. Were they going to address the property financials? How much time would it buy her while she looked for a job?

"I'll be there."

"Lovely, thank you."

Rowan propped his head up on his hand on the table. Elizabeth watched him as he stared into space and mumbled a few words to himself. The stress of what he'd been through hung years on his frame, and for the first time, Rowan Barnes looked like an old man.

CHAPTER SEVENTEEN

Elizabeth hoped the faux leather leggings weren't too much for the pub. Fargrove forced her to consider the items in her suitcase with an eye toward comfort instead of couture, which made much of what she'd packed over-the-top for the community's "casual Friday" vibe. While she would never pair the leggings with a chambray shirt in normal circumstances, it was one of the few options left that didn't make her look like she was trying too hard.

The walk to town was pitch-black, lit only by a pinprick of a moon. When something shrieked in the bushes she regretted turning down Rowan's offer for a ride, but she didn't want to put any additional pressure on him. She was independent and self-reliant, and a few days in sleepy Fargrove wasn't going to change that about her. Elizabeth tried to convince herself that cows weren't nocturnal predators with a taste for human flesh as she used her phone's meager flashlight to illuminate the uneven road in front of her blister-inducing boots. Before she knew it she could see the hazy twinkle of town ahead of her.

A cluster of men stood outside the Three Tups smoking. The fat black dog she'd seen on her first day was resting at their feet. The men were all ages, from downy-faced teens to stooped white-haired gentlemen, and they greeted her warmly as she walked up, almost as if they'd been expecting her. More than likely they'd read the dossier titled "An American Barnes in Fargrove: Similar Nose" that seemed to be circulating. A middle-aged man pulled the door open for her with a bow and she mumbled a thank-you as she waved her hand to part the thick smoke.

The pub was packed and every available stool, bench, and wood-paneled wall had a body on it. All eyes were fixed on the group of musicians sitting on a cluster of chairs at the far end of the room, not up on a stage or set apart from the crowd, but elbow to elbow with them. It wasn't what Elizabeth had been expecting when she envisioned going to see a band.

She scanned the room for Harriet or Des, hoping that she could latch onto them like

190

a life raft as she worked up the courage to talk to James again. She envisioned best-case scenarios. He'd seek her out and they'd spend the evening laughing and chatting together. Maybe they'd even make out a little, if she got drunk enough to stop her mini panic attacks. But then what? She was leaving the next day. She was sure to discover that James was even more perfect than she'd imagined, and all she'd have to show for it would be memories and a new follower.

For the first time in a long time, she needed more.

One of the musicians finished telling a story that she couldn't hear, and the group raised their instruments; a guitar, a violin, a banjo, a cylindrical accordion about the size of a loaf of bread, and a small flute. The band members were handsome, heavily tattooed, long-haired guys who wouldn't look out of place helming any paradigm-shifting start-up in San Fran. Elizabeth backed into the crowd along the wall so she could take in the music while watching for Harriet.

The first notes sounded familiar, but she couldn't place the song. Then a wave of goose bumps rippled along her arms, as involuntary as the flail from a doctor's hammer to the knee. The moment the guitar player started singing, the memories flooded back.

A North Country maid up to London has
   strayed
Although with her nature it did not agree.

"The Oak and the Ash," her mother's favorite English folk song. The band's version was slower and grittier than what she was used to, like something that might be played on a coffeehouse radio station. She hadn't heard it in at least twenty years, but the words were as familiar as a Christmas carol. Her mother had once told her that she felt like the girl in the song but hadn't explained why. Years later, after reading the lyrics, Elizabeth understood. Her mother was homesick for England.

The song conjured her mother in a way that no photo could, and Elizabeth was flooded with a memory of her singing it as she ironed her father's shirts. She could see her mother's nimble fingers rhythmically smoothing the sleeves three times before she set the iron down, and hear her voice straining as she reached for the high notes. Her encouraging nods when Elizabeth joined in. The way they sounded as they sang the ancient words together.

Elizabeth blinked fast to keep her eyes from welling up. What was it with all the tears in Fargrove? She'd always prided herself on her broken tear ducts, even when faced with Cecelia's blame-y tirades, but now it felt like she was crying every fifteen minutes. She pulled her phone out of her back pocket. No service. She considered pretending she was using it to distract from the feelings bubbling inside her but instead shoved it back in her pocket. She looked around the room at the rest of the people and noticed that not a single cell phone was casting a blue glow amid the warm light from the sconces. Every eye was trained on the actual musicians instead of a five-inch window of them.

The band worked together like a chain and gear, swaying in time with eyes shut, feeling every note as they performed it. Elizabeth bit hard on the inside of her cheek and looked down at her feet as the four-hundred-year-old song ended. Hearing it as an adult with the modern arrangement made the song's lament — and her mother's — that much more obvious. For a second after it ended no one moved, still in the thrall of the singer's final clear note. Then the room erupted in cheers, and Elizabeth found herself clapping so hard that her hands smarted.

Someone grasped her shoulder. "Fancy a pint, sweetheart?" It was Harriet. She wrapped Elizabeth in a tight hug. "So nice to see you again!"

Harriet's husband, Des, sidled up next to her and handed her a pint. "We saw you from across the room and you looked very serious. Thought you could use this," Des said.

Their kindness caught her off guard. "Thank you, next round is on me," she said, holding up her pint in a toast.

"I've never said no to a free drink, ta!" Des said as they clinked glasses.

"Look, there's a space at the Tolberts' table," Harriet interrupted, eyeing open seats near the band. She was on her way before they had a chance to answer her, using her belly to part the crowd.

Harriet pushed the dirty glasses on the table aside and rearranged the chairs so that they could all fit. Harriet gestured to the other couple, a handsome man with a close-cropped gray beard and an equally handsome woman, with shoulder-length black hair, blue eyes, and an English rose complexion. "Bess, this is Willard and Anna Tolbert. Bess is Rowan's niece."

"We heard you were visiting! Nice to meet

you. So Trudy is home now, yes? How is she?" Anna asked.

"She's on pain medication and resting, but she seems much better. And you can call me Elizabeth, actually."

"Glad she's doing well," Anna said. "We adore her. And Rowan. They're treasures. How long will you be staying with them?"

"Only until tomorrow afternoon, unfortunately. Duty calls at home," she lied.

The music kicked up again and it was impossible to talk with the band so close. This time the song was a rollicking jig alluding to what Welshmen do with their sheep when no one is around. Two men stood up and started dancing, and soon the whole room was clapping and stomping their feet. Elizabeth sat with her arms crossed, watching the action like an anthropologist regarding an undiscovered tribe. Des leaned over to her and pulled her arms apart, and with her hands cupped in his, he clapped in time to the music.

When Des finally let go of her hands Elizabeth pulled out her phone to snap a photo. Captured in the glow of sconces and dim ceiling lights, the band looked album-cover-worthy. Elizabeth envisioned the likes and compliments (*excellent composition!*) that would come pouring in after she posted it.

Willard saw her phone and gave her a stricken look. He shook his head and mimed putting it away.

"They're not allowed in here," Des said, shouting into her ear above the noise. "The publican noticed that people weren't talking to each other anymore, so he banned them about a year ago. And look" — he gestured around the room — "we're all still here. Turns out we *can* live without those things for a few hours after all!"

"Here's to that," Willard shouted, raising his glass.

Elizabeth felt her phone buzz defiantly in her back pocket as the band went on break. Now she had service, in a spot that didn't allow phones? It buzzed again, like a cranky baby.

"I have to grab this," she lied again. "I'll be back."

She ducked through the crowd and past a different group of smoking men clustered around the door. She leaned into the shadows under the eaves so that she could see the screen. There were two insistent texts from her temporary Airbnb guests, sent twenty minutes apart, wondering when the cleaners were going to show up since they had a sink full of dishes. She messaged the cleaning service and replied to the renters like a concerned concierge, then quickly checked her social media accounts. Her spotty activity was still killing her response rates, so she knelt and snapped a photo of the black pub dog sitting at the smokers' feet, framing it from the knees down. She labeled it #faithfulcompanion and posted it on Instagram, then hopped on Twitter to post a photo of Georgina from the previous day. Anyone scrolling through her feed was sure to notice the sudden uptick in dog content. Maybe that was why she was losing ground? But who didn't like dogs?

Elizabeth sped through her feed, looking for things to quickly favorite and repost, and jammed her finger on the screen when she saw the face. It was Cecelia with her faux modest head tilt and pout-grin, featured in a *Time* magazine article. She had won the Maria Mitchell Arts and Sciences Award and was to be honored in a glittery ceremony at the Smithsonian. Elizabeth's hands shook as she processed the news.

Cecelia never stopped winning. No matter that every innovation she claimed was the product of hundreds of anonymous worker bees, it was always her name on the trophy and her face in the photos. Elizabeth sped through the article. Mentions of Cecelia's volunteer work (which was actually forcing her employees to financially support or perform labor for whatever cause caught her eye), her strong ties to inner-city schools (via loaner tablets crawling with Entomon), and her devotion to the career of motherhood (thanks to two nannies and a chef).

Then it hit her. The timing of the award gave Elizabeth more than enough time to select her source to leak the photo. They would break the story the morning of the ceremony, so that Cecelia was in D.C. and far away from her troops. Elizabeth imagined the hotel room scramble as the news trickled in, with Cecelia's road minions screaming into their phones while Cecelia stormed around her luxury suite in a silk kimono.

It was such a delicious vision that Elizabeth felt the urge to buy a round for everyone in the pub, until she remembered her unemployed status. But not for long. She leaned against the wall and stared up at the twinkly sky that seemed closer than she'd ever noticed, then headed back inside.

CHAPTER EIGHTEEN

"He asked about you," Harriet shouted into Elizabeth's ear over the noise of the band. "The night of Rowan's party."

"Who? Reid?" Elizabeth tried to hide her disappointment. She'd have to walk the fine line of discouraging his interest without damaging his ego as she worked with him.

Harriet made a funny face. "Reid? He's been with Nicky for ages. You are *definitely* not his type." She laughed. "No, James Holworthy. He wanted to know all about you."

"What . . . what was he asking about?"

"Everything. Your name, why you're in Fargrove, if I thought you were nice, how long you're staying. The full download."

Elizabeth stared at Harriet with her mouth hanging open.

"So, you're interested?"

"I mean, he's . . . uh, I think . . ."

"Yeah, I know. Heartthrob central. I'd dump my baby daddy in an instant for a piece of that." She rubbed her stomach.

"Is he coming tonight?"

"He's been here all night! Back corner."

Elizabeth craned her neck and scanned the pub.

"I need to warn you, though," Harriet said. "He doesn't do long distance. He got burned by a French girl a few years ago, so he's strictly home-turf these days. You might get a quick snog out of it but don't fall too hard."

Too late.

Elizabeth didn't want anything quick with James Holworthy. She wanted time to stop so she could examine his beautiful face and explore whatever was under the blazers he always seemed to be wearing. She wanted to hear him call her any derivative of her name in his sexy voice. She'd answer to "Lizzie" if he was the one saying it.

"Look at that lovesick face. Oh, come on, then." Harriet grabbed Elizabeth's hand and dragged her out of the chair.

Elizabeth trailed behind her helplessly, watching people clear the way as Harriet plowed through the crowd to a hidden table at the far end of the pub, ending up in front of James and another man engrossed in conversation.

"James, you need to teach this American

about good beer. She's drinking Carling, for fuck's sake." Harriet nudged Elizabeth closer to the table so hard that her beer sloshed.

"Is that right," James said, eyeing the pint glass in Elizabeth's hand. Once again he looked like a street-style post with a shadow of stubble, white T-shirt, and an unbuttoned tan shirt over the top of it. And the green eyes that were locked on hers. "That's a crime given that this fine establishment has three of ours. Please join us." He scooted over to make room for them. He pointed at the guy with a rugby physique sitting next to him. "Ladies, this is Adam Phillips, he makes the Lost Dog Brewery magic happen."

"Hey, we've met." Harriet nodded at him. "Actually, Adam, Des is interested in doing some home brewing. Could you give him advice? We're right over there." She pointed across the room.

"Love to," Adam said, out of his seat before she could finish asking the question. "We've just gotten some incredible Belgian ale yeast I'd be happy to share . . ." He continued talking as he moved away.

Harriet glanced over her shoulder at Elizabeth and winked as she followed Adam through the crowd.

"That'll be the end of him for the night," James said. "Mr. Chatty Man won't shut up about brewing." Elizabeth was still standing next to the table, mute and wide-eyed. "Sit, please. Allow me to introduce you to some of my Lost Dog favorites."

Elizabeth opted to scoot in beside James on the bench instead of taking a seat across from him. Two drinks in and she was feeling bold.

"What kind of beer do you normally drink?"

"To be honest I usually *don't* drink beer. I'm more of a cosmo or martini person, but I didn't think that would fly in a pub."

"I'm going to pretend I didn't hear that," James replied, shaking his head. "Let's go about this a different way: if you had to pick, pale beer or dark beer?"

"Pale?"

"Right, that's a start. Do you like a wheaty taste?"

Elizabeth made an apologetic face and shrugged her shoulders.

"So you're an absolute beginner. Let's get to work, then. Try this." He handed her a cloudy amber-filled pint.

Elizabeth took the glass, purposely letting her fingers brush his. He watched her expectantly as she took a sip.

"Delicious." Elizabeth couldn't actually taste a thing, not while he was studying her so closely. The sound of the band and the crowd were reduced to a distant hum, and even though the light was dim it looked like James was illuminated by a spotlight.

He grinned like she'd just awarded him with a blue ribbon. "Excellent! That's our Husky Hefeweizen. It's quite good, but you've also got to try our Mad Dog Biters and our Yellow Dog Pale Ale. We've got forty-eight beers total, two ciders, and a few seasonals we swap out."

"So they all have dog names?" It was a stupidly obvious question, but she couldn't think of anything else to say.

"In one form or another, yes. Speaking of dogs, how's that pup of yours? Georgina, was it?"

"Oh, she's not mine, I'm just taking care of her for a bit. But she's good. I mean, she bites me a ton. I'm not sure she actually likes me." Elizabeth showed James the tiny wounds on her hands and forearms, hoping he'd take her hands in his to examine them. He studied them from a distance.

"That's normal puppy stuff. I remember those days with Porter."

Elizabeth was shocked that he almost sounded wistful.

"I must admit, I caught a little puppy fever when I met her," he added.

She wished he'd caught Elizabeth fever instead. "You'd get a second dog?"

"Yeah, it might be time. Porter could use a buddy." He pointed to the beer sitting in front of her. "Drink up, you've got more sampling to do."

Elizabeth obliged, taking three huge gulps. It was easier to drink than try to think of clever things to say to James. She could feel an unfamiliar wooziness coming on, which made her want to scoot closer to him and find excuses to touch him. She finished the Husky and slammed the glass on the table.

"Whoa, I guess you're a convert now," James said with an appreciative laugh. "Now let me get you a Yellow Dog. I'll be right back, wait here."

Elizabeth watched him walk away, noting how gracefully he threaded through the crowd despite his size. A back touch here, a shoulder pat there, and each person he passed turned and smiled when they saw who it was. She couldn't tell if he knew everyone in the room or if they could feel his vibe as strongly as she could and stepped aside in awe to let the godlike creature pass.

"Mission accomplished, Bess," she heard someone say.

It was Reid, grinning at her like a school-boy.

"Exchuse me?" she slurred.

"That was no market research you were doing. I know a good stalking when I see one." He slid into the chair across from her.

"Not at all, we're just talking beer," Elizabeth answered, hoping that Reid would leave before James came back. Even if there was a "Nicky" in his life, she didn't want James to think there was anything brewing with Reid.

"I wouldn't waste your last evening in Fargrove on that one. James Holworthy is picky as hell." Reid seemed to realize the insult after it was out. "No offense, I'm sure you have a lot to offer."

"I'm just . . . *drinking.* That's all. It's fine." Reid was still trying to find an angle with her, with or without a girlfriend. "So where's Nicky?"

"Somewhere around here," Reid replied, looking around the pub. "There." He pointed at a group of people a few feet away.

The woman had long brown hair with perfect beachy waves and amazing cheekbones, and she was wearing a preppy collared shirt beneath a pale blue sweater. Elizabeth could envision her in an #outfitoftheday Insta post. She was adorable, which made Elizabeth even angrier that Reid was flirting with her instead of attending to his perfectly lovely girlfriend.

"Have you two met?" Reid asked.

"We haven't. Please introduce us." The two beers she'd downed plus the Husky were taking hold and the word came out as "introdushe." She desperately wanted Reid to stop vying for her attention and hoped that being in close proximity to his girlfriend would actually remind him that he *had* a girlfriend.

Reid cupped his hands around his mouth and shouted. "Nicky!"

A handsome bearded man in a knit hipster cap and glasses turned around abruptly, then waved at Reid.

"C'mere." Reid beckoned the man over.

Elizabeth shrank in her seat, thankful for the dim room so that Reid couldn't see the mortification on her face. Was she *that* rusty at dating, to think that a happily paired-off gay man was flirting with her? She mentally scrolled through their past interactions in light of the new information and realized that nothing he'd said or done even remotely resembled interest. He'd been teasing her like a brother. She wasn't only bad at flirting, she was bad at friendship.

"So you're Bess the American Barnes,"

Nicky said, reaching out to shake her hand. "I'm Anik Sarkar, but everyone around here calls me Nicky. Childhood pet name."

"I feel your pain, I'm actually Elizabeth," she replied, taking his hand.

"But her friends call her Bess," James said as he joined them, two overflowing pints in hand.

"So what's going on here?" Nicky asked. "You trying to weaken her defenses with that stuff?"

"No, I'm trying to educate this pondwater drinker. Join us."

An hour later their table was crowded with empty glasses and Elizabeth was even deeper in the thrall of Lost Dog Brewing Company's most persuasive salesman. James didn't just describe the beers, he composed poetry about each one. He paid special attention to the beer's scent, trying to get her to notice citrus or fruity notes. He commented on the beers' color, the way they poured, whether they were "sessionable," their mouthfeel, and the lace they left on the sides of the glass. He lamented the fact that the Tups hadn't brought in Lost Dog's new saison, which was flavored with honey from Reid's hives.

Elizabeth giggled every time James said *mouthfeel*. She was surprised how much she enjoyed learning about beer and sampling it as he watched her. She tried to remain blasé and prettily posed as the evening progressed, but the potent beers were more than she was used to. She didn't know where to put her hands or how to sit. When it was finally time for her to hit the ladies' room she pitched forward as she stood up, knocking over a glass. James caught it with one hand before it hit the ground.

"Bess, you're a hazard to glassware." Reid laughed, recalling their first meeting.

"Sorry," she slurred. "Excuse me for . . . one . . . moment." She held up a finger as she tilted back and forth.

Elizabeth felt James's eyes on her as she walked away, so she arched her back and attempted to sway her hips, which made her trip on her own feet and collide with a man about to sip from his pint. When she finally reached the ladies' room she realized that she was sorority-girl drunk. She wanted to laugh hard, and hug strangers, and dance like everyone was watching. She couldn't stop smiling. James was talking to her, and he'd touched her three times! He definitely liked her. It didn't matter what Harriet and Reid had said, or that she was leaving tomorrow. James Holworthy liked her and she wasn't going to leave Fargrove without proof.

She remembered that her phone was actually working and tripped her way through the crowd to get back outside where she could connect without getting in trouble. She leaned against a side door and flipped through her socials again. A few new likes and reposts on the dog shot, but not enough. She realized that the door behind her was a pretty bright red with Gothic iron fixings, so she reversed her phone and checked the light. It was dim so she looked close to perfect. Elizabeth steadied the phone and twisted her head back and forth until she found an angle that worked and pouted her lips. She took a second shot with a giant smile.

"So you're one of those people," she heard a voice in the shadows say to her.

James. She stood up straighter and flipped her hair over her shoulder.

"One of what people?"

"One of those duck-lips social media people."

"Oh my God, I *never* do duck lips and I barely post shelfies. Selfies, I mean."

James stepped into the light. "Are you okay? You seem a little . . . unsteady. I just wanted to make sure you didn't pass out in a ditch out here."

"I'm fine. I'm barely even tipsy," she lied.

"I don't believe you," James said. He walked closer and sat on the edge of an oversized planter, balancing on it in a way that would be awkward for any other mortal. He looked like he was stretched out on a throne.

"You should follow me on my socials. That way we can, you know, keep in touch after I leave." It felt as bold as asking for his phone number.

"Sorry, can't do it."

Elizabeth shrank into the shadows. "That's okay. No problem."

"No, I mean, I don't have Instagram, or Facebook, or any of it. I'd rather live my life than perform it."

"Ouch," Elizabeth replied, and swayed a little. She slapped her hand against the wall to hide her unsteadiness.

"Hey, everyone is different. What do you say in America? 'You do you'?"

"I'd rather do you," Elizabeth slurred under her breath.

"Pardon?" James laughed.

"I mean, I'd rather live my life too, but I have followers that expect me to post stuff, constantly. And doing it in Fargrove is next to impossible because you guys have crappy service."

"What would happen if you just . . . stopped? Would the hordes come banging down your door? Would there be outcry if Bess Barnes didn't post what she ate for breakfast?"

"No, but then I wouldn't matter. I'd be invisible. No one would see me." She was too tipsy to realize the weight of what she'd said.

James leaned back and crossed his arms, not taking his eyes off Elizabeth. She couldn't tell if all the alcohol was slowing time or if the pause was as endless as it felt.

"*I* see you, Bess."

In that instant she realized that it was happening. The moment when everything around them went out of focus. Elizabeth could feel his eyes searing her. There was no doubt he saw her — he could probably see *through* her. Something radiated from him, a gravitational pull that she couldn't resist. The warmth in his voice made her legs go numb and her head feel even fuzzier. Elizabeth knew what had to happen next.

She launched herself at him.

She tried to make it sexy and feline, like a huntress capturing her prey, but instead landed awkwardly sprawled in his lap with her arms pawing at the back of his neck.

She reached up to pull his head down to meet her lips as she struggled to gain her footing and push herself closer to his beautiful face. He caught her before she tumbled to the ground and she felt him bring her closer, his arms wrapping around her like the beginning of a real embrace. She closed her eyes and readied herself for the moment when their lips would touch, hoping that the breath mint she'd popped in the bathroom was still working.

The moment never came. She opened her eyes, still encircled in his heavenly arms, and stared up at his face.

"Why won't you kish me?"

"Bess, not like this," he replied, gently pushing a strand of hair away from her eyes. He stroked her back as he adjusted his grip, and it felt like he'd lit a fuse in her spine. "Why don't we just be happy that we met and leave it at that? Thank you for listening to my silly beer talk. But maybe you shouldn't have enjoyed quite so many." He still hadn't let her go.

"I'm fine, though! I'm totally fine! Let's just try to kish, for one second. I think it'll be good. No, it'll be *great.* You'll see. Let's just . . . try. Pretty please? Please, please, please?" She closed her eyes and moved toward his mouth but ended up kissing the stubbly underside of his chin. He smelled like campfire.

"It's not going to happen tonight." He lowered his voice and stared into her eyes. "You're drunk, you won't remember anything. And if I were to kiss you, I'd want you to remember every second of it."

Elizabeth's mouth dropped open. "Oh . . ."

James put two strong hands on her arms and raised her into a seasick stance. "Now, how are you going to get back to Rowan's? Did you get dropped off?"

"I walked!" Elizabeth shouted, raising an arm in victory that pitched her off balance. "Like a boss!"

"We'll take her," Reid said, walking through the courtyard with Nicky. "It's on our way."

"Thank you, guys," James said, watching Elizabeth to make sure she was capable of remaining on her feet. "Fun night. Bess, it was a pleasure meeting you. I hope you have a wonderful life. Be good to Georgina."

It wasn't supposed to end this way. He was supposed to kiss her like in the movies. Even in her sloppy state she could tell that James wanted to kiss her as badly as she wanted to kiss him.

Elizabeth leaned against Reid as they

walked to his car. She still had something she wanted to say to James, something he needed to know. She didn't want to say it, but she felt like she had to. They were the most important words that had ever entered her brain.

"James!" she screamed.

He was about to walk back into the Tups and turned to her with his hand on the doorknob.

"James Holworthy, I think you're falling in love with me!"

CHAPTER NINETEEN

Elizabeth groaned. Puppies didn't care about hangovers, and Georgina flip-flopped on the bed beside her making little growly noises and biting at every human-shaped lump under the blankets. She remembered little from the end of the previous night other than downing a million beers with the most perfect man on the planet, and Reid and Nicky helping her find her way home.

She managed to pull herself together and force a cup of tea down her throat so that she could make it to the Operculum at nine sharp. There was no way Rowan could know how sloppy she'd been the night before, although falling up the stairs as she tried to get to her room might have clued him in. She cradled her head in her hand as she plodded down the lane and hoped that Trudy wasn't watching from her bedroom window. Major and Georgina trailed behind her, tackling each other and making noises that sounded like gang violence.

Elizabeth paused outside the door. Should she just walk in? She knocked.

"Enter," came Rowan's muffled reply.

She slid the door open and the screech startled Georgina, causing her to backpedal halfway across the courtyard. Major dashed over to Georgina and sat down next to her so that they were flank-to-flank, like a senior officer girding a young recruit for battle.

"Georgina, it's okay. It's just a door, you're fine!" Elizabeth rapped on the door with her knuckles as if to prove that it wasn't a threat. "It's all good, you can do this. You're a brave little lady, I know you are!"

Rowan stood just inside, watching as Georgina walked slowly to where Elizabeth was kneeling.

"For someone who doesn't know dogs, you certainly have fine instincts. Most people coddle scared pups, but you're jolly-ing her through her fears."

"It was the mantra of my youth. My father didn't suffer weakness." Georgina crept to her cartoon-style, extending each paw out tentatively and placing it on the ground as if it were made of molten lava.

Rowan considered this brief character sketch of his brother and then beckoned them in. "Please, sit," he said pointing to a stool next to his easel. Georgina followed Major around the studio as he ran from one end to the other, poking his nose in every corner.

"Field mice," Rowan explained. "They've got bolt-holes all over this barn. Major's going to teach your wee one to be a hunter like he is."

Elizabeth perched on the stool and looked at Rowan's work in progress. The landscape was typical of his exacting style but felt different in a way that she couldn't describe. The sky was a moody mix of purples and blues except for the moon, which punctuated the horizon like a streetlamp. She couldn't tell if the painting was depicting nightfall or dawn. The trees on the left side of the image looked skeletal, and the water mirroring the scene was ringed with algae. She could appreciate his precision and the way he invoked the rule of thirds both horizontally and vertically, but she couldn't say that she liked the painting. It looked haunted.

"What do you think?" Rowan asked as he tucked a thin paintbrush behind his ear.

"It's very good," she replied, ever the politician. "It's not like the rest, though. It's . . . I don't know how to put it in words."

"Sad?"

"Yes, I guess it is."

Rowan didn't say anything and leaned in close to his painting, so that his nose was just inches from the canvas. He pulled the paintbrush from behind his ear, slipped his glasses down from the top of his head, and contorted his arm so that his elbow pointed to the ceiling. He added something so minuscule that Elizabeth couldn't even see it.

"I never had the patience for realistic work," she said quietly as she watched him.

Rowan pushed his glasses back up on his head and looked at her in shock. "You *paint*?"

"Not in years. Not since high school. But I used to love it."

"Oh, Bess, that makes the reason you're here even more perfect! I knew that you were one of us. You come from a long line of makers. Painting, poetry, weaving — it's in our blood."

Our blood. It was unsettling and comforting at the same time. She wasn't alone.

"Would you consider painting with me?" Rowan continued, the words coming in a rush. "I have another easel, and I could set you up over there, where the light is best. I have everything you need. If you paint with oils, that is. What is your medium?"

"I used oils as well, but I don't think I can anymore. I barely remember how to hold a brush. And I don't want you to go through any trouble. I'm leaving, remember?"

"Yes, about that," Rowan said. "That's why I've invited you here this morning. I'd like to make you an offer."

"An offer?"

"Look around this studio. You noticed it the first time you came in, it's a floor-to-ceiling jumble. The time has come for me to organize, consolidate, and take stock. The retrospective has me feeling like I've got one foot in the grave, and I need to figure all of this out before it's too late." He gestured around the room helplessly.

Elizabeth wasn't sure how to answer. " 'Too late'? That's really depressing, Rowan."

"Well, it might be depressing but it's a fact. And Trudy's fall made it all the more obvious. The reality is I simply can't do the inventorying and condition reports on my own. My gallery would happily send someone to help, but that would turn my Operculum into a factory and make me a slave to deadlines. I don't want to tell them about my plans until I'm finished, so they can't boss me around. I need to work slowly, at my own pace. With someone like you." He paused. "Bess, would you help me catalog my life's work?"

Elizabeth couldn't understand what he was asking, or why. "But . . . I'm leaving, Rowan," she reminded him again. "I have to get back to the real world. To my job." She'd barely been in Fargrove for a week but the way she was losing ground at home made it feel like ages.

He cleared his throat and seemed to consider his words before speaking. "Do you have to get back, though? Pardon my saying this, but you're between jobs right now, yes? And what I'm offering, being my registrar, is a job. Temporary, certainly, but well-paying. And it's interesting work, I assure you. We might find a few nudes hidden in these stacks." He winked at her.

It was impossible. Impossible. Fargrove was sucking the life from her socials, and she couldn't commit to finding a job while she was halfway around the world in the land of spotty Wi-Fi. It felt like if she stayed in Fargrove much longer she'd disappear completely.

"I can't, Rowan."

"May I ask why not?" he probed gently.

"I have a life in San Francisco. And . . .

and, *projects.*" She thought of the photo of Cecelia waiting in the cloud like a sleeping dragon.

"Yes, you've told me. You were working on them at HiveMind, correct?"

"I worked for three hours," she answered.

"Indeed. And you were able to make progress?"

"Tons. Reid's is well under way. And I've been working on a, uh, personal project as well."

"So you accomplished work while in Fargrove?"

"I did, and —" She stopped herself. Rowan's Socratic method had backed her into a corner that she couldn't maneuver out of. The senior citizen had just schooled the tech whiz about working remotely.

"You see, my dear, it's all quite simple. You help me in the mornings, from eight till lunch, then you're free to do your computer work for as long as you like. And as for pay, we're not in London, but you'll be doing London-level archiving, so your compensation will reflect that. It will be well worth your time."

"Rowan, I know nothing about inventorying art," she replied, still hoping to convince him that it was a ridiculous idea. "I don't even know what a registrar *does.* I'm sorry, it's just not a fit for me."

He paused and then answered quietly. "I know you're capable, and I know that no one else can help me with this but you."

There was a weight to his words that she didn't understand. She couldn't say no without finding a more concrete reason.

Georgina stood up and pawed at Elizabeth, once again aware of the change in the atmosphere. She leaned down and touched the top of Georgina's head, and the little puppy's eyes darted between Rowan and Elizabeth like a spectator at a tennis match, keen to the crackling electricity between them.

"How long do you think it would take?" Anything he said would be too long, which would be her perfect reason to decline.

"That's entirely up to us. If we commit to a daily slog, then I think we could finish within a month or so. But if we detour occasionally, perhaps to pick up a paintbrush and throw some color on a canvas, well, then it might take a tad longer." He pulled the paintbrush from behind his ear again and pretended to flick it across his painting Jackson Pollock style. He grinned at her as if he could tell he was winning.

A month.

Her options played out in her mind in

quick cuts. Home, to an empty apartment and the daily battle to appear busier than she was, or Fargrove, where she could curate a life online that looked far more glamorous and important than it actually was. She envisioned photos of her sitting on the ground surrounded by Rowan's paintings, staring off into the distance. Maybe she could do something special with *Sunset over Blenheim*? It was a chance to cultivate an entirely new audience and amp her growth back up, especially when she started posting shots of Rowan's unseen works with #BarnesUnreleased in the description.

And maybe she could find a way to get through to James Holworthy while she was there.

"All right, one month. I'll do it. As long as you promise that I'll have time to focus on my real work."

"Splendid!" Rowan clapped his hands together, startling Georgina and Major. "Trudy will be thrilled, and I imagine this little lady will as well."

Elizabeth looked down at Georgina, who was playing tug-of-war with a rag trapped beneath the leg of the stool. "You win, monster, you get to bite me for a little bit longer."

CHAPTER TWENTY

"I'm chuffed to bits you're staying on, Bess," Harriet said. She took her eyes completely off the narrow road and stared at Elizabeth, waiting for her to answer while the car swerved to the other lane. The dancing hula figurine on her dashboard looked like she was twerking.

"It's going to be interesting, that's for sure," she replied, gripping tighter to the armrest as Harriet rounded a corner on two tires. It didn't matter that her belly nearly touched the steering wheel, Harriet drove like a teenage boy. "I had to do some major juggling back home to make it happen."

"I'm sure. And now you're going high class with your temporary wardrobe. Sainsbury's to the rescue. But you'll be crawling around an old barn so it won't matter what you're wearing. Might as well save a few quid."

After a few days of prep work with Rowan,

Elizabeth quickly realized that the casual outfits she'd packed were still far too dressy for the barn. When she'd mentioned it to Rowan he'd picked up the phone and called Harriet before even asking Elizabeth if she wanted to go. Rowan and Harriet negotiated pick-up and drop-off times as if Elizabeth were a child needing a ride to daycare, while Trudy quietly explained to Elizabeth that the hybrid grocery chain was a fine spot to pick up additional knickers and knockabout clothes for the dirty job ahead.

"So what happened with James at the Tups? You two looked like you were having a great time drinking the bar dry."

"We were, but I blacked out a little at the end of the night. Reid and Nicky joined us and we kept drinking, and then I don't remember much after that. Was I dancing on tables or anything?"

"Not that I saw. You looked like a well-mannered if slightly wobbly American. What's next with him now that you're staying on for a bit?"

"Probably nothing. I don't think he's interested." Elizabeth had a vague memory of James pushing her away but couldn't recall the details.

"Oh, come on. He couldn't stop staring at you the whole night. Let's have some fun with it. How about I host a little do at our place and invite the two of you and the Tolberts. Are you up for that?"

"Really?"

"We have parties all the time, it'll be the perfect cover, and then you can work your magic. You do have magic, don't you?" Harriet looked at Elizabeth over the top of her sunglasses.

"What do you mean?"

"Magic, woman! Are your feminine wiles in order? Is your flirt game strong? You don't have all the time in the world to make this happen."

"I don't have a flirt game. Maybe that's why I drank so much the other night."

"You're too cute to need liquid courage. I'll keep an eye on you. Just don't let James get going on his beers or you'll end up under a table again."

They arrived at the store and Harriet pulled a giant bag from the back seat. "Exchanges," she said, patting it. "Did you know that ultrasounds can be wrong? Turns out our little Imogen-to-be is actually an Ian-to-be. Can you even imagine our shock?"

"Unbelievable," Elizabeth answered. She realized that any other normal woman would've already asked the sex of the baby.

She struggled to find the right thing to say. "Are you disappointed?"

"My official answer is no, of course not, so long as he's healthy, and all that. My real answer? Fuck yes. I *know* girls. Poppy is a dream child and I want another just like her. I have no clue how to handle a boy! I'm having a really hard time coming to terms with it, honestly." Harriet's voice quavered.

"I'm sure you'll do fine. You'll be great, I mean," Elizabeth answered. It seemed like Harriet could successfully raise a pack of wolverines and look adorable while doing it.

"I've got no choice," Harriet answered as they entered the store. "He'll be here before we know it." She sighed. "I'm sure you have no desire to accompany me to the baby department, so let's take a half hour or so, gather our goods, then meet back here? Ring me if you need more time."

Elizabeth pulled her phone out of her back pocket and looked at it skeptically. "Amazing, I actually have service!"

"Enjoy it while you can, then. Good luck finding fashion in all of that teacher gear. I'm off."

Elizabeth immediately posted a close-up of an innocent-looking Georgina with her head resting on top of her front paws. Only she had to know that a second later Georgina launched at the phone and knocked it out of Elizabeth's hands like an angry starlet assaulting a paparazzo. A few likes trickled in, and she spent fifteen minutes giving reciprocal likes in the hopes that the algorithm would take note.

She peeked at Cecelia's Twitter feed. The last post was a close-up of Winston, who looked so unbelievably wrinkled and stained and drooly that it was hard to believe that pretty little Georgina was from the same species. But for the first time, Elizabeth could understand some of his appeal. Why had she never noticed how cute he looked with the tip of his tongue poking out of his mouth?

She smiled involuntarily when she saw the email from TechGeek waiting in her inbox. Elizabeth had ultimately settled on the site for the photo release because they promised her anonymity no matter how hard the Duchess lawyers threatened. Their long, carefully worded emails felt like a courtship, and after a half-dozen back-and-forths she finally revealed herself to them and sent the photo, making them promise not to unleash it until they had a solid strategy in place. This latest message was asking for even more details about Entomon. Elizabeth wanted to tell them to pump the brakes, but the site had assigned their best investigative journalist to the piece, and the woman seemed to want to know every detail as she assembled the story. Elizabeth couldn't decide what made her happier, taking Cecelia down or clearing her name and clawing her way back into her old life.

Elizabeth turned her attention back to shopping, settling on a few pairs of unbelievably cheap skinny jeans, simple tanks, and T-shirts, and added some sensible underwear and sports bras to the stack. Elizabeth mentally calculated the total purchase, something she hadn't done since college. She didn't want to spend more on her wardrobe than what she'd be paid working with Rowan and Reid.

A flash of yellow caught her eye as she headed to the checkout. It was a vintage-style dress covered in a ridiculous lemon print, with ruching across the bodice, thick straps, and a wide swirly skirt. It was happy and sunny and worlds apart from the black-is-the-new-black outfits she normally went for. She found her size and stuck it at the bottom of the stack before she could question why she was buying clothing in a store that also sold kitty litter.

She passed the pets section on her way to

the checkout, then made an abrupt turn back. The extra time in Fargrove meant that she would remain Georgina's keeper. Trudy had given Elizabeth some of Major's ancient hand-me-downs — the dog didn't suffer leashes — but the leather was stiff and crackled from age. The Sainsbury's options were cartoonishly cute, all pink and baby blue. She spotted a lone blackwatch plaid collar that seemed small enough and found a thin red leather leash to match it. She snagged a small bag of treats before heading to the checkout and wondered if she'd just taken the gateway drug that would lead her to becoming a crazy dog lady.

She checked her phone as she waited in line and noticed that she had a voice mail pending even though it hadn't rung. No one left messages unless something was really truly wrong. She dug her finger in her ear and listened as the cashier rang up her purchases.

"Elizabeth, dude, this is Carson Keller from VR Solutions. We talked at Mobile Expo for like a second and a half. Yo, sorry about how everything went down. Anyway, I wanna connect with you. Fantastic stuff on the horizon. Hit me back ASAP."

Elizabeth stared into space with her mouth hanging open.

VR Solutions had started out as a standard mobile gaming company, then had jumped on virtual reality technology long before anyone else. During their early years they were fierce competitors with Duchess, but once they moved to VR they were untouchable. Cecelia often made noises about getting into VR gaming and had a small department playing with the technology but didn't have anything to show for it outside of the occasional press release.

The phone call was an incredible sign. People would find out that he was interested, which meant that her shunning was about to end. Elizabeth didn't care if they planned to stick her in the farthest corner of their cube farm, it didn't matter if he was going to offer her a secretarial position, all she needed was an in. She told herself that Carson's rule-breaker reputation didn't matter. He was a tech-bro genius who had birthed enough innovation that most people looked past his frat-boy persona. Everyone at Duchess hated him.

Perfect.

She checked the date and was horrified to discover that the message had come in three days prior but had somehow gotten trapped in the Fargrove vortex before showing up in her phone. He probably thought she wasn't interested! It was just after three p.m., which meant that it was after seven in San Francisco. Elizabeth called him back before she could think twice. She got his voice mail.

"Hey, Carson, it's Elizabeth Barnes. I'm in the UK at the moment and I just got your message; the reception is really spotty where I'm staying. I'm so sorry for the delay. I'd love to chat, just name a time and I'll make it work."

She hugged the phone to her chest. Her rebound was beginning, and now she'd have even better cover when she took Cecelia down. No one would suspect that she was the photo source if she was back kicking ass in a new position with an even better company. It was all happening!

Harriet rolled up behind Elizabeth with an overflowing cart. "You found fashion, amazing!"

Elizabeth glanced at the bag sitting on the counter to make sure the lemon dress was buried at the bottom, as if it were as embarrassing as a box of hemorrhoid cream. "I'm going to be sporting some barn chic, that's for sure. And look at you, your cart overfloweth."

"Yeah, Des just got paid from a major gig, so I'm taking advantage of the money while it's here. A freelance journalist and vintage clothing store owner aren't exactly known for financial stability."

Elizabeth understood what that meant for the first time in her career. Though she was still a few months away from nightmares about being a bag lady, she could appreciate how disorienting and scary it felt to be without a stable income.

"I'm feeling particularly flush at the moment, so I'm taking you for lunch to celebrate your new position with Rowan. I won't hear a no," Harriet said as she waddled back to the car.

Elizabeth smiled at the words *new position*. The only new position that mattered to her was the one she was about to snag.

CHAPTER TWENTY-ONE

"I told you this wasn't going to be easy, Bess."

Rowan leaned against the wall with his arms crossed, smiling at Elizabeth as she walked around the studio with a cup of tea in one hand and her tablet in the other, looking more overwhelmed with each step. Major and Georgina trailed behind her like eager assistants. Working on the spreadsheet layout and talking about the process with Rowan over the prior few days had been easy, but now that it was time to start inputting the details of each work Elizabeth finally understood the full scope of what she was facing.

"I'm just in awe that there are so many. You've got paintings hidden everywhere. How fast do you paint?"

"In the old days I was a madman. Your aunt hated me for it, because I'd get the itch and keep going for hours on end.

Sometimes all through the night. Back then I was averaging about one finished work per week, plus a few smaller studies as well. Thanks to the fickle gods of art patronage, those little throwaway pieces are now valuable, so the drawers full of them need to be included in the inventory as well. It's overwhelming, I understand. And then there's this." He beckoned her to follow him through a small door on the far side of the barn.

Elizabeth peeked into the room. It was a quarter of the size of the main room, narrow, without windows and as tall as the rest of the barn. It was also crowded with paintings, but they were unlike anything in the other room.

"Portraits? You paint portraits too?"

"Used to. I haven't done one in over fifty years." Rowan walked around the room with his hands clasped behind his back. He stopped in front of a painting of a beautiful young woman hanging opposite the door like a sentry. "Do you recognize this gorgeous creature?"

Elizabeth moved closer to the painting to examine it. It was nothing like Rowan's typical exacting style and was painted with such looseness that she could see his brushstrokes. The colors were muted, as if it had been painted at twilight. The woman's dark hair spilled over her naked shoulders, which were just barely covered with rumpled white cloth she had clutched with one hand. Her chin was slightly lowered and her gaze at the viewer was direct beneath heavy eyes. Her eyebrow arched in a way that looked like she had just said something naughty. Her expression was so seductive that Elizabeth was almost embarrassed to look at it with Rowan standing behind her.

"That's my Trudy." He sighed. "The one that started it all. When your father saw it he knew exactly what was going on between us."

Elizabeth imagined her father discovering the painting. It must have broken his heart.

"Do you understand what all of this means?" Rowan gestured to the other portraits ringing the room.

"More to inventory?"

Rowan laughed. "Well, yes, of course. But this room is . . . newsworthy. I'm known as a landscape artist. The paintings in this room represent a different side of my work that the public, and more importantly, my collectors, don't know exists. There's sure to be great interest when these come to light."

"This is a big deal," Elizabeth said, almost

to herself. "Rowan, are you sure I should be the one to help you with this?"

"There's no one else I want beside me. You'll be fine, Bess."

She started to follow him out of the room and something streaked in front of her foot. Major followed closely behind it, with Georgina bringing up the rear.

"Mouse!" she screamed.

The dogs skidded, cartoon-style, into a stack of paintings and pushed their noses up against the canvases. Major whined and dug at them, and Georgina stood by watching him expectantly.

"Determined, yet perpetually unsuccessful," Rowan said. "I'm glad of it, I quite like those little things, even though they've nibbled holes in too many paintings to count."

Major raked his paw against the side of the canvases, trying to part them to get to the mouse. Georgina crowded beside him, snuffling between the paintings. Elizabeth watched until she couldn't take it and took a few halting steps toward the dogs.

"Major, stop!" He continued digging at the paintings and she looked at Rowan. "He's damaging them, get him to stop!"

"Look at you, already worried about preservation. You're a natural." Rowan chuckled. "Major, enough."

Major immediately turned to face them and plopped into a statue-like sit. Georgina ignored them and tried to force her nose between the canvases.

"I believe it's time for young Georgina to begin training. Trudy and William will help you with that. Now then, before we begin . . ." He trailed off and walked out of the small room. Elizabeth dutifully followed behind as he walked to a corner in the main barn next to a vine-covered window. He stopped in front of an easel equipped with a blank canvas and a set of brand-new paints and brushes beside it. Georgina leapt up to try to grab the rag hanging down from the table.

"Before we begin," he continued, "we paint. This canvas is yours, Bess."

The expanse of white looked gigantic and unfillable.

"Rowan, I . . ." She started to say *can't* but realized it would be rude. "Thank you."

"Sit, my dear. There's no pressure to do anything today. Settle into it slowly. Just let the brushes take you where they will. I'll be right over there if you need me. Do you mind if I play music?"

Elizabeth shook her head, imaging the calming classical that was about to fill the room. Instead, horns and drums surrounded her from speakers hidden in the eaves.

"Do you like Benny Goodman?"

"I don't know him."

"Well, then, you're about to get a musical education. Big band, swing, and a little bit of old jazz. Forgive my singing."

Elizabeth sat staring at the canvas as Rowan busied himself at his. She hadn't painted in years, and even in her peak she always found herself overwhelmed by the thought of touching the first dot of paint to the perfect field of white. She picked up one of the brushes Rowan had selected for her and examined it. The gleaming ebony handle tapered at the center and was tipped with firm, bright white bristles. She ran the brush along the back of her hand, trying to assess how the silky bristles would move the paint on the canvas. It was a quality brush, and she hated to envision the pristine handle and silver collar coated in careless layers of paint. Rowan had given her every brush she could possibly need and more, from a wisp with a few eyelash-like bristles at the end to a fat mushroom-shaped brush that was nearly as big as her fist, and every shape and size in between.

Rowan clearly enjoyed the pageantry of new supplies, and had laid out the tubes of paint in color order, starting with three shades of white on the left side of the table and working through various yellows, oranges, reds, blues, and greens to a wall of browns and blacks on the right. The variety of colors was extravagant. Back in her painting days, Elizabeth could create any hue imaginable using just the primary colors. She was both touched by Rowan's generosity and slightly insulted that he thought she wasn't capable of mixing.

She looked around the room for inspiration, and then, as if no time had passed, felt compelled to mix colors. Her fingers moved as if directed by an invisible puppeteer, squeezing the paint from the tubes onto the round porcelain palette. She quickly filled half of the twelve wells, mixing some colors with the palette knife and using others straight from the tube.

She knew immediately that the resulting colors were perfect, and she picked up a fat, flat brush and started slapping paint on the canvas, almost in time to the music. Whereas the beat seemed lost on Rowan as he leaned in inches from the canvas, Elizabeth gave in to the tempo and let it direct the brush in her hands. She worked fast, tilting her head at the image she was creating, then back at her subject across the room. Sometimes her gaze jumped back and forth between the two so quickly that she felt dizzy. She lost track of time and didn't notice Rowan standing behind her as she worked.

"Oh my," he said quietly over her shoulder, startling her out of her trance. How long had they been at it?

"Rowan! No, don't look yet, I'm not ready!" She held her hands in front of the canvas. It felt like he'd caught her half-dressed.

He gently moved her aside and inched in closer with his hand pressed to his mouth and his eyes squinted. He stepped back to take in the entire thing, then moved in again as if to decipher how she'd created the image.

"How long has it been since you've painted?" he asked.

"Forever. Please, don't look at it. It's not good."

Rowan waved a hand at her and continued analyzing her work. Elizabeth watched him and tried to imagine his critique. She'd never painted an animal before, but Major had opted to laze directly in her sightline practically willing himself to be her first subject.

It wasn't tentative, what she'd put on the canvas. Her depiction of him was bold but at the same time it captured the dog's nuances. From the way his paw curved against his chest to the way he looked asleep and alert at the same time, it was a perfect representation of the dog's spirit.

"Bess," Rowan said quietly. "You are about to go places you haven't even imagined."

CHAPTER TWENTY-TWO

"You're supposed to be taking it easy," Elizabeth told Trudy.

"I'm 'supposed' to do a lot of things, but that doesn't mean I will," she snapped back. Trudy had regained some of her strength and all of her grit in the time since the fall and had coerced Elizabeth to come to her volunteer day at Dogs Trust. They were stuffing Kong toys with food for the dogs' meals, and Trudy winced every time she accidentally used her bad arm. "There's too much to do around here. They need me."

Trudy was right. When they'd arrived in the cheery yellow foyer Trudy was greeted like a celebrity by staff and volunteers alike at the rehoming center. They fussed over her arm for a few seconds, then immediately began detailing which dogs had found forever families, which were in need of her special attention, and how she could accomplish her usual tasks with her injury.

"I'll be fine," Trudy had fussed at Lisa, the pretty blond volunteer coordinator. "I'll use a waist leash. The dogs need walking, that's why I'm here."

"Absolutely not," Lisa replied, smiling tightly as if she could tell a fight was brewing. "There's too much risk to both you and the dogs."

"Well, then, Bess can hold the leash while we walk. She's an experienced dog handler."

Elizabeth widened her eyes at Trudy.

Lisa ignored Trudy and turned to Elizabeth. "We're so happy to have you along today, but unfortunately we can't let you walk the dogs without prior training. I was thinking that the two of you could be on kitchen duty. Isn't that lovely?"

Trudy's harrumphing and banging around the kitchen made it clear that it was a rookie job well below her abilities.

"It's a perfectly perfect day outside and those poor dogs are sitting in their pens. This is ridiculous. They're treating me like I'm an invalid. I was volunteering here before they were born." She slammed a spoon on the counter and it spattered soft dog food everywhere.

"Trudy, they're just looking out for you," Elizabeth replied. "And this is sort of fun." Elizabeth had been relieved that they were

244

downgraded to kitchen duty. Although she could handle Major and Georgina, the thought of walking strange shelter dogs made her queasy. She had visions of jumping, biting, dropped leashes, and runaway dogs.

"Hey, Trudy." A woman with short dark hair and the rehoming center's telltale yellow golf shirt poked her head in the kitchen. "Can I steal you?"

"Tamsin, hello. Officially, you can't steal me because we still have a bucket to finish. But yes, please do. Get me out of this kitchen nightmare."

"Lisa gave us strict orders to keep you safe in here, but this dog needs you." Tamsin sized Elizabeth up. "You can come too."

Elizabeth's stomach knotted. Was Tamsin implying that they were about to do something unsafe? Was it a vicious dog?

They stopped outside a room away from the main floor where the rest of the dogs were, and Elizabeth hung back, waiting to hear the frenzied barks and growls from whoever was inside.

"Oh, the poor dear!" Trudy exclaimed as they looked in the window. "I can see it trembling from here."

"We just got her in yesterday and she hasn't moved from that spot. Hasn't had a drop to drink, won't even look at the food bowl. We've all tried to connect with her but she's completely shut down. I figured you could work your magic."

"Of course I will. Bess, you're coming in with me."

They both turned to look at her and she realized that she had no choice. Elizabeth worked up the courage to peek at whatever hulking beast was in the room, expecting a shaggy wolf-dog cowering in the corner. Instead she could barely make out the tiny lump of brown fur curled up on a raised bed in the corner of the room.

"I'll keep Lisa busy while you go in," Tamsin said. "Good luck."

Trudy beckoned Elizabeth to follow her into the room and shut the door behind them quietly.

"Let's sit down." Trudy awkwardly lowered herself to the ground near the door, making quiet groaning noises and pretending it wasn't an effort to do so. Elizabeth settled on the cement floor beside her.

"What now?" Elizabeth asked.

"We wait," Trudy said. She exhaled, then yawned dramatically.

The puppy slid an eye in Trudy's direction.

"And we've made contact. The yawn

always works," Trudy said, smiling. "Hello, love. We're going to be friends." She brushed her hands down her pants and looked at Elizabeth. "Don't stare at her. You'll frighten her."

Elizabeth hadn't realized that she'd been staring. "What should I do?"

"Just be calm. Feel calm. Send calm."

"Why don't we get closer to her?"

"That's exactly why she's in this mess. No one respects what she's saying. That puppy is very clearly telling everyone, 'Stay away.' Until she says otherwise, I'll listen to her."

"But how will we know?"

"It will be obvious, Bess. When she's ready to meet us, she'll tell us."

The puppy was about the size of Georgina and had light brown fur. Even though its head was nearly buried beneath its front paws Elizabeth could still see two small reddish-golden dots above each eye and an apron of the same pretty color across its chest.

"What kind of dog is it?"

"It looks to be a Rottweiler mixed with . . . maybe a chocolate lab? The coloring is lovely."

Trudy yawned again.

"Are you tired?"

"No, that's called a calming signal. It's a

little bit of dog-speak that I steal for myself in situations like this. Yawning is a way to signal that I'm not a threat." She yawned again and Elizabeth mimicked her.

"Look!" Trudy said quietly. The puppy had picked its head up and was watching them. "Let's scoot a touch closer."

They moved toward the dog slowly, and she put her head back down and looked away for a second, then looked back at them and raised her head again.

"Lovely, sweetheart," Trudy cooed. "Aren't you so brave? Are we going to be friends?"

The puppy wagged the tip of its tail and Elizabeth's heart thumped faster.

"It's working!"

"So it is. We're making wonderful progress."

They continued their slow approach, watching the puppy for signs that she was comfortable with what was happening. Trudy translated everything the puppy's body language was saying, and Elizabeth made mental notes so she could apply the new information to Georgina. Every movement the puppy made meant something, from the little licks as if she were tasting the air, to the way her eyes darted, to the position of her head and the movement of her tail. With Trudy's translation skills it was as if the puppy were having a full conversation with them.

Within fifteen minutes they were only a few feet away from the puppy, and her posture had relaxed.

"Can we touch her?"

"No, not yet. Let her make the first move."

The room was still until a tapping on the window interrupted the silence with an avalanche of sound. Lisa peered in at them.

"Bollocks. She found us. I'll go out, you stay here. Don't do anything, though." Trudy hoisted herself up as gently as she could and walked from the room slowly, leaving Elizabeth and the puppy alone.

By now the puppy was unfurled on her bed, the tucked-in nervous posture replaced by a more natural position. Every time Trudy had spoken, the dog thumped her tail. The puppy watched the door expectantly after it clicked closed.

"I know how you feel," Elizabeth whispered. "I like her too. She's nice, isn't she? I'm nice too."

The puppy wagged her tail and turned so that she was facing Elizabeth. She ignored Trudy's last instruction and instead continued what they'd been doing together. The puppy had signaled *yes,* so Elizabeth moved closer.

She looked out the window to see what was going on with Trudy and Lisa, and so she didn't notice what was happening right in front of her. The puppy crawled down off her bed and tiptoed to where Elizabeth was sitting, pausing right next to her leg. Elizabeth could barely contain her excitement.

"Hello, little friend." Once again she ignored Trudy's advice and reached a tentative hand out to scratch the puppy's chest. It had worked for Major, maybe it would work on a petrified puppy too. She scratched her for a second and heard Trudy's voice in her head reminding her to ask permission. Elizabeth moved her hand away and waited for feedback.

The puppy climbed into Elizabeth's lap in cautious, slow-motion steps then turned in a circle and tucked herself into a tight ball so that she was nestled against Elizabeth's stomach.

Victory!

Elizabeth willed herself to stay calm even though she wanted to whoop with joy. She slowly moved her hands so they encircled the puppy's tiny body. "You're safe now, I've got you," she said, trembling with excitement and hoping the puppy didn't misunderstand what her body was communicating. The puppy made a little sighing noise, the same one that Georgina always made when she was done causing trouble and had committed to sleep. Elizabeth stroked her fur and silently celebrated the magic that had just happened.

The door opened and Trudy and Lisa snuck in.

"Well, look at that," Trudy said softly, the pride evident even in a whisper. "She trusts you, Bess. You have the magic touch, so I'll go back to the kitchen drudgery and you keep up with this important cuddling."

"Well done," Lisa said. "I'm impressed. But this is just the beginning. Now we just need someone special to give her a home and work with her. I think she'd do well with another dog, to help model confidence."

Elizabeth suddenly realized why the dog's fur was so striking.

"I think I know your who new dad is going to be," she whispered to the puppy.

Chapter Twenty-Three

"Do you want to help me pull a frame from the beehives?" Reid asked. "First of the season, bound to be glorious."

Elizabeth looked up from her computer, startled back into reality by Reid's interruption. Georgina woke up on the bean sack next to Elizabeth and cocked her head at Reid. The puppy knew that he usually had something hidden in his apron for her.

"Pass. I'm not a fan of bees. Wings and stingers seem like an unfair advantage."

"My girls are harmless, tame as lambs. I promise."

Elizabeth laughed at him. She knew exactly how "tame" lambs could be.

Reid stood in front of her with his arms crossed. He wasn't taking no for an answer. "Come on."

"If I get stung I'm charging you double for your social media revamp," she said. "I'm not kidding."

She followed him past the counter with Georgina at her heels and into a stairwell that was barely wider than her elbows. Reid had to angle his broad shoulders to clear it. He looked like a giant plopped into a doll-house.

"What if someone comes in?" she asked. Georgina was so close she could feel the dog's whiskers on her bare ankles as she struggled to navigate the steep stairs.

"I'll hear the bell, eventually. Locals don't mind waiting, unlike Americans."

He opened the door at the top of the stairs and stepped into the blinding sunshine. Georgina dashed out behind him and started exploring. Elizabeth followed tentatively. The front peaked portion of the roof hid the small flat back section, where the hives were located. The six hives stood side by side, next to a chimney. They were unimpressive, just tall wooden rectangular boxes stacked one atop another, like windowless high-rise towers. Each had a ledge protruding from the bottom, where nightmare hordes of bees clumped together as if they were on an entrance ramp on a rush-hour freeway.

"This is what an information superhighway looks like in Fargrove," Reid said, pointing to activity around the hives. "Watch your head, you're right in their path."

Elizabeth turned and saw flying black dots circling toward her. She shrieked and ran back toward the door, swatting the air.

"Stop, you're fine. They won't hurt you. If you don't act like a nobhead you're nothing more than a weird-looking tree to them. Relax, Bess. Now get over here and observe the glory. I promise you're safe."

She walked to him slowly and worried as Georgina got closer to the hives. Which one of them would get stung first? The air was electrified with thrumming activity. Elizabeth stood just behind Reid's shoulder, using him as a barrier.

"My rule is you can't stop watching the hive until you see some pollen pants walking in," Reid said, staring at the activity.

"Pollen pants?"

"When a bee comes home from a successful run she's wearing the pollen on her back legs, and it looks like she has puffy yellow pants on. The color varies from butter yellow to deep orange, depending on where she's been harvesting. It's lovely to see, really."

Elizabeth moved from behind Reid and focused on the mass of bees heading into the hive. Georgina seemed to be fighting something within her DNA, curious about the buzzing but smart enough not to get too close. Elizabeth watched bee after bee fly into the busiest entrance but couldn't spot what Reid was describing. Just as she was about to give up . . .

"Pollen pants! I see them! Right there," she said, pointing to the mass.

"Indeed you do. Nice work." Reid grinned at her excitement. "It's time for me to take a peek inside, so now would be a good time to step away. Things can get hectic when I go in."

Elizabeth retreated to a safe spot. Reid started to open the flat top of one of the hives, and the bees surrounded him like a cloud. Georgina edged in closer, overcome by the excitement of what was happening. "Call Georgie. She won't like a stinger to the nose."

Elizabeth whistled in as close an approximation as she could muster to what Trudy had taught her to do to recall the puppy, and Georgina loped to her immediately. They'd only had a few quick lessons together, so it shocked her when Georgina listened to her. She hooked a finger under Georgina's collar and held her close.

"Aren't you going to wear one of those hazmat suits?" Reid was in jeans, a green

T-shirt, and his omnipresent black ticking apron. His hair was a bright beacon in the sun. Elizabeth wondered if bees reacted to the color red like an angry bull.

He shook his head. "I stopped wearing a suit after meeting with an old beekeeper in Germany. He taught me that keeping them calm is all about my connection to them. They know I'd never hurt them, so they don't hurt me." He paused and gave her a sheepish look. "Well, sometimes they do, but I've built up a tolerance to stings." He placed the top of the hive on the ledge, his movements methodical and unhurried, and looked into the heart of the box. "My beautiful girls. What you've done!"

Elizabeth strained to see what he was looking at.

"We are not worthy of this," he said as he pulled a rectangular frame out of the hive and held it up to the light.

The muted golden honey was suspended in the frame like a perfect piece of stained glass, so plentiful that it dripped down the sides and onto Reid's fingers. The bees flew in boozy rings around him, landing on his hands and forearms as if to remind him that they were responsible for the bounty.

"Have you ever seen anything so perfect?" he asked.

"I've only seen honey in plastic bears. It's unbelievable." She tried to remain calm as bees flew by her head.

"Well, prepare to have your first taste of heaven. I'll get the rest later, let's take this one down and have a try."

Reid walked toward her holding the honey-laden frame out to her, a swarm of bees trailing behind him, so Elizabeth yanked open the door and ran down the stairs with Georgina tumbling along behind her.

Reid met her by the counter. "Taste it," he said, holding it out to her.

Elizabeth reached out to touch her finger to the honey pooled on the edge of the frame, only to see a lone bee creep up from underneath. She jumped away.

"A straggler," Reid said. He walked to the door and held the frame outside, gently shaking it until the bee flew away. "Off you go, sweetheart." He came back and offered it to her again. "Okay, now try."

She dabbed her finger along the edge of the frame and touched it to her tongue. "This doesn't taste like plastic bear honey." It was sweet, but not like what she was used to. It had a depth of flavor that made her think she could taste the clover blossoms the bees had feasted on.

Reid touched his finger to the honey and looked down at Georgina. "Sit." The puppy immediately moved into position, faster than she ever had for Elizabeth, and Reid let her lick the honey from his fingertip. "A little honey is good for pups."

He disappeared into the kitchen and returned with two currant-studded triangular scones on a yellow plate, and a marrow bone for Georgina. The puppy ran back to her bean sack bed with the prize.

"I hope you don't mind yesterday's goods," he said as he handed her a scone. He took a spoon and mashed it on the honey at the corner of the frame, and the golden liquid oozed up through what looked like a thin plastic skin. Reid gently pushed the coating aside.

Elizabeth examined it. "What is that on top?"

"That's the wax cap. In order to properly collect the honey you're supposed to shave it off with a hot knife, but for this unofficial harvest we'll just work around it." He collected a blob of honey on the spoon, then hovered it over the scones, letting it run down in slow amber streams, until he'd made a glistening trail on top of each one. He pushed the plate toward her. "After you, madame."

Elizabeth was reminded of their first meeting, and how far they'd come in the past few weeks. She took a huge bite and the combination of the crumbly scone with the sticky sweetness of the honey almost made her swoon.

"Amazing," she said with her mouth full. She made little satisfied noises as she chewed. "So good."

The bell over the door jangled but Elizabeth was so caught up in the honey-coated confection that she didn't even turn to see who it was. She was starving and the scone was hitting the spot.

"Hey, mate!" Reid said. "Bess, look, it's your old friend James." There was a hint of mocking in his voice.

"Well, hello there," James said with a smile that lit up his already beautiful face. "So nice to see you here again. Reid mentioned that you're staying on for a while longer?"

Bess covered her mouth with her hand and chewed faster, kicking herself for taking a giant bite right as James walked in.

"Um-hmnf," she replied with a nod and a wave, spitting a few crumbs. Georgina dashed around the corner from the kitchen and launched herself at James, proving that he was irresistible to dogs too.

"Well, hello, you," he said, trying to pet

Georgina while preventing her from jumping up on him.

Elizabeth ran over and clipped a leash on the puppy's collar so she had more control over her. "Sorry, she's a work in progress."

"Aren't we all?" He paused and watched her for a moment like he was about to say something more but reached down to Georgina instead.

Looking into his eyes gave Elizabeth a split-second vision of his arms around her. It felt like a sense memory, like it had actually happened. Shock rippled through her. *Had* it happened?

"I met your next dog," she said without preamble. She cringed after the words came out. "I mean, if you were serious about wanting a puppy, I met one that might be perfect for you."

"Did you? And what makes you think you found The One?" He knelt and rubbed Georgina's belly, who was flat on her back and seemed just as in awe of James as Elizabeth was.

Elizabeth thought for a moment. Why did she think the dog was right for him? After all, the puppy was cripplingly shy and would need someone who was calm and kind and patient to help rehab her. Did he have the time to dedicate to a needy little dog? Would

Porter welcome a temperamental sibling? She watched James sitting cross-legged on the floor massaging Georgina like it was his job. Elizabeth peered at his ankles. He was wearing navy socks with a tiny repeating print. Dogs. James Holworthy was wearing dog print socks.

"I just have a feeling you'll like her. She's . . . special. A little socially awkward. But so adorable. And she matches Porter!" Elizabeth considered showing him the photo she'd taken of the puppy but thought an element of surprise might work in her favor.

"How do you know what Porter looks like?" James looked genuinely curious.

Reid snorted from behind the counter.

"Uh . . . Porter is a lab, a chocolate lab, right? Seen one, seen 'em all." Elizabeth mentally kicked herself for sloppy stalking.

"And where is this perfect-for-me-dog right now?"

"I met her at Dogs Trust with Trudy. She's not on the adoption floor yet because . . . uh, because they don't have the space. But I could get you a secret meeting with her." Elizabeth pretzeled herself, hugging her arms to her chest and linking her legs at the ankles.

James smiled at her, and it felt like the

sun breaking through the clouds. "If you're convinced that you've found the dog for me, I'd be happy to meet her. After all, you're pretty good at picking dogs. Look at this perfect little lump. Although truth be told I think *she* picked *you.*" Georgina was still on her back in a trance in front of James. He slid his hands beneath her shoulders and massaged them, and Georgina made a noise that sounded like a sigh.

Elizabeth watched his hands and couldn't believe that she was jealous of a dog.

"So when would you like to go?" She said it before she could think about the fact that she was asking James on a date, even though he probably didn't realize it.

"Well, we've all got Des and Harriet's dinner party on Thursday. Shall we run by Dogs Trust before, then go straight there? I imagine you'll need transportation, so I'll be your driver for the afternoon and evening."

It was as if she'd scripted it.

"Perfect. I'll set it all up." Elizabeth's heart hopscotched for a few beats as she realized the magnitude of what she'd just done. She wasn't a dog expert or a dude expert, but she'd just successfully scheduled a date with one of each. Imagining the millions of things that could go wrong with either one of them made her woozy.

Reid had his elbows on the counter, staring at them like he was in the front row at a play. "Not to break this up but your coffee's ready, James."

"Right, thanks, mate. Bess, let me know what time I should pick you up for my date with destiny. Is that what I should name this puppy? 'Destiny'?" His gaze didn't leave her eyes as he said the word, and even though they were talking about naming a dog she felt a flush creeping onto her cheeks.

Elizabeth cleared her throat and tried to act like a professional dog rescuer instead of a lovesick teenager. "Not quite. I think you'll know her name the second you see her."

"Picking my next dog *and* naming it too? I guess you know me better than I do," James said, placing his hand on her shoulder as he leaned over to grab his coffee.

The familiar sparks sizzled through Elizabeth's body. He'd touched her like that before, she was sure of it.

She just wished she could remember it.

CHAPTER TWENTY-FOUR

The cat was coming along, just in time for the Welbecks' party.

She'd cropped the original image on her phone so that it was a close-up of his face, with one eye covered by his white-tipped paw, and scraps of satin and tulle peeking out from behind his head. His leg was so perfectly blue-black that it looked like the sleeve to a shirt, with a white paw peeking out the end of it. Elizabeth wanted to alter it to include a few pops of orange since the crop obliterated some of his more impressive markings, but she also wanted to be true to the animal.

It was shocking how quickly the brush felt at home in her hand again. She became confident enough to play with her style, painting some works with the same looseness as her first image of Major, and others with the care of a scientist capturing the details of a specimen for a textbook. She'd completed a dozen paintings quickly, before she could second-guess what she was doing. Rowan had assessed each one like an art critic, sometimes praising her outright and other times making suggestions for tweaks that took her work from good to great.

She peered around the edge of her canvas at him. His moody lake painting was completed and he had moved on to an open field dominated by a sapphire sky crowded with fat clouds, which was appropriate since the song echoing around the barn was about "blue skies, nothing but blue skies." She placed her paintbrush on the edge of the trough on the easel and studied his process. He held a long dowel, tapered like a pool stick, on the top edge of the painting so that it was about two inches from the canvas, and rested his brush hand on it. This allowed him to make minuscule additions to the clouds without accidentally touching the wet paint. Were his hands so unsteady that they required the tool, or had he always used it? Elizabeth scrutinized both of his hands and couldn't detect a hint of tremor.

Helping Rowan sort through his work was an education in technique. Though he was famous for his hyperrealistic landscapes, he had stacks of impressionistic works scattered throughout the barn, not to mention the portraits in the anteroom. Learning about his artistic progression lit a fire in Elizabeth. She could see her own technique improving with every canvas. The cat was her best one yet.

Elizabeth's phone alarm went off. Before she started using it, they'd painted well past their designated time. But Rowan was paying her for her organizational skills, and as much as she loved painting with him she wanted to honor their agreement and finish the job before she headed home. At the rate they were going they'd finish in another month, two max. It didn't even feel like work, listening to Rowan talk about his inspiration and taking notes on her tablet. It was the best job she'd ever had.

The barn door screeched open and Georgina ran to Elizabeth with wide eyes and her usually happy panting mouth shut tightly, not sure if she should be worried about the noise. On most days the door stayed shut until they were done, so Georgina was on guard for an unexpected intruder.

"We talked about this," Elizabeth said in a reassuring tone. "Remember? It's all good. You've got this." Georgina did a full-body shake — which Elizabeth now knew was a canine tension breaker — and trotted off to find Major again.

It was Trudy at the door, clutching her bad arm under the elbow with eyes almost as wide as Georgina's.

"Faye," she sputtered, and gestured with her good hand. "Faye is *here*!"

Rowan dropped the dowel. "Here? What is she doing here?"

"She said she needs to talk to you and you haven't been returning her calls. She said it was important. I've made her a cup of tea to hold her off, but you must come up to the house now. Unless you want me to send her down here?"

"No, no, no, absolutely not!" Rowan bellowed. "I'll be up, tell her to wait there."

Trudy nodded and scurried out of the barn.

Rowan sighed and rubbed his eyes. "Faye's my gallerist. We've been together for my entire career. I adore her, but she's been pushy lately. I suppose this visit was inevitable. Would you like to stay here and work or come up to meet her?"

"I'm not exactly dressed for an introduction." She pointed to her paint-splotched jeans. "I definitely want to meet her, though. If you don't mind."

"Please," he said warily. "Perhaps you can be a buffer." He got up from his stool slowly.

267

Trudy and Faye were sitting in the side garden off the conservatory, chatting and smiling. Elizabeth studied Trudy as they walked closer, trying to tell if her happy expression was genuine or forced. Unless she was an incredible actress, it looked like the women shared a true friendship. So why had Rowan been avoiding Faye? What was going on?

"There you are, my dear," Faye exclaimed, jumping out of her chair when she spotted Rowan. Other than a slight limp, she looked like a tiny, white-haired Audrey Hepburn, complete with tidy low bun, white button-down shirt, and slim black pants. The only spot of color on her was a pair of narrow neon-green eyeglasses.

"Hello," Rowan said, air-kissing both of her cheeks in a way that reminded Elizabeth that he had a life outside Fargrove. "Faye Woolard, please meet my niece, Bess Barnes."

"This is such an unexpected pleasure," Faye said with genuine enthusiasm, reaching her small hand out to Elizabeth. "And Trudy tells me you're an artist as well. It runs in the family!"

"Yes, I'm Elizabeth," she replied. "And I am a finger painter compared to Rowan," she added, taking care to shake her hand as

268

if it were ancient parchment.

"Nonsense. Trudy says your animal paintings are a wonder. Perhaps you could show a few to me? Are you painting in the barn with Rowan?"

Faye didn't even know the correct name for the building. Rowan's Operculum was indeed a covert operation. "Yes, we're painting together, but I'm a beginner. Trust me, you don't want to see my stuff."

"Perhaps we could all walk down to the barn and see what's going on in there? I'm sure Rowan has all sorts of delights hidden away."

"You do not give up," Rowan said, half good-naturedly, half chiding.

"Well, in fact I do. And that's why I'm here. May we sit?"

They settled themselves in the heavy wrought-iron furniture next to Trudy, under the shade of a massive tree. Elizabeth felt unnecessary but wanted to know what was going on. Faye pursed her lips and tilted her head side to side, as if rehearsing what she was about to say before she began to speak.

"Rowan, Trudy, you've known this day was coming for quite some time. And I've put it off for much longer than I should have. But now the time *truly* has come. I am finally retiring."

Trudy began trilling before Faye had even finished the sentence. "Wonderful! That's wonderful! Isn't it, Rowan?"

"I am delighted for you. If you are ready, then it is indeed time." He looked at Faye with a wistful smile.

Elizabeth wondered what it meant for Rowan, and for herself. Would they still have to catalog his work if he didn't have a gallery space? Was she unemployed once again?

"Please don't worry, everything will remain the same. Martin will be working with me during a brief transition period, then taking over. You and Martin have a wonderful relationship, don't you?"

"Oh, yes, yes, indeed," Rowan replied.

"Except for the time he suggested Rowan find a gallery suited for people who like antiques. I believe that's what he said. 'Old lace and antiques,' wasn't it?" Trudy turned to Rowan with a sour look on her face.

Faye tittered. "That was just Martin being Martin! He was joking because Rowan has been with us longer than any other artist. He *adores* Rowan."

"Does he, though?" Trudy asked pointedly.

Faye took a sip of tea and continued as though the exchange hadn't happened. "I think my departure is going to be a seamless change for all of our artists. Of course, Martin has a few brilliant ideas for the gallery. Some up-and-coming artists, headline makers and such. But out current selection will remain, of course."

"How delightful," Rowan said softly.

"We're all very excited," Faye said, sounding like she was trying to convince herself.

Elizabeth watched Rowan and Trudy as they discussed the particulars of Faye's retirement. Something was off. Trudy focused on a button on her sleeve, trying to remove a flyaway thread, and Rowan kept shutting his eyes and running his fingertips lightly across his forehead as if he were reading Braille.

Major came trotting up to the group, breaking the tension with hearty wags and play bows for Faye. They all seemed happy for the distraction, and Elizabeth realized that dogs were the equivalent of a pinging cell phone. She looked over her shoulder for Georgina, who was usually Major's shadow, but there was no sign of her. Given the tension in the air, she was happy for an excuse to go look for the puppy.

"Excuse me, I should find Georgina. Faye, it was nice to meet you."

"Such a pleasure," Faye said without looking away from Rowan.

Elizabeth hurried down toward the Operculum, imagining what sort of trouble the little dog might be getting into.

She craned her neck as she passed the ladies' barn, thinking that Georgina might be doing some intel on them while they were out to pasture. She paused and scanned the field beyond the barn, spotting the cream-colored dots on a faraway hill with no indication that an unschooled hooligan was testing their patience. Elizabeth's heart started to pound. The property was so vast and wild that if Georgina decided to wander solo it was doubtful she'd be able to find her way home. She pictured the puppy trotting happily along without a backward glance, perhaps chasing a squirrel or bird, until she was so far away that even her superior sense of smell wouldn't help her find her way back.

It felt like the first night when she found Georgina, only this time there was a chance she *wouldn't* find Georgina.

She picked up her pace, envisioning the two naked sticks that were once an orchid sitting on the table by her door at home, and the bonsai tree she'd received as a gift that had managed to thrive for over fifty years until its premature death at her hands.

Why did anyone think that she could be responsible for a living creature?

"Georgina," she called, trying to keep her voice happy. Then she remembered what Trudy had told her during a lesson. Use the proper recall when you want her to return to you, even though Trudy had told her not to test the word in a real-life situation yet. But why teach the word if you can't actually use it?

She filled her lungs and said it loud, but with a smile in her voice, so that she didn't sound as nervous as she felt. "Here!"

She paused and waited for the pup to come dashing from her hiding space. Nothing. She attempted the two-tone whistle William had taught her but couldn't produce anything more than a puff of air.

Elizabeth poked her head in the Operculum and called for the pup, but she could tell from the stillness in the air that Georgina wasn't inside. She continued down the lane, toward where she'd walked with Trudy and Rowan on dispersement day. They hadn't talked about the land situation since that day, and even though she still had weeks left in Fargrove, she wanted to calculate how much of a financial cushion she'd be bringing home with her. The longer she waited to bring up the sale of the land the more uncomfortable it felt.

"Georg—" She stopped herself. "Here!" Her voice shook a little. She wondered if they could hear her back on the patio. Maybe William was on the grounds and had Georgina trailing him like a lovesick suitor. She continued down the lane. "Georgina, where *are* you?"

The tall grass in front of her started undulating and Georgina burst out from the greenery with a wide, grinning pant and muddy paws. Elizabeth dropped to her knees.

"I was so worried! Where were you?"

Georgina raced to Elizabeth as if they'd been separated for weeks. Elizabeth leaned down and the puppy rolled onto her back, flipping back and forth like a fish on dry land. Her stomach was wet.

"You were in the river? Naughty girl!" Elizabeth said. "You don't know how to swim." She reached out tentatively to rub Georgina's belly, ready to snatch her hand back when the needle teeth nipped it, but Georgina held still as she stroked her. "You're not going to bite me? Not this time? I guess that settles it. You really do like me."

She sat down on the weedy pea gravel next to the puppy, and Georgina crawled onto her lap. The puppy was uncharacteristically calm, allowing Elizabeth to pet her without reaching back to nip once. The noon sun warmed Elizabeth's cheeks as she leaned back on her elbows and turned her face up to the light. Her freckles were reappearing, and she could hear the scolding she'd get from her aesthetician once she returned home and made a tune-up appointment.

Elizabeth closed her eyes and realized that she didn't need mantras and breathing exercises to feel calm in Fargrove. The weight of her puppy on her lap, the scent of wildflowers on the breeze, and the pebbles pressing into her palms like shiatsu kept her in the moment more effectively than any guided meditation she'd done. She felt at peace until she remembered what was happening on the patio down the lane.

What was going to happen to Rowan? Based on Trudy's guard-dog behavior Elizabeth could tell a shift was coming, and she didn't know what it meant for any of them. The timing of Faye's retirement announcement was strange, just a few weeks into Rowan's three-month retrospective. Who was this Martin, and what was he capable of? Elizabeth felt herself preemptively hating him.

Georgina adjusted herself and did the little stretch that Elizabeth loved, pushing her front paws straight out so far that she trembled a little, then drawing them back up to her chest bunny-style.

"Don't run off like that again, okay? You scared me." Elizabeth gave her a little squeeze. Georgina made a contented sound and snuggled in closer. Even though the heat was relentless, Elizabeth liked the feeling of Georgina's sun-warmed fur pressed against her. She leaned forward a little so she could pull her phone from her back pocket only to remember that it was still sitting in the Operculum on her easel. She kissed Georgina on the top of the head and the little dog leaned back and licked her on the chin.

CHAPTER TWENTY-FIVE

James and Elizabeth stood outside the door at Dogs Trust, peeking in at the puppy. Elizabeth bounced on her toes and tried to read his face as he watched the little dog. Did he like her? Did he think she was cute? Elizabeth was too worried about her canine matchmaking to think about the fact that she was on an unofficial official first date with James Holworthy. Before he could fall in love with *her,* he had to fall in love with a tiny, needy puppy.

The puppy had come a long way since Elizabeth's first visit. She was tearing into a Kong, kicking it around the room with determined gusto. Her tail wagged and she reared back on her hind legs, waving her front paws in the air like a mime as the treat-filled toy rolled away.

James stood with his arms crossed and a little smile on his face as he leaned his forehead against the glass. He couldn't look

277

more adorable in his bright blue checkered button-down shirt and slim dark jeans. A few of the dark curls at the nape of his neck almost touched the collar of his shirt.

Lisa had graciously stepped aside to let Elizabeth do the introduction alone after a rank-pulling phone call from Trudy. Her volunteering, and more likely the generous Barnes donations, allowed Trudy to occasionally bend the rules. Elizabeth had felt awkward asking Trudy to step in on her behalf, but the moment she mentioned James over afternoon tea Trudy gave her a knowing smile and walked directly to the kitchen phone.

"Are you ready to meet her?" Elizabeth asked.

"Definitely. I cannot wait to get my hands on that pup."

"I need to warn you that she might be a little shy at first. I'd let her warm up to you before you try to pet her." Elizabeth stifled her imposter syndrome as she talked about how to handle the puppy. Hell, she'd been the first one to get through to the nervous little thing, and she'd learned a lot from dealing with Georgina. She knew what she was doing with puppies. Sort of. Like Rowan said, she had good instincts.

James followed her into the small room

and the puppy froze in place, then sank low to the ground.

"Uh-oh," James said.

"No, no, just give her a second! She'll come out of her shell." Elizabeth prayed it was true and went into full spin mode. "She's got gorgeous coloring, don't you think? She's probably a mix of —"

"Rottweiler and chocolate lab. I can see it from here. My family had a Rottie when I was a kid. She's perfection."

James crouched down and watched the puppy. She didn't move toward him and instead swung her head back and forth, assessing him through the air.

"It's okay," he whispered.

The puppy took a tentative step toward him, and Elizabeth held her breath. She thought about pulling out her phone to record their first meeting, but it was buried in her purse across the room.

James sat down and placed his hand on the ground a few feet in front of him, palm side down. The puppy kept her back paws anchored in place but tiptoed her front paws so that she could steal a sniff, stretching her body out as far as it could go. The smells were too tempting to resist, and the puppy surrendered and approached him, tracing her nose along the contours of his hand.

"That was so fast," Elizabeth said quietly. "You've got some puppy magic."

"Or I coated my hand in liver powder," James replied.

"You did?"

He chuckled and reached into his breast pocket with his other hand, pulling out a crumpled-up treat bag.

"What a great idea," Elizabeth said.

"Figured I'd cheat a little, since you're convinced that this is my next dog."

"Do you agree?" She held her breath.

James stroked the puppy, who was sitting close to him and enjoying his attention. "If it were only up to me I'd say yes, but I have a very important flatmate that needs to sign off on her too."

Elizabeth cocked her head at him. Roommate? Had her stalking failed her?

"Porter."

"Right, of course, *Porter*! Do you think he'll like her?"

"Hard to say. Sometimes puppies make him nuts. We've had a few pass through the office and he doesn't have much patience for puppy stuff."

"Well, if Georgina is any barometer for 'puppy stuff' I'd say that this puppy here is pretty chill. She seems super calm." The little dog was sniffing along James's leg.

"Sure, in this environment she's calm, but once I spring her and she starts living the good life it'll be hello, insanity."

Elizabeth leaned back against the wall. Was she failing as a matchmaker?

"So, then our next step is a meeting with Porter, right?"

"Are you in sales? Because you're working awfully hard to close this deal!" He laughed at her and the sound rumbled through the tiny room. The puppy wagged her tail and moved closer to James, as if his laugh were a siren song.

"I just had a feeling about this match. That you were the one for her."

"Is that so?" He locked on her eyes and it felt inexplicably familiar. "Tell me why you think that we're meant to be together."

"Well, she needs someone . . . special. To help her find her confidence. And you seem like you could do that for her. You and Porter, that is."

"Thank you," he replied, watching Elizabeth until the puppy swatted his hand to get him to continue petting. "That's kind of you to say. What else?"

"Obviously she's adorable."

"Agreed. I think she's stunning. Unlike anything I've seen before." James managed to pet the puppy without looking away from her face.

His focus seared her, and she felt a blush creep onto her cheeks, but she held his gaze. "She's . . . she's calm." Elizabeth finally managed to break eye contact and fiddled with the hem of her sweatshirt.

"It might be temporary. Besides, I don't think I've met her real personality yet. I think she has many, many layers."

"She seems to like you *very* much." Elizabeth held her breath as she waited for him to answer.

"And I like her very much as well. I knew it from the first moment I saw her."

The room felt like a sauna, and Elizabeth wished she could strip off her sweatshirt. They stared at each other from across the room until a knock on the window shattered the moment.

Lisa.

"Everything all right in here?" She peeked her head in and smiled. "Getting on okay?"

"More than okay," James answered. "I think we're making a real connection." He shot Elizabeth a look.

"Oh, splendid! Shall I get you a homefinding questionnaire?"

"I'm very interested, but I need to check in with my other dog before I can commit."

"Of course, that's the next step. Let's set

up a home visit."

"Can I call you about scheduling that?" James asked.

Elizabeth studied James. Why was he being evasive all of a sudden?

"Here's my card, ready when you are." Lisa walked over to him, and the puppy leapt up and scooted a few steps backward. "Poor thing. Do you think you can handle a high-needs pup?"

Elizabeth wanted to scream at Lisa. She'd been so close to making the love connection happen, and Lisa was ruining it with real-world questions about responsibility.

"It's a concern for sure," James said. "I need to know what I'm getting into, before I commit to bringing her home. My job is intense and I'd actually prefer a low-maintenance situation." He reached out to the little dog and she licked his hand. "But for some reason I really like this pup."

"Have you thought about what you'd call her?" Lisa asked.

"Care to take this one, Bess? You seem to have it all worked out."

"Look at her color," she replied. "It's right there in front of you."

"She's brown with reddish highlights." James shrugged.

"Pretend you're describing a beer," she

insisted. "Like you poured that fur into a glass."

He looked at her like she was insane, then considered the puppy. He ran his hand along her back and she leaned into his touch. "Uh, this beer is medium-bodied, a nice solid brown. It has a unique fuzzy mouthfeel . . . it's a classic . . . a classic *porter.*"

"And?" Elizabeth urged him on.

"And there are undertones of a slow-fermented golden red . . ." He scratched beneath the puppy's chin.

Elizabeth nodded at him with a huge smile.

James laughed and pulled the now happily wiggling puppy onto his lap. "Amber ale! Why hello there, Amber, lovely to meet you."

CHAPTER TWENTY-SIX

"Look at you, a quick-change artist," James said as Elizabeth pulled the thin black sweatshirt over her head.

"This is the Fargrove version of a day-into-evening outfit," she answered as she fastened her seat belt. "I didn't want to be overdressed for Amber or underdressed for the Welbecks." She smoothed the front of her blush-colored top, the first pink thing she'd owned in years. She looked down and noticed that she'd accidentally pulled it so that the scalloped edge of her thin mesh Agent Provocateur bra peeked out from the blouse. An inch lower and James Holworthy would've seen her nipple. He averted his eyes as she adjusted her top.

"You look nice," he said in a quiet voice. Once she was decent he scanned her from head to toe. Elizabeth watched him taking her in, hoping he liked what he was seeing. The unofficial first date had suddenly flipped to very official, and the air in the car crackled with static.

"My shoes!" She kicked off her sneakers and dug through her bag for the lipstick-red ballet flats she'd bought the same day she'd picked up the top. Reid had paid her first installment in cash and she'd celebrated with a mini shopping spree in town, then suffered from a case of buyer's remorse the moment she got back to Rowan and Trudy's.

"Pretty," he said softly.

She believed him, despite the spray of freckles across her nose and the waves in her hair that she hadn't bothered to tame. The way he looked at her. Like he knew something that she didn't.

"Thank you for saying that." She stared at his profile, taking in every perfect contour.

He cleared his throat and refocused on the road. "It's a quick drive, we'll be there in a few minutes. Can't wait to see what you've brought them."

Elizabeth looked over her shoulder at the oversized brown-wrapped package in the back seat. She felt a mixture of pride and embarrassment over the hostess gift she'd brought for Harriet and Des. Was it too much?

"So how much longer will you be in Fargrove?" James asked.

The dreaded question.

"Oh, a while. Rowan and I have a lot of work to do in the barn." She didn't want to give him an exact number. She didn't want to think about it either. Despite willing Carson to call or email her back every day, she still hadn't heard from him, so she focused on her work with Rowan to keep from getting depressed.

"And how long is 'a while'?"

"Long enough to have some fun!" She'd wanted to playfully avoid answering, but it came out sounding desperate and weird.

"Hm."

Silence replaced the static. She itched to take out her phone but didn't dare.

They ended up on a narrow cobblestone street that was different from the rest of Fargrove. Still charming, but more modern-leaning, lined on either side by a rainbow of flat-front homes with large double doors. There was no room for yards, so each house had a variety of potted flowers, climbing vines, and topiaries in front to add an element of green to the street.

Harriet and Desmond's home was at the very end, tucked in the corner of the dead end. It was bright blue with a fire-engine-red door. By far the happiest-looking home in a row of deliriously cheerful candy-colored painted brick façades. As James maneuvered into a tiny parking spot, Elizabeth automatically started digging through her purse for her phone, imagining which color would best complement the pink blouse. Maybe she could do a photo series? One of her in front of the pink house, then the baby blue, then the yellow.

"James, could you —" She held her phone out to him before she realized what she was asking him to do.

"What?"

She quickly threw her phone back in her bag. The split-second image of her coaching James how to snap photos while she smiled and posed was like a bad comedy skit.

"Nothing, never mind."

James pulled the package from the back seat and placed it on top of his car. He ran his fingers through his hair, then stretched, like he was getting ready for a workout.

"Can I talk to you for a sec, before we go in?" James asked in a voice that didn't match the deep groove between his eyebrows.

"Of course."

He leaned against his car and crossed his arms. The sun was setting and the fiery glow over the rooftops behind him made it hard to see his face. Elizabeth held her forearm above her eyes to block the light.

His furrow deepened. "I just want to be plain with you about everything. Tonight might get . . . crazy. The drinking. Before that happens, I want you to know that I like you, I really do . . ."

If he liked her, why was he frowning?

"I just . . . I'm not in a place where I can get involved with anyone. The brewery takes a lot of time, and if I wind up adopting Amber, too . . ." He trailed off.

Elizabeth coughed back the lump in her throat. He was using the *puppy* as an excuse to keep his distance?

"Of course, of course. I get it. You've got a great work ethic, I'm the same way. I've got a huge opportunity in front of me and I'm going to need to focus all my energy on it once I'm back home in a few weeks. So, no worries." She forced herself to sound cheerful. "Now let me at those Lost Dogs you've got in the boot!"

His face relaxed and he looked relieved. "Already calling it a 'boot' like a true 'Grover. Nice." He opened the trunk and pulled out a box filled with a mix of bottles.

She wanted to turn around and go home. The reason they were there, the entire reason why overly pregnant Harriet had put herself out to organize the little gathering, was to smooth the path between them. How could she plaster on a cheery face for the night? She needed to pull Harriet aside and tell her. Maybe she could fake a stomach flu and leave early? She definitely felt nauseous.

Elizabeth followed James to the front door, trying to hold the oversized package so that she didn't look ridiculous. He juggled the heavy box of beer onto his hip and held the door open for her, and she announced their arrival by accidentally knocking over a gong-sized metal bowl filled with lemons in the tiny foyer.

"Hey there, welcome, friends," Des said, rounding the corner, beaming at them as he stooped to pick up a few lemons.

"Sorry, I blame this thing," Elizabeth said, nodding to the package under her arm. "What an entry. At least I didn't hit a candle." The room was glowing with tea lights.

"Not at all, you've just made lemonade." He moved toward her and she couldn't tell if he wanted to shake her hand, hug her, or give her a kiss on the cheek. They danced awkwardly in front of each other for a second until Des gestured that he wanted to take the package from her. He gave her a quick air-kiss and a wink as she handed it to him, then started picking up the remaining lemons, happy to have something to do.

"Mate," James said, gracefully leaning in to chest-bump Des.

"We're all in here," Des said over his shoulder as he walked toward the kitchen. "Leave the lemons, come eat!"

"Did you get them all?" James asked, scanning the floor as he followed Des to the kitchen.

"I think," Elizabeth said as she stood up and brushed off her knees. She felt stupid and unnecessary, a clumsy, lemon-stomping party crasher forcing her way into a group of old friends. Why was she even there?

She dug through her purse and found her phone. She had service, so if she ended up alone on the couch she'd have something to do. She leaned against the wall and tapped through her accounts.

"Hello? What are you doing?" Harriet whispered to her, tiptoeing into the foyer in a pink apron covered in a repeating cat print that tented out in front of her stomach. "Is something wrong?"

"Hi, I'm fine." Elizabeth smiled at Harriet. There was no need to tell her anything; she didn't want to derail the party after all the hard work Harriet had put in.

"How did it go with the puppy?" she asked, still whispering.

"He liked her. Next step is a meeting with Porter."

"Fantastic!" Harriet clapped her hands quietly. Her pretty face was glowing. "And what about the two of you?"

She shook her head and forced a happy expression. "Not going to happen. But it's fine, no problem."

"What do you mean?" Harriet leaned in with her eyes wide.

"Sweetie?" Des's voice rang out from around the corner. "Something's burning."

Elizabeth waved her hand. "It's fine, don't worry about it. Let's go in."

The bright blue kitchen was crowded with bodies grazing around the butcher-block island. She recognized Willard and Anna Tolbert from the night at the Three Tups, along with Reid, Nicky, and a wet-haired, pajama-clad Poppy. She noticed that Anna was wearing a pretty floral dress. Elizabeth was underdressed for the first time in her life, but the room felt so welcoming and the air smelled like warm bread and garlic, and for a moment Elizabeth forgot that she was in a discount top and James wanted nothing to do with her.

"What are you drinking tonight, Bess?"

Des asked, standing over a galvanized steel tub filled with beer and wine bottles. "We've got a full assortment of Lost Dogs thanks to your driver, I know you like those!"

"Do you have any Chardonnay?" She felt small the moment she said it, but she wasn't about to drink James's beer. He shot her a look and shoved a carrot in his mouth.

"What is this giant thing you've brought us?" Harriet asked, holding up the package. "May I open it now?"

Barnabas slinked into the kitchen on cue, leaping onto the counter and posing like an Egyptian cat god. Anna scratched his head and he reared up and bumped against her shoulder.

"Of course, I hope you like it."

The room went silent as Harriet tore into the paper. Everyone leaned in to see what was inside.

"It's Barnabas!" she exclaimed. "Who painted this? You?"

She nodded and bowed her head, suddenly unsure of why she'd brought such a ridiculous gift.

Harriet took in the image with her mouth wide open, then looked at Elizabeth. "How did you do this?"

"Oh, it's nothing. It's from the first time I came to the shop, that photo I took of

Barnabas. See, there's some gray tulle and satin beneath him, to represent my dress? It's just a little expression of thanks for inviting me tonight."

"That's no 'little expression,' " Reid said. "I had no idea you were arty like your uncle!"

Everyone started talking at the same time, raving about her skill and debating where the painting should hang. She watched James as he took in the painting. He studied it quietly, nodding along with the more vocal admirers. Elizabeth took a sip of her wine and looked away. She could feel his eyes on her.

"Let's take this party outside," Harriet said, raising her voice above the ruckus. "Why do you always gather in my work space, people? And keep it down for a bit, I need to get Poppy to sleep as well."

Everyone grabbed drinks and trays of appetizers and settled beneath the glowy café lights on the patio.

"Could we commission you?" Anna asked Elizabeth, drawing the attention of the group. "We have a beagle mix that's ready for her close-up."

Elizabeth searched Anna's face to see if she was joking. "Really?"

"Yes, really."

"She's been researching artists. This is serious business for my wife," Willard added.

"I'll do it for free," Elizabeth said, her eyes wide. "I've . . . I've never gotten paid to paint."

"What? Ridiculous! Of course we'll pay you. How does it work? Do you need Chelsea to live-model for you? She's a stunner."

"It's easier for me to use photos, but I'd also love to meet her, so I can learn her personality."

"Then we'll arrange an audience with her, and I'll send some of her best pictures as well," Anna said. "I'm so excited, we're going to have a Barnes original!"

"The lesser Barnes," Elizabeth corrected.

"While we're talking art, do you have anything you can hang at the Hive?" Reid asked. "Nicky's taking down his photos and I hate naked walls."

"Wait, what? Like, a show?"

"Exactly! We'll hang whatever you have, even if it's just one painting. If anything sells I get a ten percent commission and you get the rest. It's a win-win; makes my walls look pretty and gives you some exposure. How many have you got?"

"I, uh, I might have enough. I paint fast, like Rowan. It's in our blood." She liked pointing out that they shared traits. "But . . . a *show*?"

"Indeed. You've got skills, and I've got empty walls. Perfect match. So how many?"

Elizabeth knew exactly how many paintings she had. Between her mornings with Rowan, which sometimes consisted of more painting than cataloging, and her late nights in the Operculum with Georgina at her side when she was working on something that consumed her, she'd finished fourteen paintings, and was halfway through her fifteenth. More than enough to cover the space at HiveMind. They ranged from twelve-by-twelve-inch character studies that she could turn out in a day to more elaborate paintings, like the one of Barnabas. She worked like she was on a deadline, as if she had to get through as many canvases as possible before her time in Fargrove ran out. Depending on when they'd stage the show, she could probably finish a few more.

Elizabeth hadn't considered the possibility of selling her work, but seeing the reaction from everyone made her realize that Rowan's and Trudy's praise wasn't just familial pride.

"I'll do it on one condition: don't promote me as Rowan's niece. I mean, I'm sure most people will figure it out since this is *Far-*

grove. But don't bill me that way, okay?"

Everyone booed.

"Hey, a little nepotism never hurt, but if you insist," Reid replied. "It'll be the worst-kept secret in town."

The group of them started brainstorming immediately, and Elizabeth sipped her glass of wine as they bickered among themselves about how best to promote it, whether she should title the exhibit or would it be pretentious to do so, if they should have a launch party, and if there was a launch party would it only have coffee or should they serve alcohol as well. Elizabeth glanced at James when they mentioned drinks, wondering if Lost Dog would step up to provide beer, but he sucked back his bottle and stared into space. Des offered to reach out to the Fizz to play in the courtyard. Nicky offered to help hang her works, since he was the docent of the Fargrove Historical Museum and frequently had to do double duty setting up exhibits. The entire event took shape without a word of input from Elizabeth, but she didn't mind. They doled out tasks more efficiently than any tech company she'd worked for.

"People, let's eat," Harriet said, balancing a bowl of salad on her belly as she walked to the table. "Who needs drinks? More drinks, anyone?"

Elizabeth's first glass of wine was still half full. There was no way she was blacking out again, especially since James was driving her home. She watched enviously as the rest of the group grabbed bottles and refilled glasses.

Harriet's dinner was a celebration of her culinary skills. They sat elbow to elbow at the table and passed heaping bowls of garlic-drenched pasta, crusty bread, and greens. Elizabeth sat back and watched everyone as they enjoyed the meal. Anna and Willard, so in sync with one another that they almost raised their forks in unison. Harriet and Des, ever the good hosts, making sure that glasses were filled and conversation was equally divided among the guests. Reid and Nicky, still flirting despite their years together. Everyone was having a delightful time.

Everyone but James.

He was a curmudgeon at the end of the table, downing beer after beer and chatting with Willard instead of joining the group conversation. Elizabeth never once saw him smile.

She almost felt guilty for laughing until her cheeks hurt at the other end of the table. Phones stayed facedown on the table in between the stacked dishes or in pockets. There was no discussion of sponsored content, immersive experiences, content curation, or impressions. No one took a single photo, despite how gorgeous they all looked under the strings of lights.

Harriet stood up as the group scraped the bits of Eton mess from their dessert cups. "May I remind you of the rules in the Welbeck household? Ladies, please retire to the fire pit for after-dinner drinks under the stars. Gentlemen, get going on the dishes." She threw her napkin in the air with a flourish and waddled away.

Anna grabbed her wineglass and stood up. "She's serious, Bess. The ladies did the prep, the guys do the cleanup. Come on."

The men groaned and pretended that it was all too much for them, but it was clear the ritual was well established. Elizabeth glanced at her phone to check the time and was shocked that it was midnight. She was even more shocked when an email from Carson Keller showed up as she stared at her screen. It had taken Carson ages to get back to her, but she counted on the fact that he probably had a read receipt tracker on the message, so he'd know exactly when she opened it.

"Bess," Harriet hissed from a wicker chair

by the fire pit. "Come talk to us! *What* is going on with that man?"

"Yes, what did you do to him? I've never seen James so quiet," Anna asked.

Elizabeth was so excited about the email that she could barely hear what they were saying. "I'm going to run to the powder room for a minute, I'll tell you everything when I get back."

The men were bickering in the kitchen, aprons on and sleeves rolled up, trying to decide who was better at loading the dishwasher. James stood off to the side of the cheerful group, draining another pint as Elizabeth slipped by them and out the front door. She needed silence as she processed whatever Carson had to say. She closed her eyes and crossed her fingers before she opened the email.

Two words jumped out at her.

Phone call.

He wanted to set up a phone call! Elizabeth did a little victory dance on the cobblestones. A phone call was halfway to an offer. And an offer was her ticket back. She gazed up at the stars and thanked the universe for finally delivering good news.

The door clicked open behind her. "What are you so excited about?"

It was James, looking grumpy and unsteady.

"I just got some good news."

"About what?"

"Just something back home." She wasn't sure why she didn't want to tell him.

"Ah," he said, crossing his arms. "So, are you leaving us tomorrow now?"

"No, I told you I have more work to do with Rowan. I would never leave before we finished."

"Hm." He stumbled a few steps.

"Are you drunk, James?"

"Why would you say that?" He raised his eyebrows a few seconds after he finished asking the question, as if his facial expressions were on a delay.

"I saw you down about eight beers."

"Were you *watching me,* like a . . . a . . . nanny?"

"I actually was watching you, you're supposed to be my designated driver," Elizabeth replied, enjoying the fact that she was only half a glass of wine deep and James was wasted. "And I was trying to figure out what put you in such a bad mood."

"I'm not in a bad mood, *you're* in a bad mood." His bottom lip jutted out like a little boy's.

"I was when we got here, yes. But I wound

up having a great time. I don't understand why you're not."

He paced in circles on the street in front of the carriage house, occasionally tripping on the cobblestones and trying to play it off. Between the bright moon and the light pouring from neighboring houses he was illuminated enough for Elizabeth to see the furrowed brow and his always-smiling mouth in a tight line.

She didn't like drunk James Holworthy.

He stopped pacing and stomped over to her without warning, forcing her to take a few steps back so they weren't nose to nose. She crossed her arms to ward off a shiver that rolled through her.

"Don't you *see*? It's all for you! All of it!" He threw up his hands in frustration. "Everything. The visits to HiveMind, the puppy, tonight . . ."

"What are you talking about? You're not making sense." Elizabeth fought off a flicker of hope.

He stepped closer to her, breathing heavy like he'd jogged the short distance between them.

"It's all for you, Bess," he said quietly, as if repeating the words would make her understand. "Since the first time I saw you, it's all been for you."

"The first time? You mean when we met at Rowan's party?"

"No, at HiveMind!" He stomped away, frustrated that she wasn't following his drunken logic. "I saw you there. We saw each other, right? You were checking your phone in the courtyard." He walked back and glared at her. He hadn't touched her, but the fireworks in her spine were back. "I couldn't look away from you."

"But what do you mean 'all for you'?" she asked. She could feel heat radiating from him.

"Every single thing I've done since you arrived is to get closer to you." His voice went soft. "Catching your hat? That was thanks to the wind, but I would've found a way to talk to you. Those accidental meetings at HiveMind? Those weren't accidents, Reid told me you were there. He was my lookout. And going to meet Amber tonight? I went because you suggested it. I just . . . wanted to be near you." He started to reach for her, then stopped abruptly.

"Then why did you say what you said when we got here?" Elizabeth didn't want to repeat the words, or hear him say them again.

James was quiet for a long time, like he needed to work up the courage to answer her. When he finally did, his voice was a whisper.

"Because I liked you immediately. You are magnificent, Elizabess, in so many ways." The raw emotion in his face shocked Elizabeth. His shoulders slumped and he cupped his hands against his chest. "And I *hate* that I like you."

Her heart thumped, and she rubbed her arms to smooth the goose bumps that had nothing to do with the temperature. She ached to touch him and steal some of the electricity swirling around him. "But . . . why?"

James stared at the ground and didn't say anything for a few minutes.

"Have you ever been in a long-distance relationship? Nothing but heartbreak, I tell you. Never again. My girlfriend Marion? Boyfriend in Paris the whole time. I was her boyfriend." He banged on his chest to emphasize the point, then listed from side to side and cupped his hands around his mouth to shout, "Long distance is *always rubbish!*"

Elizabeth waited a moment before she answered. "It doesn't have to be like that, James."

He harrumphed and went back to pacing in circles in the street.

"Do you want to know what I like about you, Bess? Huh? Obviously, I like the way you look." He ticked his thumb. "I mean, who wouldn't? You're a goddess. I can't think straight when you're around." He ticked his pointer finger. "Reid told me you're super fecking smart with all of his computer stuff, and to me that's a ninja combo: beauty and brains." He paused in the middle of the street and let out a tiny burp. "Uhhh . . . I like your *dog.* Georgina is a very good girl." He ticked his middle finger.

Suddenly, drunk James Holworthy was enchanting.

"Wait, wait, there's more." James threw his head back and closed his eyes for a few seconds, swaying in place, then pointed at her triumphantly. "Your art! You are a kick-ass painter. So that's five things I like: you're pretty, you're smart, you've got an awesome dog, and you are an incredible painter lady."

"That's only four things," Elizabeth said, trying to keep from laughing at his drunken math. "But that's plenty."

He mumbled to himself, counting off on his fingers. "You're right. Well, I'll come up with a fifth thing. Hell, give me a chance and I'll come up with a *million* things I like about you, Bess. A million and one things."

His voice dropped to a whisper. "A billion things."

James paused in the middle of the street and looked at her with an expression Elizabeth couldn't read. Angry? Confused? Sad? He stomped toward her in full furrow like he was getting ready to register a complaint with customer service. Every step he took set off a spark in her chest because she knew exactly what was about to happen.

Drunk James Holworthy was going to kiss her.

He came to an abrupt stop about a foot away. The furrow disappeared and his whole body relaxed, as if being in her orbit calmed him. "Hi, Bess."

He stood still, just staring at her, so Elizabeth took a step closer and placed her hand on his arm.

"Hi, James."

Elizabeth knew the kiss was inevitable, so the wait felt delicious. The pause stretched out, and they smiled at each other, sharing the moment before the moment that would change everything between them.

The door clicked open loudly enough that they both jumped, and Des peeked his head out. He looked at them and seemed to realize what he'd interrupted. "Uhhh, all okay out here? Harriet was getting worried."

"We're grand," James said as he leaned away from Elizabeth, smiling a giant fake smile. "Thanks, mate."

"There you are!" Harriet crowded Des in the doorway and looked from Elizabeth to James and then back to Elizabeth. "What's going on?"

"We were just getting some air. Someone's had a bit too much," Elizabeth said, gesturing to James. "And he's my ride."

"Really? He never drinks like this. Are you sober, Bess?"

"Incredibly."

"James," Des said. "Bess is driving you home."

"Wait a minute, the steering wheel —" Elizabeth interjected.

"Wot?" James said over her. "Never! That's not celery . . . chivalry. *Chivalrous.*"

Harriet giggled and shot Elizabeth a knowing look.

"Either you're sleeping here or she's driving you. Those are your only options."

"You lot get up too early, I'll take the Bess option." He was standing with his legs wide in an effort to stay upright.

Des looked at Elizabeth. "Can you drive on our side of the road?"

"That's what I'm trying to say. No, I cannot!"

James patted her arm. "Bess, yes you can. I bet you can do *anything.* I'll help you. I need to get home to let the P-man pee. Right? Porter needs to go out. It's close, and I'll help you."

"Think you can manage?" Des asked, looking concerned. "If not, I'll drive him and we can get Reid to take you back. But James doesn't live that far from Rowan and Trudy's, you could probably drive him home then walk from his place. Ten minutes max."

"I'll do it," Elizabeth said. "It's too much to get everyone driving this late. I just need some tips. And I think we should head out soon." She pointed at James, who was standing next to them swaying slightly with his eyes closed.

The group assembled outside as Elizabeth got settled in the driver's seat of James's Peugeot. Des and Nicky plotted the route while Harriet shouted encouragement over their shoulders. James sat silently in the passenger seat with a bemused expression on his face.

"This Uber driver is a keeper, man." He gestured to Elizabeth.

"Mind the hedgerows," Des said. "The roads are narrow. And don't forget: drive on the left!"

She nodded and backed out slowly while they watched her. Harriet had her hands pressed to her mouth, which hardly made Elizabeth feel confident.

"Drive on the *left*!" they screamed in unison as Elizabeth found the correct lane.

James laughed, and Elizabeth tried to focus on navigating as he slid his hand on top of her thigh and promptly fell asleep.

CHAPTER TWENTY-SEVEN

The headlights illuminated the windowed front door of James's cottage, making Porter's eyes glow like laser beams.

"You live here?" Elizabeth asked as she parked. The tiny white stone cottage was straight out of a Hans Christian Andersen story, the type of home where a magical grandmother might dote on her half-fairy, half-human offspring while she talked to the woodland animals.

"Welcome to the piggery!" James said as he opened the door and fell out of the car. He stood up slowly and beckoned Elizabeth to follow him. "It used to be a pig barn until I renovated it. Now, this isn't a drop-and-run, you must come in and meet Portie." He took a giant iron key off a hook by the door and fumbled with it.

"Why is your key hanging right next to the lock?" Elizabeth asked.

"This isn't to keep the bad guys out, it's

to keep Porter in. He's an ace picklock. Sometimes people stop by to visit him while I'm at work and it's easier than passing out a million keys."

James finally managed to open the door and he dropped to his knees to greet Porter. "My boy, didja miss me? Didja?" He scratched the oversized brown dog along the neck while Porter headbutted his chest.

Porter was massive, the biggest dog Elizabeth had ever seen in real life. She tried to talk herself out of her visceral fear response but couldn't stop herself from trembling.

"Go say hi to our lovely guest," James said, pointing to Elizabeth. She steeled herself for whatever Porter was about to deliver. A jump would knock her over, but she didn't want to start screaming in front of James.

Porter untangled himself from James and seemed to realize that someone else was in the room. He trotted over and danced in place in front of Elizabeth, opting to jig instead of jump. She reached out tentatively and he swooped his head beneath her hand before she could think twice, still Riverdancing with joy.

"He prances when he's happy," James said.

His fur was satin. Elizabeth stroked him

as he turned from side to side in front of her. "How much does he weigh?"

"You're petting thirty-six kilos of muscle and heart right there," James replied. He reclined on the floor with his fingers laced behind his head. He stretched almost from one end of the tiny front room to the other.

Elizabeth massaged Porter's shoulders the way Trudy had shown her, and the dog leaned into her to signal that she was very good at it. She stopped for a moment and Porter threw himself against her outstretched hands, almost toppling her. She laughed and glanced at James.

He was snoring on the slate floor.

She took the opportunity to peek around the little cottage. The high gray-beamed ceiling helped give the illusion of space in the pocket-sized home. The rock walls were painted a bright white, and there were pops of color around the place, like an Hermès orange end table by the tasteful taupe couch and a bright blue Dutch door leading out of the kitchen. She could see the edge of his old-fashioned bronze bed in a room around the corner. She'd envisioned James living in a sleek modern apartment, but seeing him filling up the space in the storybook cottage made sense too.

Porter walked to the door and whined,

but James didn't move.

"James," Elizabeth said quietly. "Porter needs to go out."

"Hmf? Just open the door and walk out with him, he'll be quick." He rolled over onto his right side and curled his hands beneath his head.

"Leash?"

"No leash. Porter is the best boy." He didn't even open his eyes.

"I guess it's you and me," Elizabeth said to Porter. "Let's go."

They walked out to the open area by the gravel driveway, and Elizabeth could understand exactly why James had made his home in a former pig barn. It was the perfect combination of wild wooded land in back and endless pasture in front. Elizabeth spotted a vine-draped trellis in the distance and envisioned the path James had carved in the untamed forest.

Porter sniffed his way around the grounds, made a few deposits along the way, and trotted back to Elizabeth looking proud. She'd never felt so at ease with a dog so quickly, especially one that looked pumped up on steroids. The dog radiated calm kindness.

"Now what?" she asked him. "Is it time for me to go kiss your person?"

Porter raced back to the front door and

waited for Elizabeth to open it. James was still asleep on the floor, curled in a ball. Porter jumped up on the couch and settled with his head on the armrest so he could observe.

She tiptoed to James and bent over him, watching him breathe. He looked portfolio perfect; he was on his side with his strong profile highlighted against the black floor. She snuck to get her phone out of her purse and then straddled him, leaning in close to his face so that she could frame the shot. She twisted her phone a few times, trying to find the right light, then snapped the photo.

The sound of the mechanical shutter startled him awake. He snatched Elizabeth's wrist, making her shriek and sending her phone clattering to the ground. Porter barked at the commotion.

"No," he said, holding on to her. "Not . . . fair."

His grip was a hot vise around her wrist, and Elizabeth couldn't tell if he was serious. He looked up at her with his eyes at half mast and finally smiled. "You are so damn pretty, Bess."

"Thank you." Elizabeth was sure her phone's screen was cracked, which overshadowed the fact that James Holworthy was slowly pulling her closer to him. "Can I just grab my phone? It sounded like it hit the ground hard."

"No, you cannot." He sat up. "Forget about your damn phone for a minute, would you? Look at me."

Elizabeth was hunched over awkwardly, still caught in his grip.

"Sit, please."

She sat down on the cold tile in front of him and he finally let go of her.

"You said something to me that night at the Tups, right as you were leaving. Do you remember it?" The short nap seemed to have cleaned some of the cobwebs from his brain.

Elizabeth shook her head and blanched. How had she embarrassed herself in front of him? The night was a haze after her fourth ale, despite the breakthrough moments of clarity she experienced when James looked through her.

"I didn't think you'd remember, but I do. I'm not going to tell you what you said, but I will tell you that you were right. And that's all I want to say on the subject right now."

Elizabeth tried to imagine what she might have said to James under the influence of the potent Lost Dog ales. That he was hot? That she'd dreamed about him? Stalked him? Every possibility was more embarrassing than the last.

"Was it something awful?"

"No, no, it was wonderful, actually." He grinned at her, but it didn't make her less mortified about what she might have revealed.

They sat cross-legged on the floor staring at each other, neither one saying a word.

"So beautiful," he said under his breath.

Elizabeth studied him back, admiring the dusting of stubble on his cheeks. His hair seemed to also have suffered the effects of his drinking, and she wanted to wrap one of his unruly curls around her fingertip. She couldn't stop staring at his mouth. The full lower lip that was begging to be nibbled and kissed.

It was time. Elizabeth leaned toward James and closed her eyes, ready for him to catch her if she tumbled off balance, but he cupped a gentle hand on her cheek, stopping her. She opened her eyes.

"Don't you want to . . ." She trailed off. "I mean, we were about to at Harriet's . . ."

"I know, and I'm so happy that we didn't."

She frowned at him.

"Bess, do you really want to kiss a drunken fool while you're completely sober? Is that the kind of first kiss we should have?" He ran his thumb across her mouth, setting off sparks at the base of her spine, so ticklish that she arched her back to disperse them. "I don't want to miss any of it. I didn't let it happen last time and I won't let it happen now."

"Last time?"

He smiled at her. "You don't remember a thing, huh? Let me take you to dinner tomorrow and I'll tell you everything that happened at the Tups. And then . . ."

She brushed her finger across his coarse cheek. "What if I don't want to wait?"

"I'm begging you." He stifled a laugh like it was an inside joke. "Tomorrow."

He stood up and offered his hand to Elizabeth, pulling her to her feet with a dancer's grace. Porter thumped his tail on the couch as they walked to the door.

She was slow to leave, unsure if she should reach out and shake his hand to say goodbye, open her arms to ask for a hug, or just wave at him. James watched her with a bemused expression as she wrestled with her options.

A familiar squawk sounded a few feet away.

"Oh my God, my phone!"

It was still where she'd dropped it, face-down on the floor.

CHAPTER TWENTY-EIGHT

"Well, good early morning to you. Painting already?" Rowan asked as he walked into the Operculum, cup of tea in hand. Georgina ran over to leap on him, then settled into a quivering sit as he folded himself in half to pet her. Major waited for his turn like a patient old man.

"You'll never believe what happened last night." Elizabeth herself still couldn't believe everything that had occurred in the past twelve hours. "I don't know what I was thinking; I agreed to an art show at Hive-Mind."

"How wonderful!" Rowan cheered, causing Georgina to leap-hop out of her sit. "When?"

"We didn't pick a date, but it obviously has to be soon so I'm trying to churn out as many as I can." She turned her small canvas so he could see the happy cow face she was working on. She didn't mention that staying busy also kept her from thinking about her date with James.

"Well, you're not leaving us for many weeks yet, so there's time."

Rowan often talked about her stay as if it were indefinite. She didn't have the heart to tell him that she'd finally managed to schedule a call with the elusive Carson Keller the next day. Everything was falling into place, which made the thought of leaving slightly less painful.

Elizabeth cleared her throat. "I have a date tonight."

"Last night was busy indeed! With whom?"

"James Holworthy. He was at your party, the beer guy."

"James! Oh, we like him, very much. Aren't you the social butterfly?"

And for the first time in her life she was. After the score-carding social life she thought was real in San Fran, the ease of connecting with people in Fargrove seemed too good to be true.

"How do you know him?" Elizabeth asked.

"How do we know James?" Rowan repeated back to her, stroking his chin. "He became friends with Reid when he moved into the area, and any friend of Reid's is a friend of ours."

Rowan settled in front of his giant canvas with Major at his feet, sipping his tea and assessing his work. Elizabeth often watched him during their morning painting sessions, not only to pick up pointers but to giggle at his conversations with his canvases. He talked to them quietly as he painted, sometimes scolding when the work wasn't coming together, other times offering encouragement and praise as a shadow or reflection took shape. Any time Elizabeth heard, *Well, then*! she knew Rowan was having a successful session.

"It's shearing day for the ladies," he said as he got started. "I guess you would call it a makeover."

"They're getting their hair cut today? I still haven't painted Rosie and Blossom! Do I have enough photos to work from?" Elizabeth slapped her back pocket and realized that she'd left her phone on the kitchen table. The case had a giant scratch on it, her reminder that everything she thought she had dreamed about the night before had really happened.

"It'll grow back, you'll have other opportunities."

Elizabeth didn't know what the growing-out period was for fleece, but she knew it was probably months, not weeks.

They painted for an hour, interrupted by Elizabeth's alarm when it was time to get to the actual work. Even though inventorying his history in the Operculum had overwhelmed her at first, she'd discovered she was perfect for the job. The advanced spreadsheet she'd created helped streamline the process, enabling them to get through stacks of history faster than either would've preferred.

They were assessing a pencil study from Rowan's river period when Major let out a warning *wuff.* Georgina leapt up from a full sleep and tipped her head, trying to determine what Major was reacting to. A few seconds later they heard wheels on the gravel, and the barking kicked into high gear.

"That'll be David the shearer," Rowan said, setting his paintbrush down and dusting off his hands. "You can't miss this, off we go."

Elizabeth looked around the barn at the remaining stacks as she followed Rowan out. Even though they worked diligently every day, they were nowhere near done.

"David's here," Trudy said, pointing her cast to the man in a sleeveless black T-shirt unloading his truck.

"Sorry for the delay, Mrs. Barnes," he said

as he pulled equipment from the bed. "Busy season." Major ran barky laps around the man with Georgina on his heels.

"Ah, well, a few extra days with the wind in their fleece was fine, I'm sure." She turned to Elizabeth. "You'll want to get close when he starts. That way you can take photos to show your friends in California."

Elizabeth hadn't posted a picture in days, and shearing the ladies was sure to be a photogenic once-in-a-lifetime opportunity. She followed Rowan, Trudy, and the dogs as David made his way into the barn. Major had brought the ladies in early, and it was almost as if Blossom and Rosie knew what the special circumstances meant. If they were nervous about what was going to happen they didn't look it. Elizabeth considered running back to the house to fetch her phone, but she didn't want to miss a moment of the strange ritual.

William joined them and shooed the dogs out of the barn so Blossom and Rosie would have one less thing to worry about. Georgina paced back in front of the open door, occasionally daring to poke her nose over the threshold. Each time she breached it, William turned to her and shook his head meaningfully, and she put her head down and stepped back until she was beside Major.

"I wish I could communicate with her like that," Elizabeth said to him. "It's like you have telepathy with her."

"You'll get there, Bess," William replied. "You've come quite far. Georgina is devoted to you, you both just need a wee bit more . . . polishing. And you need to have faith in your handling skills."

Their training had indeed come far under William and Trudy's care. Georgina responded to the full suite of basic cues when Elizabeth asked, which still shocked her given their rocky start. William didn't push Georgina's herding training, only exposing her to the sheep for short periods to assess her potential. He'd commented on her low tail when she was near Blossom and Rosie, explaining that it meant she was stable and not excitable, a surprising revelation based on what Elizabeth knew of the dog. William told Trudy the pup already had a "good stop," and Elizabeth assumed that it meant Georgina had potential.

"We begin," the shearer said. He turned to one of the sheep, which Elizabeth now knew to be Rosie because the fleece on her chest was slightly darker than Blossom's, and in a move that looked like a karate take-down, he flipped her onto her rump so that she was seated on her tail in between his legs. The shearer was strong, and handsome in a wild and muddy way. At home, a sweaty man in a dirty tank top would've been invisible, but now, after weeks in Fargrove, she couldn't ignore the magnetism of rough-hewn muscles.

"It's going to go quickly," William said, standing next to Elizabeth at the gate. "David is a wizard on the handpiece. Thirty-five strokes or less."

The shearer balanced Rosie between his legs and started shaving her low belly near her back legs, slicing through the thick fleece like he was peeling an orange. Rosie sat perfectly still in the awkward position, allowing the shearer to move the clipper rhythmically across her body. Much of the fleece came off in a large piece as he worked, leaving faint track marks in what was left of the wool on her pinkish skin.

"Does it hurt?" Elizabeth asked.

William stared at her for a moment before he answered. "Do you think these two would let anything hurt their babies?"

The shearer manipulated Rosie from one side to the other, occasionally grasping an ear to maneuver her, or tucking her head through his legs while she sat balanced on her rump. She took it all so calmly that Elizabeth wondered if losing her heavy, muckish coat felt good despite the contortions. When he flipped her onto her side she thought she saw Rosie close her eyes, as if she were getting a massage at a spa. Elizabeth was shocked by this version of the grumpy sheep. No bleating complaints, no nipping at boots, just calm acceptance of her hairdresser's work.

A minute later he was done, and Rosie looked unrecognizable. Skinny, bright white, stick-legged. The shearer gave Rosie an "atta girl" pat on the side before she dashed away. Trudy opened the gate so that she could run out to the small field just outside the barn.

"Watch this," she said to Elizabeth, beckoning her to the doorway so that she could take in the full impact of Rosie's annual makeover.

Rosie stood in the middle of the field with her nose in the air, as if reacquainting herself with the feeling of the wind on her nearly naked skin. Then she took off running, jumping and kicking joyfully.

"They revel in it," Trudy said, cradling her cast. "I just love to watch them on shearing day."

Elizabeth had never seen the stoic sheep

move with such agility. Rosie leapt and pranced her way around the small field, then made her way back to where Trudy and Elizabeth were standing.

"You look lovely," Trudy said as Rosie ambled closer. "Such a pretty girl."

It was time. Elizabeth had never been so close to one of the sheep, but after weeks of watching them from a distance as Georgina worked them, she felt like she understood them better. They were confident creatures that walked the line between bowing to authority and bucking it, often literally. They were observers and deep thinkers. They played favorites, opting to follow William on some days and Trudy on others. And there was no denying it: they were adorable. She needed to paint them quickly, with their before and after looks, so that she could include them in her show at Hive-Mind.

Instead of half stepping behind Trudy for protection as she normally did, Elizabeth held her ground while Rosie snuffled around her feet. Rosie looked up at her, twitching her ears, and seemed to ponder how to interact with the nervous acquaintance at close range.

"You do look very pretty," Elizabeth said. "It's like you just broke up with your boyfriend and you needed a new style. It suits you."

She reached out her hand and Rosie stepped closer, so Elizabeth tentatively scratched the top of her head between her ears. When she stopped Rosie bowed her head and leaned gently against Elizabeth's leg as if to say, *Do go on,* so Elizabeth scratched with more gusto. She was surprised to discover that petting Rosie felt very similar to petting Georgina, Major, or Porter. And based on Rosie's reaction, she was very good at it.

"Finally," Trudy said with a sigh. "You're finally friends. I've been waiting for this since the first day you met them. Now just try to rid yourself of her."

Elizabeth laughed and headed back inside the barn to watch the shearer prepare Blossom. Rosie followed close behind them, bleating jealously.

CHAPTER TWENTY-NINE

"Why are we here?" Elizabeth asked as they pulled up to James's cottage. Was he fast-tracking their date, starting with dessert?

"I have to show you something." He smiled at her. "I think you're going to like it."

Elizabeth watched for Porter's happy face in the window, but he didn't appear. James almost ran to the front door and swung it open without unlocking it.

"Come." He beckoned. "This way."

He led her back to the bedroom, and she worried about what had him so excited. Was this the part where she found out he was a sex maniac with handcuffs attached to his bed? Was he going to show off a dildo collection?

Porter woofed at James as he walked in the room, and for a moment she couldn't see past James's broad shoulders. He stepped to the side and there in front of him was Porter dancing beside a small dog crate covered with a blanket.

"You did it? You brought her home?" Elizabeth's eyes filled with tears. She dropped to her knees and peered inside the crate, and Amber's little face emerged from the shadows. "I can't believe it! How did you make it happen so quickly?"

"It helps to be an F.O.T., a friend of Trudy. That woman runs the place! They let me speed the process since I was there with her blessing. And yours too, of course. Lisa thinks you're amazing."

"Can we let her out?" Elizabeth was so excited to see Amber out of the shelter that the compliment didn't register.

Porter was still dancing in place next to the crate, pausing to peek inside at his new sister and then resuming his choreography. He barked again, as if to get them to hurry up.

"Of course we can! Hey, Amber," he said softly. "Come see your guardian angel. She's the reason you're here."

Elizabeth bit the inside of her cheek. She'd done a full face for the first time in ages, lashes and all, and she didn't want to start the evening with runny eye makeup.

Amber stepped out of the crate and looked around. She shook off, and Elizabeth remembered that Trudy called it a *level set* or a way to signal stress or arousal. Porter danced beside Amber, bopping his nose on her small body every few steps. The dog was overjoyed with his new sister.

"How's it going?" Elizabeth watched Amber closely as she sniffed her way around the room, trying to remember everything Trudy had told her about canine stress signals.

"It's only been a few hours, but so far so good. Obviously Porter adores her." He gestured to his dog, who was play-bowing in front of Amber over and over, trying to get the puppy to play with him. "And she seems fine. A little overwhelmed, but that's to be expected."

Amber walked to Elizabeth with Porter dancing beside her.

"Hello, friend," she said softly. "Isn't this great?" She scratched her under the chin and the pup wagged her tail. Porter nose-bopped Amber again and the little dog turned abruptly and yipped at him.

"Whoa!" Elizabeth said. "Look who's boss!"

"Yeah, that's happened a few times. Total role reversal. Porter is acting like a lovesick dope, and she's acting like the grown-up. Let's get them outside for a potty trip and then go. I'm starving."

"Wait, you mean we're not going to stay here and play with them all night?"

"We'll have plenty of time for that." He paused. "Well, for a few weeks at least."

It was his first long-distance wisecrack of the evening. Elizabeth wondered how many times it would come up throughout their date.

"Besides, she's exhausted. Porter and I ran her ragged. Look," James said, trying to change the subject.

Amber was splayed on her side, pawing Porter's nose as he tried to entice her to play.

"Let's have a quick dinner and finish the night here," Elizabeth said before she realized what she was implying.

The Blue Boar gastropub was nearly empty when James and Elizabeth arrived. The two men sitting at a table turned to stare at them when they walked in, then went back to ignoring one another in favor of the television.

"I'm sorry that we're mixing business and pleasure," James said as he led her in. "I promise the food here is amazing. It'll be a good night."

Elizabeth didn't mind that James was piggybacking a customer service visit on their evening. The Blue Boar had finally taken on two of Lost Dog's beers after months of James's wooing, and he was checking in to see how they were performing on what was sure to be a busy night. She was eager to see him in action.

The gastropub wasn't ancient and quaint like the Three Tups. It had a soaring tin ceiling, chalkboards with impressive lettering describing the day's specials, and a show-stopping rough-hewn wooden bar that ran the length of the room.

"I'm afraid we have to sit at the bar," he said quietly. "I can pick up more that way. And I'll need your eyes and ears as well."

The flat-capped bartender smiled widely when he spotted James and reached out his hand. "Welcome back, good to see you, mate! Checking up on us, eh?"

"Not at all, just a friendly visit for a bite. Rory, this is Bess."

Rory gave her a once-over, his eyes lingering on her short floral skirt. "So nice to meet James's lady. I can tell already you're far too good for him."

"Oh, I'm not . . . we're just . . ." Elizabeth wasn't sure exactly what they were.

"Bess has relatives in Fargrove, but she lives in the States. She's heading back soon."

Two mentions.

"Well, I hope you'll have fun while you're here." Rory winked at her. "Now, what are you having?"

She squinted at the tap handles down the bar. "Do I see the new saison on tap? I'll have that, please."

"A fine Lost Dog Sealyham Saison for the lady. And for you, sir?"

"The same." James turned to her with a huge smile. "You remembered. I mentioned the saison to you at the Tups and you remembered."

"That's basically all I remember. So about that night . . ."

"Yes, that night. All in good time." He winked at her.

Rory pulled their beers and chatted with James, and as they talked Elizabeth began to understand just how important the social aspect was to his job. The deal was officially closed — the Blue Boar already had his beers on tap — but to keep the orders coming he had to make the staff like him and the liquids he represented, so that when someone asked them to suggest an ale, a Lost Dog would be the first to come to mind.

She didn't mind letting him work. She understood a strong work ethic far better than most. James was driven and proud of his product, and after watching him finesse Rory and his cohort behind the bar, it was clear he was very good at what he did. Too good, as Rory wouldn't leave them alone. But when the bar started to fill, Rory had to get to work and they were finally able to focus on each other.

"Do you do events for the brewery?" Elizabeth asked him.

"Sure, we do, loads of them. Trivia nights are popular, of course. Sometimes we'll do tap takeovers at new accounts to introduce our stuff. Support local band launches, that sort of thing."

"Have you done any *at* the brewery?"

"Never. Why do you ask?"

"I was just brainstorming while you guys were talking. The most popular events at my old job were the ones held on campus, because people loved seeing behind the curtain. I just thought it could be cool for you guys to do the same thing. Invite your fans and favorite clients so they can see the heart that goes into the Lost Dog label."

"We're not really set up for that sort of thing. We've got a tidy spot, but it's not consumer ready. Where would everyone pee?" He was staring into space with a frown as if envisioning hordes of people urinating in front of him.

"Outdoor loos for hire, like at Rowan's party. You could try it once and see how it goes. If it's terrible, then don't do it again. But I think it would be a great way to build loyalty, James. Tours, tastings, sell a bunch of T-shirts. Create your own hashtag for social media stuff." She shrugged and sipped her beer.

"Hm. I'll bring it up with the team. But I promise we're done with beer talk for the night, okay? It's bad enough I dragged you here on a work call. You must think I'm the most boring person in the world."

"Business is never boring. I love it. I live for it."

He grimaced. "That's sort of sad, Bess. Business? There's got to be something else that you love and live for. What are you going home to? What do you miss about San Francisco?" He traced the condensation on the side of the glass. "Or should I say, who do you miss?"

The weight of the question after talk of firkins and casks and a brewer's true vision caught her off guard. Then the realization that she didn't know how to answer it made her tongue-tied.

"Well, obviously I'm excited to get back to work. I've been working while I was here, of course, but it wasn't exactly in my area of expertise."

James nodded thoughtfully, still manipulating the glass in front of him. "So that's all you're excited for? Work? No friends, family, pets, boyfriends?"

She started to switch into spin mode, but for the first time ever she opted for honesty. "My work didn't really give me much time for friends," she said softly. "Or boyfriends." She gave him a meaningful look and he glanced at her out of the corner of his eye, as if gauging her truthfulness. "And as for family . . . well, all that's left is what's here. My mother died when I was twelve, and my father died six months ago. No siblings."

He turned to her, sympathy etched into his face. "I'm so sorry, Bess. You must still be grieving. Losing a parent . . . losing *both* parents . . ." He trailed off and shook his head, then reached over and rubbed her back. It was so comforting, so genuine. Elizabeth couldn't remember anyone touching her that way as she dealt with losing her parents.

"My mom passing, yeah, it was awful. Right when I needed her, right when all that adolescent girl stuff started happening. I was so mad at her." She smiled and tried to play it off but couldn't control the telltale prickle in her nose. She focused on the two barmen stacking glasses.

"And your father? How's . . . that going? I mean, how are you?"

"I'm fine," she answered quickly. "We weren't close. Not at all. He never even told me about Fargrove. I didn't know Rowan and Trudy existed, so that should give you some idea as to what I was dealing with. But I've learned more about him while I've been here. It's given me a new perspective on him, I guess."

"That sounds like . . . what's that word? Closure?"

"Sort of, yes. I see him differently now." She didn't mention that she still couldn't quite forgive him.

James nodded, took a long gulp of his beer, and seemed unsure how to proceed.

"Your turn," Elizabeth said overly cheerfully. "Now let's talk about *your* painful stuff."

"What pain?" He looked baffled. "Nothing to complain about here. I've got a great job, amazing mates, two perfect dogs . . ."

"One word: Paris."

He crossed his arms and leaned away from her. "Oh, *that.* Or should I say, her."

Elizabeth nodded.

"Marion was here for six months. She worked for a wind turbine manufacturer

337

and was here setting up a remote office. We were together almost the whole time, and we planned to stay together after she went home." He glared at his beer. "Reid was the one who told me what was going on. She kept posting pictures on her social media and there was always this . . . guy in the background. Obviously, I was clueless. I literally just upgraded from a flip phone." He pointed to his iPhone peeking out of his breast pocket. "She posted a video thing of her kissing the guy, and I guess it was supposed to disappear after a certain amount of time, but Reid snagged it and showed it to me. So that was it."

"I'm so sorry, James. What an awful way to find out." His hatred of social media took on a new dimension.

"It was." He took another swallow of beer and avoided looking at her. "Live and learn."

The words hung between them, the weight of what they meant casting a shadow over what had started off as a perfect night. But the pub filled, their meals appeared, and they managed to keep the conversation focused on the dogs, avoiding too-serious topics like dead parents, cheating exes, and looming departure dates. James scooted his chair closer to Elizabeth as people lined up for drinks. Even though the room was buzzing with activity, the air around them seemed soundproofed.

Rory appeared in front of them. "Another?" He pointed at their nearly empty pints.

"We're taking it slow tonight, we're good for now, mate. Thanks."

There would be no alcohol to blame for whatever happened between them.

Elizabeth scraped up the last of her butternut squash curry. The night was going quickly, and she needed answers.

"Can we talk about the Tups now? What did I do? Harriet said she didn't see me dancing on tables, so what was it?"

They were locked in on each other, leaning in close with their shoulders touching and staring so intently that neither one noticed Rory quietly trying to get James's attention.

"I'm sorry to disturb," he said, clearing his throat. "James, could you try this? Someone said it tastes off." He held out a quarter-filled pint glass.

"My bitter? That's unlikely, it was just delivered yesterday." James took the glass and drank the amber liquid in a single swig, then made a face. "Oh. Well. That's not right at all, is it? I'll sort it out. May I go down to the cellar?"

"We'd appreciate it, thanks."

James looked like he was already working through the possible scenarios before he'd even stood up, then seemed to remember that Elizabeth was there with him.

"Would you like to join me in the cellar?"

"I don't know, would I? It sounds ominous."

"It's actually quite interesting. Come, it's the heart of the pub, and not everyone gets to see it." He grabbed the empty pint glass off the bar and took her hand.

She followed him down a narrow flight of stairs, down a brightly lit hallway to a cramped room with a low ceiling filled with silver kegs and octopus tubing that threaded into the ceiling.

"This is where the magic happens," he said gesturing around them.

"It's *freezing* in here," Elizabeth said, hugging her arms close to her chest.

"That's how they like it," James said, patting one of the silver bullets.

"How can you tell which keg is yours?" she asked.

"They're casks, and trust me, I could find ours with my eyes closed even if I hadn't been here for the install."

Elizabeth walked around the room and

340

followed the lines up through the ceiling. "That's the bar above us?"

"Indeed it is. Taste this." He handed her the pint glass, which he'd filled directly from the cask. He watched her intently.

"It's fine, right?" he asked.

"Delicious."

"So, the problem is not with Lost Dog, but with the Blue Boar's dirty lines. If they don't regularly flush the lines that carry the beer to the taps, they end up with dodgy brew. Now I have to tell Rory to step up his housekeeping." He leaned against the wall and crossed his arms. "Awkward."

"He seems to like you, and I'm sure you'll approach it gently." Elizabeth hugged herself to ward off the chill.

"I'm quite good at being gentle," James said, half to himself and half to her. He was staring at the floor, deep in thought.

"Brrr," Elizabeth said quietly. She didn't mean for it to be audible. Though she was freezing, she didn't want to leave the cramped little room. She liked being alone with James with the clueless crowd just a few feet above their heads.

"You're cold! I'm so sorry," James said, snapping back into the present. He walked over to her and rubbed her arms from her shoulders to her elbows, setting off trails of sparklers on her skin. "Better?" He didn't suggest leaving to warm up.

"Not really," she replied as a series of images flip-carded through her mind.

The red door.

James sitting on the planter.

His hands on her arms.

"Oh my God, I threw myself at you at the Tups!"

James laughed. "You remembered!"

"I'm mortified. I *never* drink that much." She could feel her cheeks getting hot. "Did I actually kiss you?"

"You tried. It landed here." He pointed to his chin.

"I can't believe you still want to talk to me." She shook her head. "Wow. Sorry."

"Now why would you be sorry? What man doesn't want a beautiful woman begging for a kiss?"

"I *begged*?"

"You did." James nodded, his warm hands still wrapped around her arms. "Now it's my turn. And I'm going to quote you." He lowered his voice to a husky whisper. "Let's just kiss. Let's just try it."

He stood close, his green eyes locked on hers. She searched his face for any sign of teasing, but he looked like he wanted to devour her. He didn't move.

Elizabeth stood up on her tiptoes, grabbed the edges of his collar, and pulled him closer. If he wouldn't make the official first move, she would.

"Please, please, please," she whispered with a little smile.

They paused for a second as if sharing a joke, then touched their lips together. Elizabeth shuddered, partly from the chill in the air and partly from the jolt of his soft lips finally settling on top of hers.

Within a second she was no longer cold. Locked in his arms, Elizabeth felt like she was surrounded by sunlight. She pressed her body even closer to his and he locked his arms tightly around her waist as they kissed. She nipped his bottom lip and he responded by kissing her harder, like it was a contest that he needed to win. James wrapped his hand in her hair and tugged gently so that her neck was exposed, then nibbled, licked, and kissed his way from the hollow at her throat to the secret spot behind her ear. Her knees almost gave out.

"I waited too long for this, but it was worth it," he whispered, sending a fresh wave of heat through her body.

He ran a hand down her back, detouring to the curve of her hip. His fingers teased the hem of her skirt, slipping underneath as they kissed and skimming along the bare skin of her thighs. She pushed her hips against him, signaling that he was welcome to explore. James traced slow circles on her leg, each one moving slightly higher, until his fingers hit lace. She silently begged him not to stop.

"James?" A loud voice echoed down the hallway. "All okay down there? How's the Mad Dog?"

Elizabeth leapt away from James and slapped her hands over her mouth, eyes wide.

"It's all good down here, Rory," James called back, bending over at the waist and breathing heavily. "We're coming." He mouthed, *No, we're not,* and Elizabeth laughed.

"Nice timing, Rory," she whispered to James. "But we should go up. I don't want to get a reputation as the whore of the Blue Boar. Not that I want to stop . . ."

"Your honor is at stake, I understand," he replied. "Let me just grab a taste of Mad Dog for Rory so I can make my case." He pulled her into a final embrace, locking his lips over hers for a moment, then pushed her away as Elizabeth's hand started exploring his waistband.

They walked through the narrow halls in

the cellar and right before they got to the bottom of the steps, Elizabeth grabbed James into another melting kiss.

"Shall we settle up and leave?" she asked.

"Definitely."

Rory was waiting for them at the top of the stairs, and Elizabeth hoped that her flushed cheeks and messy hair didn't give away what they'd been doing. She went back to her seat at the bar to allow James privacy as he dealt with the dirty-line issue.

"He tried to get us to stay for another as a thank-you, but I can't wait another minute," James whispered to her once he was done. "Besides, I want a clear head for what I'm about to do to you. Let's go."

Elizabeth raised her eyebrows in mock shock. "What *are* you going to do to me?"

He grabbed her hand and pulled her off her bar stool.

"Let's just say I might get you to beg again."

CHAPTER THIRTY

"What's the latest with you and James?" Reid asked from behind the counter. "He popped in this morning before you got here and turned scarlet when I asked about you. Are you officially a thing?"

Elizabeth was trying to concentrate on the last round of edits on Reid's updated website but found her mind wandering to the night before with James. Tangled in his sheets all night doing things that made her sweat and moan. His morning stubble tickling parts of her body that she was still blushing about hours later. She'd evened up the begging score, making James plead with *her* not to stop.

"We're . . . having fun."

"That's it?"

She prayed that wasn't all they were doing, but James had racked up five sarcastic comments about being long distance by the time she left that morning. She wondered how she could convince him to stop joking about it as she leaned down and petted Georgina, who was sleeping on her coffee bean sack upside down after an exhausting training session with William.

"I really like him. A lot."

"No kidding. You've been stalking him since you arrived."

"Stop."

"Just calling it like I see it," he replied, then disappeared into the back room.

She refocused on his website. She was close to beta testing and wanted to be able to tick one project off her list of unfinished Fargrove business before things started to get serious back home.

Home.

Elizabeth typed faster, trying to ignore the inkblot that spread inside her any time she thought about going back to her aggressively minimalistic apartment. She could hear the echo of her keys hitting the narrow metal table in her front hall. At least she wouldn't have to worry about the box anymore.

Georgina rolled onto her back on the bean sack next to her chair, splaying her legs out. Elizabeth studied the puppy, noting the new freckles accumulating on the naked part of her belly. If only she could be more like

Georgina and just . . . be. There was no way for Elizabeth to "just be" in San Francisco, and she got exhausted thinking about going back to her old routines, from work to exercise to the endless, joyless happy hours with subpar beer.

What *was* she going back to? A career that had been her everything and the money that came with it. A gorgeous apartment. Her social media accounts and the dopamine hit that came with every new like and follower. It was the life she'd worked hard for, and the only one that made sense to her.

Her phone alarm chimed, reminding her that she had five minutes before her scheduled call with Carson Keller.

"Reid, I've got a call, I'm going on the roof!" She ran past him, holding up her phone. "Watch Georgie for me!"

She dashed up the narrow stairs and onto the roof, thankful that the mild day hadn't turned it into a sauna. Elizabeth focused on the perfect blue sky and tried to visualize a positive outcome as the minutes passed. She closed her eyes and thought about how Cecelia's face would look when she heard that Elizabeth had clawed her way back into the cool crowd.

A shrieking bark shattered her brief meditation, then scratching on the door. Georgina had followed her to the roof, more than likely because Reid had gotten tied up with customers. She didn't have time to run her back down, and she wasn't about to listen to barking and scratching during the call, so she ran to the door and let her out.

"Please be good," she pleaded as Georgina jumped on her. "No shenanigans, this is important!"

Georgina trotted off in the direction of the hives.

"Stay away from the bees, Georgie!"

She dialed the number and crossed her fingers as it rang, taking cleansing breaths until he picked up.

"Carson Keller. Go."

"Carson, it's Elizabeth Barnes, so great to talk to you finally."

"Yeah, no kidding. You're impossible to reach. Are you playing hard to get?"

"Not at all, just busy. You know how it is."

"Do you live in the UK now? You've been gone forever."

"Not even close, just a quick trip." She knew that the lie wouldn't register, that he was so wrapped up in his own world that she could tell him it had only been two weeks and he would've believed her. There was no way she was going to admit she'd been unemployed and hiding in Fargrove for nearly a month and a half. "I had some family business. Do you know Rowan Barnes?" She didn't throw his name around casually, but the situation called for her big guns.

"Is he the guy who started that new music app? What's it called?"

"No, no, he's an artist. He's pretty famous over here." Rowan was pretty famous everywhere, but unless Carson was one of the tech entrepreneurs who threw his excess earnings at art, there was no way he'd recognize the name. And she couldn't imagine Carson Keller investing in tasteful landscapes. "He's my uncle and I had to help him organize his collection." She realized that it sounded very far out of her wheelhouse. "I, uh, developed a registrar spreadsheet to catalog his collection. I think it can be transitioned to an app."

"An app, huh? Can you get it scalable? Cloud-ready?" Carson immediately focused on the one aspect of the conversation that made sense to him.

"Of course." The thought hadn't even crossed Elizabeth's mind.

"Let's put a pin in that and revisit it later. Anyway, you've probably heard we're expanding. We all know that the next great frontier in VR is —"

"Medicine," Elizabeth interrupted. Her heart started thudding in her chest. "Yes, it's amazing what's being done in medical research with the technology."

"Sure, yeah. Medical VR is important. But we want to stay in a vertical aligned with our core competencies, so we're actually looking to expand into VR gaming for kids."

"That's fantastic. So educational-type games?"

"Not exactly. There's already a glut of that sort of play, and that's boring anyway, so we're looking to do games that turn kids into little addicts. Get 'em hooked while they're young. Right now we've got two we're setting our sights on: Blood Hunter for boys, and Shop Diva for girls."

Elizabeth laughed at the ridiculous names.

"I'm serious. They're testing off the charts."

"What ages?" Elizabeth kept her voice measured.

"We start at age three. Let's get to the good stuff. We're thinking veep of comm. Now, before I make any promises you gotta run the gauntlet first, because there's still some stink connected to your name. But we know what you're capable of. We've been watching you."

She was officially back. Not only was it a

way in, it was a way in that was at least two pay grades above where she'd been before. Cecelia would lose her mind.

"I'm interested. What's next?"

"We're wire-framing. Let me give you our dark site so you can see what we're up to. It's not go time yet, but when we're nimble one of us will reach out to you to start the interview process. That is, if you can get back to San Fran."

Elizabeth heard a shriek from the other side of the roof. Georgina dashed to her, stopping to rub her paw on her nose. She wiped her face back and forth on the ground, then rolled onto her back, dragging both paws along her snout.

She'd been stung.

She tried to call Georgina to her without making noise, but the dog was too stressed to do anything but fuss with her painful snout. Elizabeth ran to her and tried to figure out what to do, stroking Georgina to try to calm her with one hand while pressing the phone to her ear with the other.

"Elizabeth, you still there?"

"What? Sorry, Carson, yes. I think the call dropped out for a second. Spotty service over here in nowheresville. Of course I can come home. Say the word and I'm there."

"Perfect. Won't be too long and you'll be

back in the real world, kicking ass and taking names."

"Can't wait. I look forward to next steps." The words caught in her throat as she said them.

The second the call disconnected she threw the phone down and examined Georgina's muzzle. It was already starting to swell, and Georgina was clearly hurting. Elizabeth picked her up and kissed the top of her head.

"Oh, sweetie, I'm sorry. They didn't mean to hurt you, it's just what bees do. Let's go talk to Uncle Reid, he'll know how to help."

Elizabeth held Georgina tightly as she carried her down the steps and cooed to her, trying to keep the pup from focusing on the painful sting.

"I've got you, don't worry. I'm here, little one, I'm here," Elizabeth whispered.

But she wouldn't always be, and Georgina wouldn't understand why. The realization was an unexpected gut punch. Would her dog think that she was being abandoned for a second time? It didn't matter if Georgina ended up with Rowan and Trudy, or Reid, or James. Every option was great but also terrible, because none of them were her.

Georgina whimpered and nuzzled closer, and instead of blowing away the storm clouds the way her snuggles usually did, the move sent a fissure through Elizabeth's heart.

CHAPTER THIRTY-ONE

"He's so handsome," Trudy whispered as James got out of his car and readied his dogs in the back seat. He was stunning even in a simple navy T-shirt and shorts.

"Isn't he?" Elizabeth agreed as he headed down the gravel lane to the barn with Porter and Amber kicking up pebbles next to him. It had been a little over a month since their first *official* official date at the Blue Boar, and seeing him still made her feel as nervous and fluttery as the first time she'd spotted him at HiveMind.

"What are you on about, Trudy?" Rowan asked. "Is your eye wandering?"

"Never, my love." She winked at Elizabeth and cradled her newly cast-free arm.

Georgina and Major dashed from the Operculum to greet Porter and Amber, already fast friends. The dogs spun around each other, sniffing bums and play-bowing, then took off into the brush with hostess

Georgina in the lead. After back-slapping hugs and a quick catch-up with Rowan and Trudy, Elizabeth and James set off on their hike.

"I've hiked nearly every inch of Fargrove, but this is the first time I've gotten to explore this property," James said as they walked down the lane. "It's gorgeous."

"It's really special," Elizabeth agreed. "Wait until you see the river."

She hadn't been back to the river since the dispersement, but for some reason the walk there felt familiar, as if they'd visited it the day before. Elizabeth made her way through the dense growth with ease, keeping pace with James in her sneakers. After walking everywhere since arriving in Fargrove and experiencing all sorts of surprises along the way, including a lost cow with prehistoric horns and long brown bangs standing in the middle of the road, and a man in a top hat driving a tractor, nothing about her surroundings fazed her.

The dogs crashed along in the woods, always circling back as if Elizabeth and James were two-legged deadweights that couldn't keep up. Amber and Georgina led the pack, an adorable girl gang with speed that put their older male buddies to shame. Major brought up the rear, occasionally looking worried when the group became too spread out.

They ended up in the clearing near the old grist mill ruins. Her father's property, and for the moment hers.

"This is incredible," James said. "It's paradise. Look at the way the light filters through the trees. And the river! It's wider here than any other place in Fargrove. It's just a trickle in some spots."

He walked around the space in awe, like he was checking the amenities in a luxury hotel suite.

"And a mill as well? Phenomenal. Look at that craftsmanship. Four solid walls, still standing after all this time. Throw a roof up there and someone could move in tomorrow."

"As of this moment, I own this little patch of paradise." She was almost embarrassed to admit it.

"Seriously?"

She nodded. "It was my father's but I think I'm going to sell it back to Rowan and Trudy. They want to keep it in the family."

"I wouldn't be too quick to do that, Bess. This is a magical spot. Why not keep it?"

"I need the money," she blurted out, regretting her honesty the minute she said it. Talking about the real world with James made their fairy tale seem even more un-likely. "I mean, my situation is changing, but still. The money from selling it will help." She was vague on purpose and James knew exactly why.

"What do you mean? What situation is changing?"

The one off-limits topic when they were together was her departure date. Elizabeth never mentioned it, and James's digs about her leaving had finally stopped. Being more specific about her "situation" would break the spell.

"Where are the dogs?"

"Don't ignore the question. What situation?"

"I'm serious, I can't hear them!" Elizabeth cocked her head and made a worried expression, even though they both knew the dogs were fine.

"You are so transparent, Bess," he said. "Porter, here!" Within seconds the sound of sixteen paws crashing through undergrowth echoed around them.

The pack of dogs tumbled to them looking like they'd been up to no good, with muddy paws and wet bellies. They stood shoulder-to-shoulder in size order: Amber, then Georgina, then Major, then Porter. After checking in they took off on another adventure.

"They're living their best lives," Elizabeth said. "So happy."

"Aren't we all?" James replied, sounding like he was anything but.

She knew she needed to change the subject and lighten the mood, so she pretended she was about to peel off her T-shirt. "Shall we skinny-dip? I'm boiling."

"Nah." James was staring into space with an expression that Elizabeth couldn't read.

Elizabeth walked over and stood in front of him. "Stop," she said softly. "Just be here with me now, okay?"

"I *am* here."

She put her hand on his cheek and gently turned his face so that he had to look at her. "No, you're not. You're thinking about —" She stopped herself from being specific. ". . . the future."

He shrugged.

Every time James retreated, the vise in Elizabeth's chest cinched tighter.

"We'll make it work. We will. I'm not her, James, so don't punish me for her mistakes."

"You have to understand why this is hard for me. Trusting again."

"Of course I do." Elizabeth reached around his waist and clasped her hands behind him, locking him in close to her so the feeling of her body pressed against his would make him stop talking about it. She nestled against his solid chest, and when he finally relented and rested his chin on top of her head, she sighed.

"I hate the thought of you leaving," James said.

"Then don't think of it. Just kiss me." Elizabeth leaned away from him so that she could see his beautiful face. "I'm begging you."

It worked every time. He smirked and lowered his lips onto hers. Two seconds later all she could think of was pulling her T-shirt over her head so that he could get more creative with his kisses.

The cavalcade of dogs returned as they groped one another, and James groaned when one of them started barking manically.

"Porter, enough."

The other dogs joined in and took off through the bushes, past the grist mill.

"They're on a scent. Porter and Major should be fine, but Amber and Georgina aren't as trustworthy. Come on." He grabbed Elizabeth's hand and ran after the dogs.

They found them gathered around a giant tree stump. Porter stood barking at it while Major ran in circles around the stump.

Georgina and Amber were next to each other digging the loose dirt so fast that their heads were already beneath ground level.

"What was it?"

"Probably something small and furry. They'll never get it, don't worry. They're fine."

James walked on and Elizabeth trailed behind him until they reached a clearing at the edge of the property.

"I've lost my bearings, which never happens. The sun is there, so that's east," he said pointing in the distance. "The village must be that way." He pointed in the opposite direction. "And what's that? A road?" He put his hand above his eyes to shade them and squinted.

"We're so far out in the wild I have no idea where we are."

"A trick of the landscape. Look through the trees across the way. That's Yeldham Road, also known as the road to Fargrove. We're a lot closer to civilization than you know."

CHAPTER THIRTY-TWO

Rowan had told her to dress smart, that they wouldn't be spending the morning in the barn, but he hadn't told her where they were headed.

Elizabeth's "smart" clothes were hanging in the back corner of the wardrobe in her room, beautiful relics of her San Fran life ready to be called into battle at a moment's notice. Her black sleeveless peplum top, skintight white pants (which were tighter than normal around her waist), and black heels made her look ten feet tall and lethal. After spending so much time in grubby jeans and T-shirts, it felt like wearing a costume.

"Look at the fancy lady!" Trudy exclaimed as Elizabeth walked into the kitchen.

"You're not used to me in my armor," Elizabeth replied as she filled her teacup from the black-and-white kettle. "Please tell me what's going on today. I'm not great with ambushes."

"You're going to see the retrospective, at the museum. Rowan hasn't gone yet. Faye Woolard will be there, along with *Martin.*" She spat the name out.

It made sense that Rowan had kept the trip to the museum a secret. When Rowan had invited Elizabeth to assist with organizing his legacy, he hadn't counted on her intense drive, cultivated from years of seven-day workweeks. As they made their way through the stacks of paintings, Elizabeth quickly transformed from confused newbie to taskmaster, with a cataloging system that was as efficient as anything a gallerist might use. Rowan had expected a slow stroll down memory lane, but Elizabeth held him to a strict timeline. Telling her about the meeting prior to it would've prompted a barrage of questions and strategizing that she knew he didn't have the heart to consider. Now he'd only have to deal with Elizabeth's planning during the drive into London.

"Why aren't you going?" Elizabeth asked Trudy.

"I cannot stand that gormless face of his, and I don't hide it well. I have a feeling that no matter what you think of him, your training will prevent you from physically recoiling from him, as I do."

"Well, my training has failed me in the past." She shrugged, thinking about the disastrous interview that had led to her new world order. She tried to imagine what an impolite Trudy might look like. Perhaps she'd only kiss Martin on one cheek, or she'd forget to say *Thank you* when he held the door for her. "Is he really that bad?"

"Oh yes," Trudy said, nodding. "He thinks he's the bad boy of the art world, and that Rowan's paintings are too old-fashioned. He only likes shocking art. Beautiful landscapes just won't do when you could have paintings made with used syringes."

"And without Faye there to keep him in check . . ." Elizabeth trailed off.

Trudy pursed her lips and busied herself with the kettle. "One for the road, dear?"

Elizabeth held out her cup for Trudy to fill and gulped it down. "This is going to be quite a day. You're okay to watch Georgina?"

"Glad to." They both looked at the canine scrum. Georgina was on top of Major, biting his cheek and rearing back.

"She's such a monster," Elizabeth said, shaking her head. "I don't know how he tolerates her."

"Bess," Trudy said quietly. "Help Rowan today. This isn't going to be easy for him. Martin is . . . well, you'll see."

"Is there something I should know?"

"Faye said nothing was going to change when she left, but Martin is already making waves. He's quite eager to see her gone. You'd never know they were mother and son."

"Oh, you're kidding, I had no idea they're related. This is going to be a nightmare." Elizabeth mentally prepared to go to battle with Martin Woolard.

"Take this," Trudy said, holding out a silk scarf.

Elizabeth looked at her questioningly.

"He wants to drive the toy. His Austin-Healey. It'll be top down if he has anything to say about it, and this will protect your hair."

Elizabeth recognized the bridle pattern immediately. Hermès. Sometimes she forgot that her wellie-wearing aunt and uncle were also incredibly posh. She leaned down to pet Georgina and Major and hurried out the door.

Rowan was waiting for her in front of the house, leaning against a beautiful car Elizabeth had never seen before and staring off into the distance. He was dressed up in a blazer and pressed slacks.

"This car is incredible," Elizabeth exclaimed. The low-slung convertible was a steely blue-gray and looked like something out of a 1960s spy movie. It was small enough to feel playful, with a front grille that resembled a cheeky smile, while at the same time sleekly elegant.

"My pride and joy," Rowan said. "Ready?"

He didn't say much as they made their way out of Fargrove and eased onto the busier roads on the way to London. Elizabeth peeked at her phone, still watching Rowan out of the corner of her eye. Being in work clothes made her feel one step closer to her old life. She had service, and the tantalizing notification icons stretched all the way down the screen, but it felt wrong to focus on her phone with Rowan stewing right beside her. She was sure she could steal away to check in at some point during the day.

"How do you feel about the retrospective?" Elizabeth asked. She wanted to get Rowan talking so he'd stop frowning.

"It's awakening the ghosts. Dredging up memories. And you here at the same time? It's fate."

"Why do you say that?" Elizabeth asked.

"A retrospective is a life's story, told in art. Every painting is a memory. And some of the memories I carry are difficult to bear. But with you here, well, perhaps I can silence some of them."

"Are you talking about my father?"

"Your father, yes, and others."

Elizabeth waited for him to continue, but he turned on the radio and adjusted the volume so big band battled the breeze whooshing in the convertible. She adjusted the scarf on her head and worried that her crazy-woman hair would throw her off her game for the Martin Woolard confrontation.

Rowan eased the car through the streets of London as if he did it every day. Being back in a city after the time in Fargrove made Elizabeth's pulse race. London was a true city: beautiful, busy, vibrant.

Almost too much so.

They parked in a tiny hidden lot near the museum and walked to the main entrance side by side. Rowan looked so nervous that Elizabeth spontaneously linked her arm through his as they walked toward the entrance.

"Don't worry, I've got your back. You haven't seen me in business mode."

"What you're doing to me in the barn every day isn't business mode? Oh, I pity Martin." Rowan chuckled and shook his head.

Two women with white hair and white shoes approached them tentatively as they got closer to the museum. "Sorry, excuse me? We're so sorry to disturb you but aren't you . . . ?" The woman trailed off and pointed toward the museum. Elizabeth looked at the front of the castlelike building and was thrilled to see a giant banner with a slice of *Sunset over Blenheim* blown up, overlaid with the words *Rowan Barnes: Shifting Landscapes.*

"Yes, you've caught me at the scene of the crime," Rowan replied, bowing his head and smiling.

Both women started gushing at once. "Brilliant! May we take a photo with you? Would you mind terribly?"

"Of course, I'd be honored."

The shorter of the two women thrust a phone into Elizabeth's hands, and she dutifully snapped several photos of the trio. Rowan looked sheepish and pleased at the same time.

Elizabeth stared at him slack-jawed as they walked away from the women. "You're a celebrity!"

"It only happens when there's been news. My face has been in the papers to promote the show, that's all. When we hit the pub afterward, I'll be as invisible as the town drunk, trust me."

Faye met them at the door leaning on a

brightly colored cane.

"Quick, before more people recognize you," she said with a laugh. "That's why we scheduled this tour before the museum opens."

Elizabeth fell in step behind them, still in shock over the scope of the retrospective. She had barely even taken in the grand building when a young woman in a black dress and distracting earrings rushed up to them.

"Rowan, welcome! Lovely to see you again, we are so thrilled that you're finally here to see the show."

Rowan introduced Elizabeth to Charlotte Ainsworth, the curator and driving force behind the exhibition, and the four of them stood in the lobby making awkward small talk while a room full of Rowan's works beckoned from beyond the oversized doorway. After holding the studies that gave birth to *Sunset over Blenheim* in her gloved hands, she couldn't wait to see the real thing in person — though in this setting, Rowan's work belonged to the world, not just the two of them.

It was clear they were waiting for Martin Woolard, which made Elizabeth immediately dislike him. Cecelia was also prone to late entrances peppered with faux apologies. Arriving late reinforced the idea that nothing could happen until she was in the room.

Elizabeth heard clicking footsteps and a voice echoing through the empty museum before she saw the man who had to be Martin Woolard. "I'm well aware that he's hard to reach, that's why I'm asking *you* to do it. Lightbender. By the end of today."

He entered the room with the posture of a well-trained butler, hands clasped behind his back and shoulders squared. Based on Trudy's comments Elizabeth was prepared for a strung-out man-child, but Martin was the picture of British propriety in a fitted high-buttoned suit with a vest just peeking out from underneath.

Martin walked toward the group with his hand out, smiling in a way that Elizabeth recognized. Practiced, not genuine. "Rowan. The man of the hour."

Rowan smiled warily and shook Martin's hand. "And the clock is striking midnight. Please meet my niece, Elizabeth."

Hearing him call her by her full name was as obvious as if Rowan had screamed *Mayday.* But Elizabeth was ten steps ahead of him, already profiling Martin and preparing for war. His expensive Italian shoes had a heel on them, which meant he was sensitive about his height. His head was bare on top but there were wisps of hair straining forward from the base of his skull, which meant that he wasn't bowing to baldness without a fight. His nails were buffed to a glossy sheen, which meant he was vain. He stood in the center of the group, directly in front of Faye. He was desperate to come out from under his mother's shadow.

Martin turned his attention to Elizabeth. "The American. Welcome to London." He nodded in her direction, then turned away, but Elizabeth took a step closer to him and held out her hand defiantly so that he had no choice but to shake it. In an instant Elizabeth could tell exactly why Trudy hated him. If she took one thing with her from Duchess, it was that no man would ever treat her like her hand was unworthy of shaking.

Martin had no idea what was in store for him.

"Let's head in, shall we?" Charlotte the curator said as they walked into the cavernous room. "So far the show has gotten wonderful feedback. People are still so inspired by your work, Rowan." She gestured to a huge painting dominating the entrance to the exhibition. "Now, you'll notice that the first painting we encounter is *Nightfall,* and I must admit that I pulled rank and placed it here because it's my favorite. It's a significant work because of its size, of course, but also because it's your only painting depicting complete darkness. May I ask what inspired it, Rowan?"

Martin began speaking before Rowan could even open his mouth, peering at the group over the top of his glasses. "This came right after Rowan's *Twilight* series, so it was a natural progression from the encroaching darkness in that series to the full black in *Nightfall.*"

"Actually, *Nightfall* came before *Twilight,*" Elizabeth interrupted. "Two years before, in fact. And Rowan painted his *Jardin* series in between, which, as I'm sure you know, Martin, was an explosion of color. Am I right about that, Rowan?" She knew that she was.

"Indeed you are, Elizabeth."

The name again.

Charlotte led the group around the exhibition with a mix of nerves and enthusiasm. She knew Rowan's work inside and out, but Elizabeth knew more. She'd seen the pencil sketches and hastily painted studies of the famous works hanging in the bright white room. She knew that a fight with Trudy had inspired *Storm Clouds.* That he hated *The Bend* and had happily sold it to a collector so he'd never have to see it again, though it hung along with the others, on loan for the show. And most importantly, she knew that he had a secret collection of portraits that would knock the art world on its collective ass.

Elizabeth could see Rowan's masterpiece at the far end of the room. Charlotte had set the room perfectly, forcing people to walk through his entire career before arriving at the work they were all there to see.

"Ah, my old friend," Rowan said quietly when they finally stopped in front of *Sunset over Blenheim.* "So good to see you again."

He moved in close to his canvas, studying his own painting as if it were the first time he was seeing it. Elizabeth hung back, mentally framing the image of the master in front of his famous work. But the slump in his shoulders made it clear that it wasn't a joyful moment for him. Elizabeth walked over and stood next to Rowan, a human shield between him and Martin.

"Remind me to tell you about the stars someday," he whispered to her, pointing to three bright points of light in the sky.

"Just one more to see, over here, please," Charlotte said, moving the group to the painting directly across from *Blenheim.* Martin trailed the group, tapping on his phone. Elizabeth wanted to kick him for his disrespect. The very man the museum was celebrating, Martin's own client, was in the room with them and he was acting like he was a bored high schooler on a group tour.

"Martin, did you know that Elizabeth is a painter as well?" Faye asked him, trying to get her son to rejoin the group.

"Pardon?" He looked up from his phone with an annoyed expression.

"My niece paints too," Rowan said. "She's quite the talent."

"Isn't that nice?" Martin turned to Elizabeth and gave her a patronizing smile. "I'm so happy you have a little hobby. Paint by number, I presume?"

Elizabeth was so caught off guard by his rudeness that she couldn't think of a thing to say. Her face got hot and she clenched her fists until she could feel her fingernails leaving marks in her palms.

Charlotte stopped in front of *Cumulus,* the giant cloud painting that was one of Elizabeth's favorites, and pointed to a minuscule black shadow in a tree. "Rowan, I think this is the only living creature in your entire catalog. A raven. Why didn't you paint more animals?"

"Rowan paints what he knows, locked away on that farm of his. Trees, sky, river, plants, no people, no animals," Martin said in a singsong voice, as if he weren't delivering a string of insults. "You prefer the company of landscapes over living things, yes? Slightly hermitlike, I'd say. I'm surprised we even got you here, my friend."

It was the last slight she'd stand for. Elizabeth blurted before she could censor herself, just like at the disastrous interview, "Is that what you think, little man?" Martin's face looked like she'd slapped him. "Rowan Barnes might have a few secrets up his sleeve. Have you ever been in the Operculum? No? Well, I have, and I know every inch of what's in it. Just you wait and see what's coming. You're going to lose . . . your . . . *shit.*"

Faye gasped and Charlotte looked half amazed and half horrified. Elizabeth realized what she'd just done and turned to see Rowan's reaction.

He stood a few feet away from the group with his eyes squinted and his hands pressed to his mouth. For a moment it looked like he was crying, and Elizabeth wanted to run over to hug him and apologize. She took a step toward him and realized that he was holding back giggles and tears of joy.

CHAPTER THIRTY-THREE

Trudy clutched her bad arm as if the stress of the situation made her bones ache. She hadn't stopped asking Rowan and Elizabeth questions since they'd arrived home from the museum. They were gathered on the patio in the fading summer light, a candle casting a glow on the trio.

"Everything is fine for now, please stop fretting," Rowan said, leaning back in his chair. Major sidled up to him and filled in the space between his feet. "Unless Bess's 'little man' comment pushed him over the brink."

"I have a blurting problem in high-pressure situations," Elizabeth said. "I'm so sorry, I cannot believe I said that."

"It was poetry, my dear. And well deserved," Rowan answered.

"Bess, what do you think is going to happen?" Trudy was fixated on figuring out their next steps, so they could be rid of Martin and Woolard Gallery as quickly as possible.

Elizabeth weighed her words before opening her mouth, watching Georgina stalk a spider that was making its way across the bricks. They all knew the truth, but it was up to her to make it real, to say what no one wanted to say.

"Martin is going to work his way through the Woolard Gallery like a tornado. He wants to erase every bit of his mother's legacy, and that means getting rid of Rowan. He has no respect for his career. It's an unbelievably stupid move, but after meeting Martin I'm not surprised."

Trudy made an exasperated noise. "I knew it! Isn't he horrid?"

"The absolute worst. I know exactly why you hate him," Elizabeth replied.

They sat in silence. Georgina lowered herself into a deep crouch, paused, and then leapt on top of the spider.

"What happens now?" Elizabeth asked. "What should we do? I mean, what should you do?"

"I have a gallery in mind. They've been courting me since the beginning of my career. And they'll do my portraits justice."

"Tempus Gallery?" Trudy asked.

Rowan nodded and stared into the distance, exhausted by the late-stage drama he was facing.

"What did you call him again, Bess? Wee man?"

"Little man," she corrected. "It was horrifying."

"Oh, I wish I could have been there," Trudy said with her eyes shining.

"Speaking of being there, I'm going to excuse myself. I need to go down to the Operculum for a bit. My little show is coming up fast, and after seeing all of Rowan's stuff I'm feeling inspired," Elizabeth said.

"It's a lovely symmetry, isn't it? My career is in its twilight and yours is just unfolding," Rowan said.

"Stop it. You are nowhere near twilight. Your stamina puts mine to shame. And painting is hardly my career."

Trudy reached out to grasp Elizabeth's hand as she stood up to leave. "You may have no choice in the matter, my dear."

Elizabeth gave Trudy's hand a squeeze and called Georgina to her. The pair walked down the lane side by side, and Elizabeth's thoughts shifted to the turmoil Rowan was facing. It didn't seem fair that he was being forced to make such major changes at his age.

She pulled the screeching Operculum

door open and reflexively looked down at Georgina. The little dog took a half step backward but held her ground as the door wailed along the track. "Good girl," she said. "Brave girl."

To her, the barn smelled as delicious as a cinnamon roll. Every time she walked in she felt tingly and invigorated. She was excited to put the finishing touches on the painting of Porter and Amber before her show, since it was going to be a central piece. James had no idea that she'd set up a photo shoot with the dogs one morning when he was in the shower.

It still stunned her that her easel was right next to the one that gave birth to master-pieces. She walked around the barn, look-ing at Rowan's works with new eyes. Being surrounded by them every day normalized them. A sketch here, a forgotten painting there — they were just items that needed a description and number. But seeing his art in an important room in grand frames almost made her scared to walk among them in the Operculum.

She remembered seeing a study for *Night-fall* leaning against the wall in the portrait room and wanted to examine it now that she'd stood before the grand finished prod-uct at the museum. Rowan had taken to organizing on his own while she cataloged works on her tablet, though his version of organizing was more about shifting things from one corner to another. More than a few landscapes had migrated to the portrait room, even though she'd begged him to keep them separate. She worked her way through the stack that had materialized where she had last seen the *Nightfall* study, and the pile next to it. Landscapes on top of portraits on top of landscapes. More mess to organize.

Georgina scuttled from corner to corner, hoping to trap a mouse. She knew that once they went into the Operculum she had to entertain herself.

Elizabeth was ready to give up on finding the study when she noticed a half-hidden canvas in the farthest corner of the room, behind a support beam that ran low to the ground. It was covered with a brownish cloth. Rowan was a horrible caretaker of his own works, leaving them exposed to the tiny art critics who chewed holes and the dust from the ancient wood and stone, so she was surprised that he had taken the time to shield one of his paintings. She made her way back, brushing aside spiderwebs and bending over as the ceiling dipped lower, until she had no choice but to kneel and shuffle her way into the tight space.

No one had touched the painting in years. She worked her way out of the corner and back to the table they'd set up and placed the painting on top of it.

She remembered her gloves right as she was about to lift the cloth. The painting was sure to have suffered damage after resting in the vulnerable spot for so long, so rather than add the natural oils on her hands to the problems she was sure to find on the canvas, she slid on a fresh pair of cotton gloves. She took a deep breath and slowly lifted the cloth.

It was a portrait of a beautiful woman in profile, wearing a simple full white slip. Her head was down, and her raven hair spilled over her shoulders. Elizabeth flipped into registrar mode, studying the woman's face so that she could summarize the painting's mood. The woman's expression was happy, proud, hopeful. She looked like she had a secret.

The rest of Rowan's portraits were loose and expressive, but the one of the woman was painted carefully, as if he wanted to spend more time than usual with the model. Rowan had mentioned that he always posed his subjects and that everything in the portraits, from the person's clothing to the way they held their hands, held keys to the work's coded messages. The black-haired woman was the first portrait Elizabeth had seen posed in profile. Her hands were clutched against her stomach, one on top of the other. Elizabeth traced the woman's line of sight and realized that her downcast eyes fixed on her hands. She looked closer and noticed that the woman's stomach was slightly rounded.

Goose bumps prickled the skin on her arms. The woman was newly pregnant. She looked closer at the raven-haired woman, then glanced at the portrait across from the door, the one Rowan had shown her on her first day in the Operculum.

The woman in the painting was Trudy.

Elizabeth tried to make sense of it as a thousand scenarios played out in her mind. Maybe Trudy had a twin sister. Maybe it was just the slip of fabric hanging at an odd angle. Maybe she was a little chubby the day he painted it. Because if it *was* Trudy and she had been pregnant, the painting's legacy was heartbreak. Then she remembered what Trudy had said to her the night she came home from the hospital. "I wish you could've known your cousin . . . our little bird."

It was true. Rowan and Trudy had lost

their baby.

She looked back at the heartbreaking image and wondered how she was going to introduce it into the cataloging process. Rowan told her the backstory for every painting, so how could she transition from asking him about a fishmonger delivery driver painting to the image of Trudy? Should she tell him she found it while they took their morning tea, before they headed into the Operculum? Should she let him discover it in a stack? Nothing felt right, because the moment he saw it the story would be fresh again. And as much as Elizabeth wanted to understand what they'd been through, she was reluctant to reopen the old wound. She hated to see Rowan unhappy.

Elizabeth reverted to her typical avoidance strategy and crawled back to place the painting where she'd found it. Georgina scooted into the tight space with her, always at her side and ready to assist. They sat side by side next to the painting, each staring off into the distance as an owl hooted a melancholy soundtrack.

CHAPTER THIRTY-FOUR

The crowd at HiveMind was thinning as Elizabeth's show came to a close. The fact that she'd even had a crowd was mind-blowing, but her three months in Fargrove had cemented her as a part of the community. She'd worried that people would only show up to gawk at Rowan, but he'd walked unnoticed through HiveMind the entire evening while she was the focal point.

"Eight paintings. I can't believe I sold eight of them. To strangers! I don't think there was one pity purchase." Elizabeth felt like a millionaire.

Harriet propped her swollen feet up on the edge of one of HiveMind's signature yellow chairs and scowled at Elizabeth. "Why would anyone pity-purchase? Your stuff is wonderful. I'm honored to have a Bess Barnes original hanging in my house. I can say I knew you when."

The little red *SOLD* stickers next to her

paintings looked like lipstick kisses. She'd sold two paintings of the happy cows that she passed every day on the way to Fargrove, a six-by-six study of a rabbit she'd spotted in the field by the Operculum, a portrait of Floyd the black lab mascot from the Tups, a hedgehog in a knit cap, a sleeping fox, a close-up of a runaway rooster that ended up in the courtyard outside Hive-Mind, and the owl that she heard every night during late-night painting sessions.

"Where's Georgina? I think you've painted every creature in Fargrove, but not your own dog. Why is that?" Harriet asked.

"I'm not sure. Maybe I'm too close to my subject?"

The truth was she was afraid to try.

Harriet closed her eyes and rubbed her stomach, and Elizabeth was reminded of the painting of young Trudy. They were about to begin work on the portrait room and she still didn't know how to broach the painting of Trudy with Rowan.

Des walked up behind Harriet and massaged her shoulders. "Shall we?"

"I don't want to leave, but it seems Ian does. He's cranky tonight." She placed her hands on her lower belly and huffed as she stood up. "Lovely evening tonight. I'm so happy for you, Bess." Harriet leaned down and gave Elizabeth a kiss on the top of her head.

"Thank you, Harriet," Elizabeth said, grabbing her hand before she could waddle away. "For everything."

Elizabeth leaned back against the couch and scanned the stragglers. James was chatting with the band in the courtyard, Willard and Anna Tolbert were looking bleary-eyed on another couch across the room, and Reid and Nicky were gathering pint glasses and mugs. It was the first time that evening there was no one waiting to talk to her about her inspiration or process.

She took advantage of the momentary solitude and pulled her phone from a pocket hidden in her lemon print dress. She was surprised to see more notifications than she'd had in weeks. Her posting had decreased as her daily workload increased, but she knew she'd be back to optimizing her accounts with perfectly curated content soon enough. She'd make up for lost time.

She tried to imagine what she'd post about when she returned home. Shoes, of course. Cups of coffee. Filtered selfies. Inspirational quotes. The dog and sheep content was about to drop from eighty-five percent of her feed to zero.

A bunch of the notifications were tagged

photos from the show by a photographer from the local paper. She surveyed the images quickly to make sure she actually *wanted* to be tagged in them. There was one of her in profile in front of her painting of a muntjac deer with a crowd of people around her. Another photo showed her standing between Rowan and Trudy, with Rowan's arm draped around her shoulder and their heads bowed into one another, as if strategizing a play for a rugby match. Another showed her leaning against the counter in between Reid and Nicky holding champagne glasses, with Harriet and Des visible behind them. She hadn't been aware of anyone taking her photo, so none of them had her wearing her practiced grin and head tilt. She looked so happy that her wonky eye wasn't even noticeable.

Elizabeth reposted a few of the photos in the hopes that Cecelia would see them, then posted a shot of her field mouse painting, the one she'd painted for Rowan that referenced *Sunset over Blenheim* with her version of the twilight sky visible through the window of the Operculum. She hashtagged it #agoodnight and #RowanBarnesTribute. Then she checked Twitter and almost dropped her phone.

The top trending story was Entomon.

Elizabeth did a quick search and was horrified to discover that TechGeek had published the story without warning her, and worse yet, they'd done it while she was still in the land of spotty cell service! They'd sworn they'd wait until Elizabeth was home and employed before they went public. After all, her disastrous interview had been the first public mention of Entomon, and she was counting on the interview requests and gossipy lunches to come that would allow her to spin her firing. Yet there it was, *her* photo, breaking the internet without her.

She started to tremble.

"Hey, you okay? What's going on?" James asked, sitting down across from her as if he'd been summoned by a distress flare.

Elizabeth pushed her phone farther away, like it was contagious. She was so upset she could barely speak so she pointed at her phone. "Bad news. I'm processing."

"Do you want to talk about it?" He took her hands in his and it felt like she'd popped a painkiller. "You're all red. What's going on?"

Elizabeth shook her head and her eyes filled with tears.

"Bess, what? Is it me? Did I do something?" The telltale furrow appeared, along with a frown.

She shook her head again and blinked fast. "Work."

"Oh." He leaned back in his chair and his face relaxed. "Do you want me to leave you alone?"

For a change she didn't want him to play therapist and make her feel better. She wanted to seethe, hate-read every detail of Cecelia's undoing and beat herself up for not being the one to make it happen. She was already drafting a raging email to Tech-Geek.

"Yes. No." She slammed her hands on the table. "Fuck, I don't know."

"Just tell me. What's got you this upset?"

Elizabeth shook her head, then rubbed the back of her hand along her nose to wipe away the snot. She stared down at the table.

"Fine, I'll leave you alone." James started to stand up. "But I think you'll feel better if you tell me." He hovered at a half stand.

"All right, all right," Elizabeth snapped at him. "Sit."

James plopped back into his seat.

"Remember how I told you I left my old job?"

He nodded.

"Well, that wasn't the whole story. I was fired." Elizabeth's cheeks burned as she said the word.

His eyes went wide.

"*Unjustly* fired. I made a mistake during a live interview that cost me my job. Normally what happened would've gotten me a reprimand, but they fired me because my company was trying to cover up this potential story about the spyware in their latest release. Firing me was like their smokescreen, so they could divert attention from what was really going on. I was sacrificed." Elizabeth felt herself winding tighter again. "She took everything from me. My career, my reputation, my money."

Talking about it wasn't helping at all.

"Who is 'she'?"

"My boss, Cecelia. I actually thought she was my friend at one point." Elizabeth barked out a laugh. "I knew nothing about friendship. She screwed me over, but I was planning to screw her back. Harder."

"So what happened?" James asked carefully.

Elizabeth reached for her phone, scrolled to the article, and threw it to James. "See that photo of Cecelia at the top? That's mine. *I'm* the one who was able to link everything together with that photo. *I'm* the reason TechGeek has an Internet-breaking story, but they released it before, uh," she hesitated, reluctant to bring up going home.

"Before I was ready."

James cocked his head. "Now why would they do that?"

"No clue." Elizabeth fell back against her chair. "Maybe they were tired of waiting for me to be ready."

"Well, if you own the photo, can't you sue them or something? Or come out publicly and say it's yours?"

"My reputation is destroyed at home. It would make me look even more desperate if I got on Twitter and started crying about the photo." She slammed her hands on the table. "Ugh, I want to punch someone!"

"Bess, it's over. And maybe that's for the best," James said softly. "Why don't you sneak out the side door for a few minutes. Look at the stars, take a breath, then refocus on all of these people who are here for you now."

Her face flushed. James had a way of reframing situations with just a few words, and sometimes she hated him for it.

She grabbed her phone. "I'll be back. Don't tell anyone, okay?"

"Of course not. I'll be packing up; come find me when you're ready for a hug."

She wanted to punch him for being so kind in the face of her anger.

Elizabeth snuck out the side door to the

small courtyard near HiveMind's bins. She sat on the upside-down bucket behind the door that Reid used when he needed to hide out from customers and immediately questioned his sense of smell. The odor of hot garbage was overwhelming, but she pulled out her phone and started to speed-read through the article. She was berating herself for not staying on top of her TechGeek contact when the door swung open and slammed into the wall next to her.

"Grrrahhhh," Reid shouted, holding two massive bags of trash in the air above his head. "I . . . am . . . BIN MAN!" He shrieked and jumped when he saw Elizabeth. "Holy shit, you scared me! What are you doing out here?"

" 'Bin Man'? Awesome superhero persona."

"Why is our star artist sitting out here among the spent coffee grinds?"

"I'm dealing with some stuff from home."

"Fargrove is your home, so whatever it is can wait. Back inside, m'duck." He pointed at the door.

"Reid, I just want to —"

"*In.* Now." He gestured with two hands like an airport worker.

"Wow, someone's been drinking tonight."

"Indeed." Reid held the door for her, then

followed her back inside. He came to a stop in front of the painting she'd done for him, hanging in a place of honor near the counter.

"Ladies and gentlemen, may I have your attention, please," Reid said. There was no one inside the shop. "Here we have an early work of Miss Elizabeth Barnes. This was painted during her red period" — he pointed at his hair and winked — "as a tribute to her favorite coffeeshop owner, who also happened to be a dear friend. You'll notice a tiny bee wearing a crown and standing on the edge of the yellow mug. This pollen-collecting flying insect is the source of all life, and Barnes wisely made it the focal point of the work. Thank you for coming to my art talk, I won't be taking questions." He bowed to a nonexistent audience.

Elizabeth finally gave in and smiled at him. It was hard to be unhappy in Reid's presence.

"I love it, Bess, thank you so much," he said sincerely, draping his massive arm around her shoulder.

"Did you notice the little secret in it?"

Reid stepped closer and examined the painting. "The mug! It's all cracked and glued back together!"

"In honor of our first meeting."

"Oh, did I hate you at first, you snobby American."

"And I thought you were a clumsy, grumpy ginger. But look at us now."

"Look at us now." He smiled at her and touched his head to the side of hers. "And since you're basically my sister you won't mind me asking you to help me clean up some damn dishes."

Elizabeth chuckled and started clearing off tables while he went outside to start putting the café tables away. Staying busy helped keep her mind off the news, so she loaded up a tray and headed for the kitchen.

James walked in behind her with a bucket filled with melted ice and bottles of beer. "That was a drinking crowd. I've barely anything left." He watched her carefully, trying to gauge the level of support she required. "You okay?"

She nodded and walked to him with her arms out, and he dropped the bucket on the counter and hugged her tightly.

"I don't want to talk about it right now," she whispered. "I shouldn't waste this perfect night. I'm fine for now." Being in his arms made it so. "It was a good night, wasn't it? Everyone had fun, right?"

"It was a *perfect* night," James said. "I'm

so proud of you."

The word stopped her in her tracks. No one had ever said it to her. "Really?"

"Yes, really. Why wouldn't I be? You're incredibly talented." He kissed the top of her head. "And hot as hell." He leaned in and nibbled her earlobe.

"Don't." She squirmed and tried to move away from him as the James-fireworks exploded along the back of her neck. "You know what that does to me."

He took her face in his hands and kissed her gently.

"Do you really want me to stop?" He pulled away slowly as he kissed her, but she stood on her tiptoes and followed his mouth. "I'm trying to stop but you're not letting me," he mumbled against her lips.

Elizabeth tangled her fingers in his unruly hair and held him in place so that his soft tongue could continue making her knees weak.

"Could we, really quick?" she whispered hoarsely as they kissed. "I mean, I can lift up my dress, and you could . . ." She started unbuckling his belt and hooked her leg behind him, drawing him closer to her.

James groaned as her hand grazed his zipper. He grabbed the sides of her lemon print dress and pulled it up, then turned her around so she was pinned against the sink with her ass pushed up against him. He had his finger hooked on the edge of her lace thong, about to pull it to the side when the door opened.

"Oh, my sweet *Jesus*!" Reid screamed, putting his hand in front of his eyes. "Sorry!"

Elizabeth fell to her knees behind the counter while James struggled to zip his pants up.

"Carry on, mate," Reid said as he backed out of the room. "It's fine!"

Elizabeth looked at James in horror. "What just happened?"

James doubled over with laughter. "My best friend and your employer caught us pre-shag in his spotless kitchen."

"Did he see my butt?"

"Maybe a cheek, yes."

"Oh my God. Is he going to tell everyone?"

"What do you think?"

"I think I'm never going to leave this kitchen."

"No, we should face the music right away. The longer we wait the shaggier it seems." He pulled her up from the floor, and they walked out of the kitchen to Reid leading a standing ovation.

CHAPTER THIRTY-FIVE

"Chelsea buns — these look like professional-grade baked goods. I'm impressed!" Harriet said as she pulled back the red polka-dot cloth napkin on top of the basket. Georgina stood on her hind legs to trace the scent trails from the buns, dancing back and forth to keep her balance. Elizabeth shook her head at the puppy, and Georgina reverted to all fours.

"Trudy did most of it, I just helped with the kneading." It had been Trudy's idea to send Elizabeth over to the Welbeck home with food. She knew nothing about the protocol for the birth of a child, and she was happy to have Trudy advising her. She arrived with treats for now, a crock of pappardelle they had prepared together for the Welbecks' dinner, and a huge bouquet of summer flowers that Elizabeth had picked and arranged herself.

"Let's tuck in. I go from podged to famished in an instant thanks to this one." She gazed at the baby nestled in her arms in a pale green blanket. Harriet, illuminated by a skylight, looked like Renaissance art, all flowing locks and maternal tenderness. Elizabeth wanted to snap a photo but realized her phone was buried in her bag on the table in the entry hall.

"One week old, can you believe it?" Harriet beamed at her son as she munched on a bun. "This is your Auntie Bess. You're the reason I had to leave her art show. Yes, love, you just had to make your appearance that night! She's your American auntie. And she's *desperate* to hold you, Ian. I can tell!"

"No, that's fine. He probably wants to be with you. And what about germs?" Elizabeth flapped her hands in front of her and leaned away from Harriet, as if to imply that she was too weak and untrustworthy to be allowed to hold a newborn.

"Are you worried about getting them or giving them? He's been passed around like a library book; take the child, please. Even Poppy holds him. I bet Barnabas could do it, if he had thumbs." Harriet leaned her head back against the couch to where the cat sat watching over her, and he rubbed his head against her hair and hitched his tail in the air.

Harriet handed the baby over before Elizabeth could move away. He was swaddled tightly, with no flailing limbs to worry about, but his tiny head peeked from the top of the blanket completely unguarded. Elizabeth held him awkwardly in front of her and hoped that he wouldn't twitch in his sleep. She'd mastered puppies, but a human was an entirely different sort of baby.

Georgina stood at attention at Elizabeth's feet, once again moving her head back and forth in the air to make sense of the strange new scent. Georgina inched closer to the baby, as if she could tell that the tiny human required a cautious approach. She buried her nose in a bit of the blanket that trailed down, trying to place the newest member of the two-legged tribe.

"Babies aren't contagious, Bess. Bring him in close to your body. You might find that you like the sensation."

Elizabeth moved the baby toward her torso, cantilevering him slowly so that his head rested in the crook of her arm. She wasn't sure what to do with her other hand, so she placed it on top of him, then underneath him, then opted to grasp onto her wrist to make her grip around his tiny body more secure.

She looked down at baby Ian and realized

that it was the first time she'd ever held a newborn, and it was just as nerve-racking as she'd imagined it to be. Everything about the baby looked fragile and impermanent. His froth of black curls, his gossamer eyelashes, the tiny fingernails on the hand curled in a defiant fist next to his cheek. How did anyone manage to keep these things alive?

"Isn't he a carbon copy of Des?"

Elizabeth looked down at the sleeping baby and could only see an adorably wrinkled alien, without an identifiable trace of either parent except for his light brown skin. She sidestepped the question. "He's incredible."

"I know." Harriet sighed. "He's utterly perfect."

"What does Poppy think of him?"

"Love-hate," Harriet replied with a shrug. "When he's quiet she treats him like her doll, but the second he starts yowling she runs away with her hands over her ears. She's a little jealous, so she's out with Des and his parents running some errands. Barnabas, on the other hand, finds him fascinating. They nap together. It's absolutely storybook."

"Do you feel better about the whole . . . boy thing?"

"No question. The moment I held him I knew he was meant to be mine." Harriet stared hungrily at Ian resting in Elizabeth's arms, so she took the opportunity to hand him back.

"Now on to you," Harriet said as she adjusted the baby close to her body. "How are things with James?"

"Perfect. Like, movie perfect."

"I'm thrilled. I think it was love at first sight for both of you; stupid James just had to get past the distance thing. Have you talked about what you're going to do once you leave? How you'll manage?"

"No. That subject is off-limits. I want to talk about it, but he won't."

"He was hurt really badly by that Marion girl. Screwed him up for a long time. Just go easy on him." Harriet shook her head. "We all wish you could stay. I've loved getting to know you. I'm going to miss you so."

"Me too." The familiar roiling in Elizabeth's gut kicked in, but she worked to calibrate her thoughts to the positives she was returning to. Career, financial stability, success, recognition. Her *real* life. She sank into the couch and tried to summon excitement for her next chapter.

The baby started to mewl, and Harriet reached beneath her blouse and bumped around, then flipped the green blanket across her chest and moved Ian beneath it. Elizabeth averted her eyes.

"Let's not think about your departure just yet, Bess. Let's keep the Fargrove magic in your life until the last possible second." Harriet seemed to warm to the topic, perhaps lulled by the sleepy infant at her breast. "Life here is made up of the beautiful unexpected, you know? Like when a stranger walks into a shop and becomes a dear friend. Like when you pick up a paintbrush and capture the *soul* of a creature. I think you'll always carry a bit of the Fargrove magic with you from this point on. You're one of us. You always have been."

Elizabeth scooted closer to Harriet and reached for her hand. "Thank you so much for . . ." she began, and gave Harriet's hand a squeeze. "Well, for being my first real . . ." Elizabeth's bag pinged from the other room and the second she heard the Face-Time ring tone she knew who it was.

"Shit!" Elizabeth shouted, then slapped her hand over her mouth. "Whoops, sorry, baby Ian. I need to take this call," she said as she ran out of the room to grab her purse. "Is there a quiet spot?"

"The loo by the front door!" Harriet yelled to her.

Elizabeth snagged her phone and ran into the bathroom with Georgina at her heels. "Go back to Auntie Harriet, she needs to talk to you!"

She didn't want to miss the call, so she answered and hoped it would take a few seconds to connect, pointing her phone at the floor so she could steal a moment to compose herself.

It was time for her guerilla interview.

Carson Keller believed that scheduled interviews gave candidates too much time to prepare and put on a game face that didn't reflect their true selves. The guerilla interview allowed him to catch candidates off guard and made it easy to weed through people who couldn't rise to the challenge of being pithy in their pajamas with sleep dust in their eyes, or when drunk at a club at two a.m. Every potential VR Solutions employee knew a guerilla interview was coming, they just didn't know when.

"Yo, Elizabeth Barnes! You know what this is, right? I've got Spencer and Walden here too." Carson didn't bother to mention their titles, correctly assuming that everyone already knew them. He swung the phone around and the two boy-men waved.

Elizabeth smiled and waved back. "I've been waiting for this! Hi, gentlemen, nice to see you. This should be fun." She adjusted the phone so that it was slightly farther away from her freckled face, but not so far away that they could see that she was in a bathroom sitting on a toilet.

"Hi, Elizabeth, Walden here." The image on her phone switched to the three of them sitting side by side in a glass-walled conference room. "Really excited to learn more about you. Gonna jump right in and get started. First question: this might sound like a nightmare situation, but envision that you're on a planet with no Internet service. How do you keep your followers engaged?"

They knew. They'd been stealth-following her and could see that her feeds were silent for days at a time. Her infrequent posts of dogs, sheep, and paintings were gorgeous, but they didn't align with the #womenwhowork brand she'd spent years cultivating. And going off-brand was an unforgivable sin for someone in her position.

Elizabeth gracefully sidestepped the question, referencing cave paintings and then spinning her answer so that she talked a lot but didn't really say anything of substance. She mentioned user-generated content and affiliate marketing, and the rest of the buzzwords came flooding back. She could filibuster like a dodgy politician. She'd hadn't worked on strategies for VR Solutions even though she knew they'd ask, so she cobbled together a version of the plans rolled out at Duchess, hoping that they wouldn't catch on that they were recycled.

The interview continued for thirty minutes while the men asked bizarre questions about horse-sized ducks and expanding hot dogs and talked about their plans to create screen-addicted children. Ian yowled in the background, but by that point Elizabeth knew she'd aced the interview.

"Hey, before we wrap up, can we talk about Cecelia for a sec? Totally OTR, off the record." Carson's habit of translating acronyms made it pointless to use them. "I mean . . . wow, man. You were like a total insider. What happened with that shitware?"

Anything she told him would be far from OTR since Carson gossiped like a teenager. Elizabeth realized that if she played it right it was a chance to attach her name to the photo of Cecelia. But was he giving her a loyalty test? To see how she'd react if VR Solutions' dirty secrets ever came out?

"I think we're all curious," Elizabeth evaded in a measured tone. "But everything I know was covered in the TechGeek article. Besides, I'd rather focus on what's ahead for VR Solutions." She swallowed hard to keep from saying anything more.

"Bummer, I was hoping for the deets. Anyway, I have one more question for you." Carson paused like he was about to announce the winner on a reality show. "Do you want the job?"

She froze. This was it. Even though they all knew she was perfect for the position, Carson was making it official.

"I do. *Very* much." She forced herself to look excited even though she wanted to flip around and get sick in the toilet she was sitting on.

"Fantastic! Then it's done. We need you back in ten days, so finish up your family crap and get on a goddamned plane, okay? Paperwork is on the way."

"Thank you so much, I'm really excited to get started." She sounded sincere and her face looked exactly like someone who had just received the opportunity of a lifetime.

Carson did the "hang loose" hand signal and disconnected the phone.

Elizabeth leaned against the toilet and envisioned telling Harriet the news. They'd hug and talk about . . . what, exactly? How she wouldn't have to shop for clothing at a supermarket anymore? That she'd make more money in a month than Des made in six?

She waited for the euphoria to kick in as the rest of the Welbeck clan crashed through the front door and Ian howled a greeting from Harriet's arms.

CHAPTER THIRTY-SIX

"Rough going today?" Rowan said, looking at Elizabeth's canvas.

She'd sketched in the guidelines for her painting, possibly the last and most important one she'd do in Fargrove, but she couldn't move beyond the simple first step she normally sped through. The official departure countdown was on and she had eight days left. She still hadn't painted Georgina.

"It's just not flowing today." Elizabeth set her paintbrush on the edge of the easel. "I was hoping to get a jump on this one before we started working."

"Don't worry, your muse will return."

"I don't have a muse, Rowan. I'm just throwing paint on the canvas. I'm not like you."

"You are very much like me, young lady," he chastised. "You are an artist. And you have more raw talent than I ever had."

"Please. You're a genius. I paint silly pictures of animals. So do a million other people who are more talented and have been doing it for longer than me."

"So artistic worth is determined by years invested?"

"You know what I mean."

They sat in silence. Elizabeth pushed the paint around on her palette and wished she had the courage to start. She looked over at Georgina, who was sleeping upside down in a sunbeam.

"I was thinking we should turn our full attention to the portrait room today," Rowan said quietly.

His words hung heavy in the air. Neither one had wanted to suggest it, each for their own reasons, but now there was no avoiding the inevitable. The portraits were all they had left, and with Elizabeth's very concrete departure date looming they'd have to work at double speed to get through them in time.

"I'm ready when you are," Elizabeth said with as much cheer as she could fake.

She didn't want him to know that she wasn't ready for the end. That she loved the predictability of their days together. That watching him paint over his shoulder was like a masterclass in technique. That she couldn't envision how painting would fit into her life in San Fran. And that once she returned home, she wasn't sure how to represent a company that she was embarrassed to elevator pitch.

"Since you're all set up at your easel I'll do some dabbing myself before we get our heads down." Rowan switched on the music and the tension in the room dissipated. He'd been working on a new painting and he'd made Elizabeth swear not to look, but she knew it was a rendering of her father's land at the River Dorcalon. He wanted her to always have the piece of their shared history, even after she sold it back to them.

Elizabeth set her paintbrush down and stared at the top of Rowan's head, just barely visible over his canvas. How was he going to fend for himself without her there as a buffer? What was he going to do when she left?

"Are you nervous, Rowan?"

"Why should I be? The paint is dry, many of my subjects are long gone. The public will either like them or they won't. I can't do anything about it."

He was right, as usual.

"Are you excited to be going home?" Rowan asked. "I can't believe it's so soon."

Her mouth went dry. Hearing Rowan call

San Francisco her home felt like an insult, though she wasn't sure why. "I am. I'm a little worried about you, though . . ." she trailed off.

"Oh, pish posh. I'll be fine. And you'll be back for visits, yes? There's a certain young man who's counting on it, I'm sure."

"Definitely. And I need to keep up with this little one, so she doesn't forget me." She walked over to Georgina and rubbed her belly. Georgina stretched out beneath her hand, arcing like a diver before hitting the water. "Can I please get you set up with Skype or FaceTime? It's easy and so much better than just a phone call."

"We'll see." It was the answer he gave when he didn't want to really answer. "Which one should we launch with? Which portrait should be the one printed in all of the papers? They always select one work that becomes synonymous with this sort of unveiling, so tell me which one it should be."

"There are so many options," Elizabeth started blurting before she could think about the magnitude of what she was about to bring up. "I discovered a work and I think it's very special."

"Did you? Is it the man in white? That was always a favorite of mine."

"No, I haven't seen that one yet."

"Hm. The old lady by the window? She's Mrs. Nevers, a neighbor from long ago with an exceptional nose."

"No, the one I'm talking about is of Trudy."

"Well, that one is a bit too cheeky, I think. We need something . . . more tasteful."

"No, I'm talking about the other one. In the white slip."

Rowan put down his paintbrush and bowed his head so that he was completely hidden behind his canvas. "You've found it. Our little bird," he said softly. "That's the portrait I've been looking for. I was worried my mice friends had found it first."

"It's amazing, Rowan." She didn't know what else to say.

"I think it's my best. That was the last portrait I ever painted."

"Will you tell me about it?" Her stomach twisted as she waited for his answer. There was a chance Rowan would say something noncommittal and move on to talking about the weather.

His sigh was heavy with hurt. "I knew I'd eventually have to. I haven't been able to find that painting for all these years, and I knew that when we came upon it, you'd have questions. You see, there's more to the

412

story about what happened with your father. More than we told you."

Elizabeth's fingertips went numb. How was her father involved with the baby? She imagined the possibilities and none of them were good.

"Sit." He gestured to the stool in front of his easel, and then dragged his stool out from behind it so that they were facing one another.

"Clive was living in Boston," Rowan began slowly. "Our father had a heart attack and died, very unexpectedly, so Clive came back for the funeral. By then Trudy had fallen pregnant, but she was only a few months along. We weren't telling anyone yet. It was our beautiful little secret." Rowan smiled at the memory.

"Everything about my relationship with Trudy was still raw for Clive. He never stopped loving her. Seeing us together, helping one another through our grief, broke his heart. I think he felt very alone. Then he caught me giving Trudy's stomach a pat and he knew. He knew that he would never win her back.

"He drank to drown his sorrows. We didn't know it, but the morning of the funeral he'd had so much vodka. And your father wasn't a drinker."

413

Rowan cleared his throat and wiped the corner of his eye. The decades-old story was fresh again.

"He insisted on driving us the day of the funeral. He wouldn't hear a no. Trudy and I were too caught up in our own sadness to notice how unsteady he was, how . . . angry he was." Rowan paused. "Sadness and drink are a frightening combination."

Georgina had found her way to Elizabeth and pawed at her to get into her lap. Elizabeth pulled her up, happy to vent some of the tension she was feeling by giving the puppy a deep tissue massage.

"We had an accident, Bess. A car accident on the way home, with your father at the wheel. Trudy took the brunt of it. She was badly injured." He ran his hands above his forearms. "Have you ever noticed that she never wears short sleeves, even on the warmest days?"

The moment he said it she envisioned Trudy's collection of pastel linen shirts, all with sleeves never rolled higher than her wrists.

"She was scarred particularly badly along her arms. Even though they faded over the years she never wants to see them, because the scars are a reminder of all we lost."

"You mean . . ."

"We lost our little bird that day." Rowan bowed his head. "The three stars in *Blenheim*? That was us. I painted *Blenheim* in a burst of joy when we discovered Trudy was pregnant. I finished it as we mourned the loss."

"We tried again. We were hopeful. For so many years. But it wasn't meant to be for us."

She wanted him to stop talking, so that she wouldn't have to think about Trudy aching for the child she could never have. For a moment she felt the weight of baby Ian in her arms and Trudy's pain became hers.

"Did my father . . . did he go to jail?" She choked on the words. So many hazy parts of her history were snapping into focus.

"It was a different time. It was just a car accident. But he didn't need prison. He jailed himself. When he found out Trudy had lost the baby he left. We tried to reach him, to say that we'd forgiven him, but he wouldn't return our calls or letters. That was why he cut off all contact. The accident changed us, but it ruined him."

And Elizabeth finally understood.

Her father believed his love cursed the people around him. First Rowan, Trudy, and their child, then her mother. Did he think that by loving Elizabeth he'd end up hurting her too? Was his distance a way of ensuring her survival?

Elizabeth placed Georgina on the floor and walked to Rowan with her arms open, and they cried together for everything they'd both lost on that day so long ago.

CHAPTER THIRTY-SEVEN

Georgina, Porter, and Amber came running from the back of the house and screeched to a stop in front of them.

"Beggars, the lot of you," James said as they licked their chops and danced in place in the hopes that Elizabeth or James would share their breakfast. "No food from the table, you know that."

"I think Georgina is teaching them bad habits. Rowan slips her stuff now and then, so she thinks everyone eating a meal owes her food."

They were sitting at the cheerful turquoise table on the little stone patio in front of James's cottage, finishing off the fresh strawberry and hazelnut crepes he'd made. Once the dogs realized they weren't getting anything they took off on another adventure, chasing something that only they could see.

"I've never seen a Lost Dog T-shirt look so good," James said, giving her a lecherous once-over. "And I like the pants-free aesthetic as well."

"You look pretty good yourself, even if I did steal the shirt off your back." Elizabeth leaned over and kissed him, running her hand down his chest. "Shall we go back in and . . ." She wiggled her eyebrows at him.

"I definitely need to work off that breakfast, but I want to talk to you first." He gave Elizabeth the look that signaled that she was about to get interrogated.

"What?"

"You tell me. You've been weird."

"Weird how?" She suddenly felt overfull, the crepes a brick in her stomach. She'd tried to bring up her departure date the night before but the moment never felt right. To talk about what was just a week away would've brought their joyful night to a bickering end.

"Overly happy. It looks like you're posing for a never-ending selfie."

Elizabeth picked at the crumbs on her plate. She pulled her legs up on the chair and slid the oversized T-shirt over them, as if she needed protection from the conversation they were about to have.

"I've been meaning to talk to you." She couldn't look at him.

"So, I was right? Something is going on

with you?"

Elizabeth nodded, and James leaned back in the chair and crossed his arms, his face immediately in full furrow.

"When? When are you leaving?"

"The fourteenth." She whispered it.

"When were you planning on telling me?" He was frighteningly calm.

"Today, I swear. Well, actually I tried to tell you last night but you . . . well, I didn't want to ruin the moment. I just found out, James. It all happened really quickly, like phone interview, then, *boom,* immediate offer. I'm still in shock." She hoped that he couldn't tell that she'd been sitting on the news for days.

"Are you happy about it?" The line between his eyebrows deepened.

"I sort of have to be. I've been unemployed for way too long. It's like a black hole on my résumé. I need to make money. I need to get back to my real life."

He sat up a little straighter. "This isn't real life? Here with me?"

"James, this is a fairy tale. I'm not this lucky in my real life." She made a sweeping gesture that took in his cottage and the rolling land surrounding it. "Look at this place. Look at *you.* I mean, you're not going anywhere, of course, but Fargrove is basically Disney World. It's an amazing place to visit, but how could I make a life here?"

"Maybe you should ask the people who do it every day?"

"What would I do here, James? Work at HiveMind? Be Rowan's assistant forever?" She realized how angry she sounded, so she softened her tone and leaned closer to him. "You have to understand. I've got an apartment and bills and a career to worry about." It was the truth, but it still made her nauseous to say it.

"Of course you do."

She scooted her chair closer to his and put her hand on his forearm. "I'm not losing you when I leave." Just saying the words made her want to cry, but she pretended to be strong. "We're going to make this work, James."

"Are we?" His mouth twisted into a frown. "Let's walk through our future, shall we? Just for fun, let me explain what I envision it's going to be like. You go back and your life goes on. You work your high-powered job, which, if I remember correctly, involves fourteen-hour days. I stay here and work my silly little beer job —"

"James, stop."

"Let me finish! I work my job and wait for the moment when we can connect *by phone.* Calculating the length of your day and the time difference, that puts our calls at about . . . uhhh, two a.m. my time. So, we have scintillating middle-of-the-night conversations for a few minutes every few days and it's a romance for the ages." He tipped his head to her.

Hearing him lay it out made it seem too real.

"It won't be like that."

"No, it actually gets worse. One night you'll go to one of your fancy work cocktail parties and meet some guy who has a billion followers on Instagram or started a company in his parents' garage and now he owns an island. You'll take cute food photos together and talk computers and you'll eventually realize that a backward beer salesman with zero followers in a fairy-tale town has nothing at all to offer you. *That's* how it's going to work."

The insults ripped through her.

"Do you know me at all?" She didn't care that she was yelling. "How much have I been on social media since we've been together? I'm scared to even take photos of us because you hate my phone so much. I think I have *one* picture of us. Technology has a place, and don't pretend you don't use your phone for work all the time because

I see it. It's not that hard to send a quick text, James."

"That's different. And that's not what I'm talking about."

"Okay, so to be fair let's talk about how *you'll* end up with someone else. You'll go to one of your 'chat up the bartender' visits and belly up to the bar. A pretty girl who looks perfect without makeup and drank Guinness in her baby bottle will catch your eye. She can tell a witbier from a hefeweizen with her eyes shut, and she'll order an obscure reserve cask special and you'll ask her to marry you on the spot. Oh, and you'll go hiking on your honeymoon with Porter and Amber and her ten rescue dogs."

They glared at each other, but Elizabeth broke first.

"I don't want what's left of our time together to be like this. Please, James."

He wouldn't look at her, so she went over and forced herself onto his lap, snuggling into his chest until he had no choice but to wrap his arms around her.

"We'll make it work, I promise." She traced kisses along his stubbly cheek and down to his mouth.

When he kissed her back he felt like a stranger.

CHAPTER THIRTY-EIGHT

The breeze coming off the hills tamed the midday sun. Elizabeth shielded her eyes with her forearm, watching Georgina in the distance as she schooled the sheep-ladies. Working with her dog enabled Elizabeth to forget about everything else and focus solely on the job of coaching Georgina to move Rosie and Blossom around the field. It was better than meditation.

Elizabeth blew her whistle, attempting to replicate the perfect two-tone sound that William made when he blew into his. Georgina stopped running after the sheep and plopped into a down as if her belly were magnetized to the ground. Elizabeth whooped and looked back at William and Trudy, hoping that they'd seen their perfect execution.

"Well done!" It was William's version of the highest praise.

Elizabeth and Georgina's training had

turned a corner. The puppy still didn't listen to her with the same intensity she gave William, but the telepathic connection was finally happening between them as well. Georgina kept one eye on the sheep and the other on Elizabeth, ready to perform a move as the tones came out of the whistle.

The sheep had fallen in line as well. Georgina was faster than Major, and occasionally unpredictable, so Rosie and Blossom minded her as if they were worried about her motives. Major seemed to enjoy watching Georgina work. He went through the motions in miniature, moving left, right, around, and down next to Trudy, like an eager father coaching his child from the sidelines. He grinned and wagged his tail the entire time he watched Georgina at work.

"That's enough for today," William called out. "Bring her by."

When Elizabeth reached them Trudy smiled at her and gently grasped her chin. "Look at you," she said as she leaned in to examine Elizabeth's cheeks. "I haven't noticed these freckles before. You look like a fresh Welsummer egg, all tan and dotted. Charming."

"Not sure I'm in love with that comparison, but okay," Elizabeth said. She'd seen the encroaching spots when she leaned in close to the mirror. The first thing she needed to do when she arrived home was schedule a full-body plucking, lasering, and bleaching overhaul.

"You look like a healthy farmer's daughter," William said. "A real working lass with mud on her boots. Let's get some calluses on your hands and you'll be ready to tame the land."

"Me?" Elizabeth laughed. "Put me in front of a computer and I'll give you fifteen straight hours. Put me in front of a hedgerow and I'm worthless."

"Would you like to spend some time learning about plants before you go?" Trudy asked hopefully. She sounded like Rowan the first time he'd asked her to paint.

"That sounds lovely, but I'm not sure there's time." Elizabeth imagined standing beside Trudy in her beautiful garden as she pointed out the various herbs, snipping sprigs for the evening meal with a pair of shiny scissors. She thought about William walking amid the roses, naming each variety with both the Latin and the common name, and advising her how best to prune them for maximum blooms. It made her heart ache.

"Of course, we understand," Trudy said,

and William nodded solemnly.

"How are you going to ship Miss Georgina back with you?" William asked.

Elizabeth stifled the gut clench. "We've talked about this, William. She has to stay in Fargrove. She would hate San Francisco." Elizabeth watched as Major and Georgina dashed through the field, tripping, rolling, and wrestling with each other like they were doing a choreographed dance.

"I was sure you'd change your mind," William said quietly. "She's *yours*, Bess. No matter how she abides me, or how well she minds Trudy, *you* are the one she loves. Her eye is always on you. Have you noticed that? You make a move and she's trailing behind you. She is your shadow." He sounded like he was scolding her even though every word was a compliment.

Elizabeth bit the inside of her cheek. Everything he said was true. The truth was that she couldn't imagine walking through the world without her companion at her feet, but she also couldn't imagine Georgina finding a happy life in San Francisco. There were no sheep, open fields, or friendly relatives waiting at home.

Elizabeth knew of people at Duchess who had oversized, intense-looking dogs. They talked about multiple dog walkers and full days at daycare centers while they worked long hours, their dogs' schedules so packed that they rivaled an Ivy League–bound kindergartner's. But she also heard about doggie psychologists, and canine Prozac for anxiety disorders, and the occasional "found him a more suitable home" stories. She couldn't imagine bringing Georgina all the way to San Fran only to give her to someone else. At least she knew she'd be happy in Fargrove. She just needed to figure out which option would be Georgina's final home.

"I adore her, you know that," Elizabeth said, keeping her voice even. "But her life here . . . it's perfect. I can't give her this. You know she's not cut out for city life. My schedule is hard enough for me, let alone a dependent. I hope you understand that I'm doing this for her. It's not that I don't love her back, it's that I love her too much to force her into my world."

"Well, I'm very unhappy about it," Trudy said, sounding more angry than sad. "For both of you. What kind of life are you going back to anyway, that you wouldn't subject a dog to it?"

"Trudy," William admonished.

"Please don't make this any tougher for me than it has to be." Her voice broke as she said it.

"Who is going to take her, then?" Trudy asked gently, as if she finally realized that she was pushing too hard. "She's more than welcome to stay here, of course. Reid also said he'd be happy to make her the official HiveMind mascot. And what about James?"

"I don't think James can handle another dog. Three dogs would be a lot of work for one person." Elizabeth wasn't sure if James would want a canine anchor to bind her to him.

"My only concern about keeping her here is her age. Major is an old man and he doesn't need much to tire him out. Georgina is so young and if she doesn't get enough exercise she might run us all ragged. And Rowan and I are going to be busy for the next bit as we settle in with Tempus and deal with the portrait news."

"What about a joint custody scenario?" Elizabeth asked. "Reid could pick her up to spend the day with him at HiveMind, then he could drop her off here at the end of the day when she's all worn out."

William nodded. "That way I could keep working her as well."

Trudy pursed her lips. "That sounds like the best solution. And when you come back to see us she'll be here to keep you warm at night, as always."

Elizabeth envisioned returning for a visit. Would Georgina immediately recognize her, or would she treat her like any guest on the property? Would there be a getting-to-know-you period, or would they fall into their routines immediately? Thinking about the possible scenarios of their first reunion made her heartsick.

They watched Major and Georgina wrestle and chase, completely locked in on each other with their usual comic intensity. Elizabeth turned to head back to the house and before she even had a chance to blow the whistle, Georgina was in step at her side.

CHAPTER THIRTY-NINE

"This is better than I'd hoped for," Trudy said softly to Elizabeth, stopping in front of Rowan's portrait of a pensive man in round glasses titled *Weary*, the representative image they'd selected for the portrait reveal.

"So, you're pleased, then?" Tempus Gallery owner Luis Leal asked, plucking at the edge of his black turtleneck as he eavesdropped. "Rowan, are you happy?" The tall, thin man nearly quivered with nerves.

"Luis, it's wonderful. I can't thank you enough."

"You're here, Rowan!" Luis laughed and gestured to the paintings surrounding them in the pristine white room. "And we cannot believe our luck."

The joyful marriage between Rowan and Tempus Gallery was one more check mark on Elizabeth's predeparture to-do list.

First, the breakup with Woolard Gallery.

Then, the empty Operculum.

And finally, Rowan's portraits in their beautiful new home.

They walked through the gallery in a reverent silence. Each painting was surrounded by a halo of light, and coupled with the glow reflected from the gleaming black floor, the images looked like they were hovering a few inches above the walls. The subjects seemed ready to turn and have conversations with the viewer.

"Rowan, I don't mean to push, but if you ever change your mind about the paintings you've reserved . . . well, let's just say we've had interest in your entire catalog, sight unseen," Luis said.

Both of the paintings of Trudy remained in the Operculum, along with a few other favorites. Elizabeth knew it was unlikely they'd ever leave.

A pretty woman in a green jumpsuit peeked her head around the corner. "It's hit the news. It's officially out."

Tempus had timed the news of Rowan's portrait reveal perfectly, first announcing that they'd be representing him after his "long and fruitful partnership with Faye Woolard, formerly of Woolard Gallery," then hinting that there was an even bigger announcement to come. The operation was airtight, so the entire world was seeing

Weary online for the first time together.

"Do you mind if I check . . ." Elizabeth held out her phone.

"By all means, do what you must," Rowan said. "Let us know what the masses think about my little paintings."

Elizabeth walked through the graceful arched doorway to the lone chair in the lobby. Before she looked for reactions to the announcement, she pulled up Woolard Gallery's Twitter feed. Sure enough, in the past fifteen minutes they'd tweeted eight times, highlighting Martin's new roster of "subversive, modern, daring young artists." He was tweeting like a desperate politician, doing everything he could to draw attention away from Rowan's incredible announcement.

Elizabeth smiled and started scrolling through the feedback about the portraits. It was universal gobsmackery. No one could believe that Rowan Barnes had kept such an incredible secret.

"Bess?" The young woman in the green jumpsuit said. "We haven't formally met yet, I'm Amelia Davies. I do PR for the gallery."

Elizabeth walked over to shake her hand. "Hi, so nice to meet you. Thank you for everything you've done. Rowan is thrilled. We all are."

"You don't even know," Amelia replied.

"I've never seen Luis happier."

"Have you been checking?" Elizabeth held up her phone.

"Nonstop, and it's incredible. This is like the highlight of my career." She paused. "Speaking of careers, Rowan showed me some photos of your work."

Elizabeth blanched. Sharing her work in Fargrove was one thing; showing it to someone at the epicenter of the art world was quite another. "You're kidding me."

"They're good! They're really good, actually." She smiled warmly. "I have some friends who just started a new gallery. It's small but it's already getting attention. I think you should talk to them."

It was too farfetched to even consider. Elizabeth made animal paintings for friends that ended up over fireplaces and cash registers. Amelia was clearly caught up in Rowan fever and wasn't thinking straight.

"Thank you. I'm sort of mortified, but thank you. I'm getting ready to go home, in a few days actually. I don't know how . . . I mean, I'm not going to have the chance to paint once I leave. That's really kind of you to offer, but my painting career is basically over. And it was just a hobby anyway." She shrugged.

"Really? Well, that's a shame, I think they

would've loved your work." She reached into her pocket and pulled out a business card. "Promise to ring me if anything changes."

"Promise," Elizabeth said as she took the card.

Amelia left and Elizabeth leaned back to stare at the giant purple-tentacled glass sculpture hanging from the ceiling.

In three days, she'd be home.

CHAPTER FORTY

Town was quiet, so Harriet took the opportunity to rally her crew, put the *Gone Swimming* sign on the Siren's front door, and join Elizabeth and Georgina on a walk. They strolled along the cobblestone streets, stopping to chat any time someone peered into Ian's carriage, and laughing as Poppy tried to draw attention away from the baby. Elizabeth was pleased to discover that she remembered nearly everyone's names, and that they greeted her as warmly as they did Harriet.

"So, tomorrow?" Harriet asked as they walked along the bumpy street.

"Tomorrow." Elizabeth nodded, suppressing the familiar wave of nausea that rolled through her any time she talked about leaving.

"We should've had a party for you! What was I thinking?"

"Harriet, you've done more than enough

for me. Stop."

"Have you said all of your good-byes?" Harriet drove a baby carriage the same way she drove her car, staring at Elizabeth instead of the road in front of her. The carriage careened off a step, jostling Ian. "Whoopsie!"

"I'm working my way through them. I told Reid I'd drop in today so we could figure out the Georgina hand-off details." The gutpunch of tears caught her off guard. "Oh my God, this sucks." She sniffled and rubbed her eyes.

Harriet stopped pushing the carriage and pulled Elizabeth into a hug, which made Poppy run over and join in and Georgina leap up on their backs, yipping and pawing at them. The tearful moment shifted into laughter.

"Did you enjoy your time in Fargrove? Was it worth the trip?" Harriet asked when they finally continued walking.

"I can't even put it into words." She swallowed hard and sniffled.

"Okay, okay, let's talk about something else. Let's talk about . . . coffee! I'm desperate for a cup since Ian is nocturnal." The baby let out a disgruntled scream from his carriage. Poppy ran to Elizabeth and grabbed her hand and skipped along beside her, pretending that her baby brother didn't exist. Barnabas and Georgina trailed behind them, and the effect made them look like the circus was coming to town.

The courtyard in front of HiveMind was empty, which Elizabeth knew would make for a jittery Reid. Even though his business was strong, the occasional slow times made him crazy. She tried to imagine what busy-work he'd conjured up to keep from focusing on his empty shop. Perhaps he was on the roof communing with the bees?

"Barnie, you stay here," Poppy said to her cat when they reached the door. Barnabas responded by rolling onto his back in a patch of sun by the door. "Maybe we'll bring you a sweet, if you're a good kitty."

Georgina forgot her manners and scratched on the door, eager to get to Reid. HiveMind was as much her home as Reid's.

The group burst in with a clap of chatter and laughter, catching Reid off guard.

"Hey, love, we're here to make you work!" Harriet bellowed at him. "Get off yer arse, man." Poppy held her hands to her mouth and giggled at the word *arse*.

"Look at all of the beautiful women," he said as Poppy ran behind the counter to give him a hug.

"Cup of chocolate?" Poppy asked shyly.

"One hot chocolate coming up. And I have a lovely new espresso for the grown-ups. And a crusty bread bone for Georgina."

Elizabeth dropped Georgina's leash, and the dog dashed behind the counter to pester Reid for goodies.

"What about Barnie?" Poppy asked, and pointed to the window, where the cat sat watching.

"Hmm, how about some leftover waffle for the adventure cat?"

Poppy jumped up and down and clapped her hands.

"Bess, I've worked out the Georgina details with Rowan and Trudy," Reid said, suddenly serious. "She's going to spend the day with them tomorrow after you leave, and then on Monday she'll punch in here with me."

"Are you sure it's not too much? The back-and-forth?" Elizabeth focused on the logistics to keep from getting overwhelmed by what they were mapping out. The care and feeding of *her* dog.

"Not at all. I'd miss having her around. And besides, she's good for business. Everyone loves her. She's going to be employee of the month for life."

Reid knelt next to Georgina to rub her shoulders and she threw her head back,

438

smiling and panting at him with her front paws dancing. Anyone looking at them would assume that they were a dog-human team, bonded for life.

"Aw, Bess. It's okay," Reid said when he noticed Elizabeth's heartbroken expression. "She'll never forget you, I promise. You will *always* be her person." He leapt up, threw his massive arms around her, and picked her off the ground in a bone-crushing bear hug. "And you will always be my sister, you damn Yankee."

CHAPTER FORTY-ONE

"They clearly enjoyed the hike," Elizabeth said as a symphony of canine snoring seeped in through the closed bedroom door.

James was spooned against her naked body, gently stroking her arm in a way that both lulled and enflamed her. She thought she didn't have the energy for another round, but the more he petted her the more likely it became.

"It was the only way I could guarantee a night of peace. Otherwise we'd be dealing with whining at the door."

"So you're saying we took a sex hike?"

"Four miles of hilly terrain with three off-leash dogs means I can have you without interruptions for the entire night. Yes, it was definitely a sex hike."

Elizabeth rolled over so she could see his face. Illuminated in the moonlight, he looked like he was made of pale blue porcelain. She traced along his lips, trying to

440

commit the sensation to memory.

"You are perfect," she marveled. "How do I even deserve you?"

"I'm so far from perfect, Bess. Stick around, you'll see." He gave her a wry smile, realizing what he'd said after it was too late.

They stared into each other's eyes, not saying a word.

"I want you to know something," Elizabeth said, rising onto her elbow. "Before I go, I think it's important that I say this." Her heart felt like it was beating off rhythm, and she wondered if he could hear the irregular thumping.

James reached out to smooth her hair behind her ear. They both knew what was coming.

"I've never met anyone like you. I've never had anyone make me feel the way you do. It sounds weird, but my skin needs to be close to your skin. It's almost . . . chemical."

He nodded.

Elizabeth pulled the blanket higher across her chest like a shield as she readied herself to say the words.

"I know it hasn't been a long time, but that doesn't matter. I just —"

James grabbed her hand and pulled her close until they were inches apart.

"Bess Barnes, I love you."

He rolled on top of her and crushed his mouth on hers before she could respond. She wanted to say it back to him, but she didn't want to stop kissing him either.

A metallic sound from the other room pierced the silence.

Porter let out a test woof, followed by a questioning bark from Amber. Georgina erased any canine doubt by launching into a full-throated barking fit, and the other two dogs joined in.

"What's going on?" James asked angrily.

"My phone, that's someone FaceTiming me. I think it's work."

"But it's after eleven!"

Elizabeth shot him a look as she leapt out of bed with a blanket wrapped around her. The dogs barked at her with worried expressions as she tiptoed to the phone and pulled it out of her purse.

"Shhh, it's fine," she told them.

As predicted, it was Carson Keller. There was no way she could skip the call, not with her first day so close. She answered the phone and placed it on the orange end table so that it was facing the ceiling as she ran around looking for the shirt she'd ripped off a few hours prior.

"Carson, hey," she called out from across the room as she pulled James's T-shirt over her head instead. "Gimme one sec." She ran her fingers through her bedhead, licked her finger and swiped the runny mascara from under her eyes, and picked up the phone.

"There you are. Looking good, Barnes."

"Sorry, it's late here."

"You ready to get out of . . . what did you call it? 'Nowheresville'?"

"Did I say that? I don't think I said that." She laughed nervously and looked toward the bedroom. "What's up?"

"We gotta go over some planning and I figured it was easier to do it live instead of going back and forth. Then I need to go over your schedule with you. I've got you booked solid on your first day."

"Is that right? Wow, jumping right back into the fire." It was probably for the best. Being busy would keep her from thinking about anything but work.

"I won't take too long tonight, half hour max."

"Uh, okay. Just give me a minute."

She muted the phone and ran back to the bedroom. "Sorry," she whispered.

James turned over in bed so that his back was to her. "Try to keep your voice down, please."

Elizabeth ran back to the phone and unmuted it. "I'm here. Shoot."

The sound of Carson's voice filled the tiny cottage no matter how low she turned the volume. Georgina watched her for a few moments, then whined and pawed at her to signal that she wanted to climb on Elizabeth's lap. Elizabeth sat the phone on the edge of a shelf, adjusted so Carson couldn't see below her shoulders, and carefully pulled the little dog up.

Georgina maneuvered herself until she found a comfortable spot on Elizabeth's lap. She made her little contented sighing noise, and Elizabeth tried to absorb some of her dog's calm as Carson droned on.

CHAPTER FORTY-TWO

Georgina followed Elizabeth down the hallway, pawing at her overstuffed suitcase. She could tell Georgina wasn't playing based on how she had her ears plastered back. Elizabeth didn't know how to comfort her, because if she knelt down to pet Georgina she'd wind up weeping. She had five good-byes to get through — canine and human — and it was too early to start crying.

"I'm just going on an adventure, Georgie," she said, making her voice sound cheerful. "Don't be sad!"

They walked to the kitchen together, where Trudy stood looking out the window with a cup of tea in hand.

"He'll be here soon. I'm sure James planned for traffic. Although you missing your plane wouldn't be the worst thing." The corners of her mouth turned up in a wicked smile.

Rowan strode into the room, all business.

"Copies of the land transfer paperwork will be mailed to you, Bess. Once that's settled we can begin the sales process," he said. "We'll see to that. And I'll have your paintings shipped too. Of course, we're keeping the one of Major, as well as the one with the field mouse." He leaned down and petted Major, who looked as concerned as his people.

"You don't have to send the paintings, I won't have the time to do anything with them."

"Well, that is a sin." He shook his head.

"He's here. James is here," Trudy said, her voice thin. Major let out a test woof, then looked up at Trudy with his ears back.

Elizabeth waited for the usual barking fits as the sound of wheels on stones got louder, but Major and Georgina were too keyed into the vibe in the room. They paced faster when James's car came into view, but never uttered a sound beyond a few questioning grumbles. Elizabeth had been counting on the hubbub of a normal greeting with James to make the final good-byes less painful, but her self-appointed therapy dogs were too good at their jobs.

Trudy opened the door and Major shot out silently. Georgina turned to look at Elizabeth and waited until she'd rolled the suitcase to the door so that they could walk out together. It was a feat of patience well beyond the dog's typical behavior, especially when a favorite person had just arrived on the scene.

But nothing about the past twenty-four hours had been typical.

James jogged up to take the suitcase from her. "Hello, all set here?" His voice was overly chipper, and Elizabeth could tell he was putting on a show for Rowan and Trudy. She knew that underneath he was still boiling at her over the call from Carson. He'd been asleep by the time she got back into bed nearly an hour later.

James made a fuss rearranging the back seat of his car and loading the suitcase slowly so that Elizabeth could have the final few moments alone with Rowan and Trudy.

She turned to them, drunk with sadness. "I don't even know what to say."

Trudy stepped to her and cupped Elizabeth's cheek in her hand. She looked pale, the navy hollows beneath her eyes more prominent. "You are *magic,* Bess Barnes. Every minute with you was a delight, my dear. Your room will always be ready for you, and your dog will always be waiting for you."

Trudy pulled her close and pressed her

cheek into Elizabeth's shoulder as they hugged. When Trudy stepped away she dabbed her eyes with the edge of her long sleeve.

Rowan began with a heavy sigh. "I cannot thank you enough for everything you did for me, Elizabeth. You are the reason I was able to move on to Tempus. Now, I hope that you will continue to cultivate your own gift. You are a rare natural talent. Don't let it lie fallow." He took a breath. "I'm not sure, though, if the Operculum will ever be quite the same again. It feels so empty, and when I look over to your easel and you're not there either . . ." He broke off as his eyes filled with tears. He cleared his throat and stared at the horizon, like a passenger on a boat trying not to get seasick.

"Why did you just call me Elizabeth?" she asked.

"Did I?"

"You did."

He reached out his arms to her. "Well, come hug this dotty old man, I'm clearly going senile."

She stepped into his embrace and was reminded of her first day in Fargrove, when she was forced out of her comfort zone and into a world that was foreign and wild and bursting with love. She now knew that sending her there was her father's final gift, and a way to make up for his lifetime of failures.

"It's time," Elizabeth said, untangling herself before they became more emotional. "Thank you both, so much. I . . . I love you."

"And we've loved you since before we knew you," Trudy said, her voice cracking. "You are family."

The word took her breath away. Family had only ever meant biology and heartbreak. But now she understood.

Elizabeth leaned down to pet Major, and he pushed into her hand like no amount of petting from her would be enough. He paced back and forth in front of her so she could stroke him on both sides of his body, then leaned up against her legs and stared at her face with eyes that told her everything he was feeling. She took a deep breath, then reached for Georgina.

The good-bye. She had to keep it together in front of everyone.

Georgina darted just out of reach. "Georgie." Elizabeth laughed nervously, trying to keep the moment light. "Now's not the time to play games." She reached out again, and Georgina stepped farther away, refusing to even look at her. Elizabeth shrugged, trying to play off the hurt that made her head throb. "It's probably for the best, right? I don't know if I could take a Lassie-style good-bye."

Elizabeth squatted down to try one more time. "Can I pet you, Georgina?" The dog backed up and then sat next to Trudy. She felt like she'd been disowned.

All she wanted was to run her hands over her dog one last time, so that she could memorize the texture of her fur and quickly count the spots on the top of her head. She wanted to squeeze her in a smothering hug until Georgina squirmed to get away, but she wasn't about to chase her around to make it happen.

"She understands," Trudy said, trying to comfort Elizabeth. "Don't worry, she knows."

Elizabeth choked back the lump in her throat and walked to the car where James stood waiting. She took one last look at the sprawling fields, then down the lane to where she'd first met the ladies, at the Operculum, the house. She tried to memorize the place that had come to feel like her home.

She got in the car and slammed the door. James didn't even look at her as he started off down the driveway. The moment the car moved, Major launched into a fit of barking, chasing behind the car. Georgina joined him, and the two dogs raced down the driveway. Now she was just someone to be barked at, an about-to-be-stranger.

Elizabeth watched them in the rearview mirror. It made them feel distant, like she was watching a movie. To turn and look over her shoulder would be to realize that they were right there, just a few feet behind her, trying desperately to catch up to her.

They neared the end of the driveway with the dogs still in pursuit. Elizabeth bit hard on the inside of her cheek, but the tears pooled in her eyes anyway. She was about to tell James to stop the car, to keep them from running into the road, when she saw William standing at the edge of the property. He raised a hand to her, stoic as ever, as he whistled the familiar tone, so shrill she could hear it through the closed window. Major immediately peeled off and headed to William. Georgina trailed behind the car for a few more steps, as if in disbelief about what was happening.

The little dog paused, then ran to William, but never stopped watching the car as it disappeared down the road.

Chapter Forty-Three

They were surrounded by people at Heathrow, which made it hard to have a good-bye that felt anything other than rushed and analyzed.

"Is your suitcase locked? And do you have snacks with you?" James asked. "They barely give you a bag of nuts these days."

"Yes, I've got emergency Toblerone ready to go."

"What time do you arrive?"

"Tomorrow morning at six our time. I mean, your time."

"Okay," James replied.

"I'll call you," Elizabeth said. "Or is that too early?"

"I'll be up. I think the dogs and I are going to be out of sorts for a few days while we adjust to . . . the changes. We'll probably hike."

"Great, then I'll call you to tell you I've arrived."

"Um-hm."

It felt impossible that they'd run out of things to say to each other, but they stood in silence and watched people with worried expressions rushing around the airport.

"I'm sorry I answered the phone last night."

"It's work." He shrugged. "Duty calls, literally."

The next morning had been a rush to get her back to Rowan and Trudy's so she could finish packing, and between her anxiety about leaving and James's surliness about the call, the time never seemed right to finish what she'd started saying to him.

"The security queue is getting pretty long, you should get over there."

"Okay." She struggled with how to give the words she needed to say to him the weight they deserved. The cold light of Heathrow made every exchange feel clinical.

"James, last night I wanted to tell you . . ."

He cut her off for the second time. "Don't say it, Elizabeth. Not now."

"Why not?" Anger and confusion swirled in her chest. "Why can't I tell you that I —"

"Stop." He put his hand up. "This isn't the time."

"James, why are you acting like this? I feel

like I'm being punished. I'm sorry, but that was my new boss. What did you want me to do, screen his call?"

"Bess, I get it. Your job is your life, you told me as much, and if that's what you want, it's fine. I just don't want to invest more of myself if you're going to end up married to your career. I mean, it would be tough enough if we lived in the same city, but add an eight-hour time difference and it's over before it's begun."

"I'm confused," Elizabeth said with a shaky voice. "Are we going to try this or not? Because I'm not following you."

"I don't know what we should do." James stared at the security line as more people stacked on. "But you really need to get over there, you're cutting it close as it is."

Her hands shook as she grabbed her carry-on, half rage, half fear. "You have great timing, you know that? Breaking up with me right as I'm about to get on a red-eye?"

His face softened, and he finally reached out to her. "I'm not breaking up with you, Bess. I'm sorry."

She stood her ground and resisted when he tried to pull her closer. "Thanks for making this even worse. I don't know what to think, James." She blinked back furious tears.

"I'm sorry. I don't know either." He forced her into an awkward hug. She held on to her bags, refusing to respond.

She pulled away from him. "I'll let you know when I arrive. Thanks for driving me."

"You're welcome."

They had nothing left to say to one another, so Elizabeth turned to walk to the security line. She hoped that he'd call her name or run to catch up with her and say something that would make their final moments together less awful. She looked over her shoulder and he was still standing where she left him, watching her.

"James Holworthy!" she screamed, with tears streaming down her face. "I want you to know that I love you!"

CHAPTER FORTY-FOUR

Elizabeth walked into the conference room where the rest of the skeleton crew had already gathered. They were in the red room, where the walls had been coated in gleaming car paint until they were almost reflective. That, coupled with the dozens of tentacle pendants hanging from the ceiling, gave everyone in the room an unflattering orangish hue to their skin.

"Hey, Barnes, welcome," Carson said. "Okay, we're all here now, let's get to it."

Elizabeth looked around the room as Carson launched into his thoughts on their presence at the upcoming Worldwide Virtual Reality Expo in Vegas. They looked like any other scrappy start-up, recently flush with VC funds. Carson, Walden, and Spencer were in typical tech bro gear, in their limited-edition sneakers and black-framed glasses. The only other woman in the room, Anne from accounting, looked equally cool.

It was hard to imagine that they were in the business of corrupting children.

Elizabeth was still failing at trying to re-frame what had been bugging her since her initial discussions with Carson. Even though she knew little about children, aside from her tentative friendship with Poppy, when she'd looked at the sample screens of their launch games she knew that they were aw-ful. They'd renamed Blood Hunter to Clown Hunter and added a counting feature that made it seem like it was educational. But it was still a first-person shooter game that armed boys with a water pistol to "waste" scary clowns. And Shop Diva was nothing more than a consumerism game about ac-cruing goods and taking selfies. Elizabeth envisioned Poppy wearing the VR headset, accidentally stepping on Barnabas as she worked her way around the boutique that only she could see, trying to find the perfect pair of sparkly leggings.

"You still with us, Barnes?" Carson asked, snapping his fingers to get her attention.

"I'm all in," she replied, even though she had no idea what he'd just said.

It had been a foggy three weeks since she'd returned to San Francisco, and not just because of the jet lag. The culture shock of going from Fargrove back to her old life hit her in unexpected ways. The tea she'd learned to crave was no longer enough to get her day started. Her old battle-armor clothing felt like costumes. She sketched on any scrap of paper that landed in front of her, wishing she were painting instead. She had no time to finish reading the book about the secret lives of sheep she'd bought in the Fargrove bookstore, even in the few moments before she turned off the light each night. And she wished to hear the pitter-pat of paws when she arrived home every day.

Georgina.

The dog was the only Fargrove resident who was still daring her to try to forget about her time there with physical reminders. She still found strands of Georgina's fur in unexpected spots, like trapped between the teeth of her makeup bag and poking through one of the wool socks Trudy had knitted for her. Now, when she passed dogs on the street, she watched them interacting with their people like a jealous stalker. Because she knew what it meant to be loved by one.

She'd kept up a halfhearted correspondence with Rowan and Trudy via email. They refused to video-conference with her, which didn't really matter because they were always in bed long before she was available to talk. Reid sent her texts with photos of Georgina around HiveMind and news of what was happening in Fargrove. Harriet sent video messages of Poppy and Ian wrapped in towels after bathtime, and photos of the family posed together. It always took her a few days to respond.

And James.

They acted like cordial acquaintances, always exceedingly polite when they connected. Their conversations focused around what the dogs were up to, what his hikes had been like, and how many new accounts he'd signed on. Elizabeth skirted around talking about exactly what she was doing at work, focusing instead on safe topics like her new colleagues and the campus amenities. Talking to him always left her feeling worse than not talking to him.

But she was back in her real life, and she was back in a big way. Now that she had a shiny new title at what was rumored to be the next category disruptor, it was as if the disastrous interview in Vegas had never happened. Duchess had been dismantled and auctioned off, and Cecelia had disappeared from social media while prosecutors figured out what they were going to do with her. The last photo Cecelia had posted on Instagram, just a few days before the leak, was of her hugging her daughter and Winston. Elizabeth had stared at the image until she'd memorized the details.

"Did everyone see that wireframe?" Walden asked, bringing her back into the moment. "Hey, Barnes, you see it?"

There was a good chance she hadn't seen it, since there were 230 unopened emails in her inbox. "I did," she lied convincingly. "Looks great."

"Remember," Carson said. "We're going to create our buzz through relationships with influencers and their parents. The kid vloggers on YouTube, the moms that pimp out their Jaxons and Reighlynns on Instagram. We give them a free headset and game pack and they're gonna eat this shit up."

One of Elizabeth's first responsibilities was working on a launch party where the attendees were well-known social media influencers, all under age ten. All of the kids had more followers than Elizabeth and knew how to create content that put hers to shame. There were Instagram toddler models wearing lip gloss and off-the-shoulder tops, professional toy reviewers where every post was #sponsored, unboxing pros, tiny sketch comedians, and a six-year-old fashion blogger who was setting trends on playgrounds across the country. As expected, all of the parents were insufferable.

"Okay, it's all good, y'all. Back to work," Carson said, smacking his hands together with a clap that made Elizabeth jump.

They started to disperse, but Carson called to Elizabeth.

"Barnes, check this out," he said, beckoning to her before she could get away from him. She followed him to the stairwell that overlooked the lobby, where a team of men were struggling to mount something on the wall.

"I'm getting into art!" Carson said, with shock in his voice. "I actually commissioned this thing. You know art, right?"

"I do."

Elizabeth studied the piece, a twelve-foot-tall neon display. Since it wasn't plugged in, she had to squint to make out what it was.

"It's Ted the Clown," Carson said. "That's Ted after he's been torched by a pistol. See the hair and nose?"

Elizabeth could make out the mascot skeleton with the red fright wig and nose, and the oversized bow tie around its bony neck. She could see the outline of the clown's legs and arms, so when it was plugged in it would do his ridiculous death dance.

"Have you ever seen anything like it?"

Elizabeth took a steadying breath before she answered. "I have. That's by Light-bender."

Chapter Forty-Five

The young woman walking in front of Elizabeth was oblivious to the fact that there were other people on the sidewalk around her. She was studying her phone and pausing every few steps, and each time Elizabeth attempted to move around her the woman managed to splay her elbows so that there was no room to pass.

Elizabeth was heading home after an evening meeting with the party planner for the launch feeling overwhelmed. The suggested "hubs" for the event — the party planner's word for the various activity stations — were overwhelming. Did they really need a DIY cotton candy cart, six pedicure chairs, a retired military tank, a faux tattoo bar with an actual tattoo artist, a balloon pit, a live-feed photo booth, and a "real" unicorn in addition to the immersive real-life versions of Clown Hunter and Shop Diva? It felt like too much, but the planner insisted that they consider adding more, like a petting zoo with exotic animals.

Elizabeth pulled her phone from her purse as she shadowed the oblivious woman. Her socials hadn't picked up much momentum since she'd been back despite her half-hearted attempts to create content. Whitney was back to "yaasss queen"-ing her posts, which Elizabeth didn't bother to respond to. It wasn't that she couldn't find images or stories to post, it was more that she just didn't care to keep up with it. Nothing seemed compelling.

The woman in front of her continued to dominate the narrow sidewalk. When she stopped suddenly to pose for a selfie she caught Elizabeth off guard, and caused her to slam into the woman's back. The jolt made both of them stumble on top of one another for a few steps, and as Elizabeth attempted to regain her balance her phone flew out of her hand. It bounced on the ground with a heartbreaking smash and skidded into the street like a skipped stone, just in time for a passing car to crush it as if it had been aiming for it.

"Fuck!" Elizabeth screamed. She dodged another car that wasn't slowing down and managed to grab the phone before a third almost hit her. No one seemed to care that she was in distress, not the passing cars, or the stupid woman who had caused the pileup in the first place, who stood on the sidewalk with her camera pointed at Elizabeth.

"Are you *filming* me?" she screamed at her. The woman shrugged and tapped her phone's screen, then walked away.

Elizabeth tried to slow her pounding heart. She was scared to look at her phone. When she finally flipped it over, it was worse than she'd imagined. The glass looked like it had taken a bullet and had pulled away from the phone's base so that the guts were exposed around the edges. She pushed the power button and nothing happened, not even a spark of an attempt to turn back on.

It was too late to think about it. She'd have to go ten hours without a phone. Six months prior Elizabeth would've tracked down a technician to triage her phone immediately. Now it didn't seem necessary. Work could wait.

The adrenaline of the near-accident had finally subsided by the time she arrived at her apartment. She opened the door and was almost leveled by the smell of bleach. No matter how many times she told the cleaning lady to lighten up, the woman still used enough to make Elizabeth's eyes water even when she arrived home hours later.

She flipped on the light and saw a wood crate leaning up against the console table that the cleaning lady had probably signed for. Her heart fell. She knew exactly what it was based on the way it was packaged and the multiple airmail stickers.

She was starving and her feet hurt, but she decided to open the package before she'd even put her bag down. After all, she'd been waiting to see it for ages. She'd envisioned how Rowan had chosen to depict the patch of land by the river for months, and it was finally time to see his version of the River Dorcalon.

Elizabeth opened the wood crate with an expert hand, using her house key to pop the edges at just the right angle to ensure that the pieces slid apart easily. The painting was in a cardboard box inside, with an envelope taped to the outside. She skipped the letter and opened the lid of the box. The canvas was nestled facedown in gray egg-carton foam, something that they'd never used before and was probably a technique he'd picked up from Tempus. She flipped the canvas over.

It wasn't the river.

It was a portrait of her, standing in front of her easel in the Operculum. His first portrait in fifty years. Rowan had mapped out every nuance of their daily lives together. How she tipped her head as she studied her work. The dab rag she tucked in her belt. The smudges of paint on the front of her jeans. The beam of light that danced across the top of her head at eleven thirty every day. The painting was a marriage of the freedom of his early portraits mixed with the realism of his landscapes. He'd captured her in the thrall of creation, and because of that, and because he'd painted her with love, she looked more beautiful than she looked in her most filtered selfie.

Her eyes traveled around the rest of the painting, taking in the details. He'd painted every part of the Operculum, and had hidden little surprises to delight her, like one of Trudy's shawls draped over her stool, and *Sunset over Blenheim* hanging on a distant wall even though it was actually still hanging in a museum.

She studied the rest of the works he'd chosen to hang on the walls of the Operculum. The painting of Trudy with naked shoulders peeked through the doorway to the portrait room. The sad painting he'd been working on when she arrived was leaning in a corner with a drape covering most of it, and the happy blue-sky painting hung above it. She squinted at a portrait that was hanging near her and was delighted to discover that he'd captured James in miniature, laughing and holding a pint up in a toast.

She noticed he'd painted a mirror on the wall behind her reflecting part of what was on her canvas, even though there were no mirrors in the real Operculum. She took the painting to the light so she could see it more clearly. Her eyes filled with tears the moment she realized what he'd done.

It was Georgina on her canvas. Elizabeth had wondered why he'd chosen to leave the dog out of the work since she was always nearby when she was painting, but it was a conscious decision, and a pointed comment. Rowan was telling her that he wasn't a painter of animals, Elizabeth was. He didn't feel it was his place to attempt to capture her dog, since no one could do it better than she could. And it was a reminder that during her time there she'd painted every animal she'd encountered except for the one she loved the most.

She put the painting down, walked back to the box, and tore open the envelope.

There were three lines.

Fargrove isn't the same without you.

You will always be welcome here.
You are missed, and loved.

CHAPTER FORTY-SIX

Elizabeth settled into her seat, arranging her water, wrap, and snacks just so, and tucking the sheep book in the pocket in the seat in front of her. Departure time was looming, and it looked like the seat next to her was to remain empty.

It was hard to sit still. She pulled the book from the pocket and hunted for where she'd left off, weeks and weeks ago. Her bookmark tumbled out, a scrap of paper from the Operculum that Georgina had stepped on, leaving a perfect blue paw print. She wondered how much bigger the paw was now.

A purse landed on the seat next to her, and she looked up to find a woman smiling apologetically at her. "This is me, sorry," the woman said, as if she were imposing even though she'd actually paid for the spot.

"No problem," Elizabeth replied, flicking the edge of her light pink wrap from the armrest.

The woman eased herself into the seat and Elizabeth studied her out of the corner of her eye. She was a mix of Midwestern mom and kindly librarian, all cardigan and softness, and Elizabeth knew that if the seat next to her had to be occupied, she couldn't have asked for a better option. She envisioned the offers of moist towelettes and tabloid magazines to come.

"So," the woman said to Elizabeth with a kindly smile. "Is this trip business or pleasure?"

"Um, both, I guess."

"Well, I'm meeting up with some girlfriends. We've been friends for thirty years, if you can believe it." The woman scrolled through her phone and showed Elizabeth a photo of her with two other white-haired women wearing giant smiles.

"Wow, that's wonderful. You're lucky." She showed the woman a photo of her next to Harriet, from the dinner party. "This is my best friend."

The woman peered at the photo over the top of her glasses. "You'll be friends forever. I can tell. So where are you from, sweetheart?"

The plane hadn't even begun to taxi and they were already getting to the heavy stuff.

"I don't exactly live anywhere yet. I'm in

the process of moving."

"Oh, moving is the worst! I don't envy you, honey. Where are you going to end up?"

Elizabeth swallowed the doubt spinning inside her. She was doing this; there was no turning back. "It's a small town, called Fargrove. West of London. It's where my family comes from."

"You're moving to *England*? Aren't you the luckiest?"

She felt like she was. And part of her felt like she was making the biggest mistake of her life.

"What do you do?" the woman asked.

The question. What *did* she do?

"Well, that's in flux at the moment. I've been in tech forever, but I'm also . . ." She forced herself to say the words. ". . . an artist."

"An artist! What kind of art?"

"I paint. It's sort of in my blood. My uncle is an artist . . ."

The woman cut her off. "That'll help. He probably knows folks and can give you pointers and such."

Elizabeth smiled. Oh, he knew people. She stared out the window as the plane began its taxi, but the friendly interrogation wasn't over.

"Do you have a place to live already?"

"I'm going to stay with my aunt and uncle for a bit. I've got a little spot where I'm going to fix up an old stone house."

The woman harrumphed. "We built our first house and let me tell you, it was a nightmare. I wonder how hard it'll be over there? Zoning and contractors and all of that?"

"I'll have lots of support, thankfully." Reid was already lining people up for her to meet who could help her tame the land by the river.

"Sounds like you've got everything all figured out. A gal with a plan!" The woman chuckled.

For the first time in her life, Elizabeth *didn't* have a plan. Rowan and Trudy were allowing her to rent the land back from them for a pound a year, so she had the cushion of the sale of the land to them to carry her through as she found her way. She had a rough idea of what her new life was going to look like, but there were no goals to hit or milestones to measure. She'd set up a meeting with the gallery Amelia Davies had told her about, but that was it.

Any time she thought about her move to Fargrove, she flip-flopped between euphoria and white-knuckle terror.

"Is there a special someone in this plan?"

the woman asked, leaning forward to hear the juicy stuff.

"Yes, a couple of them, actually."

Her seatmate raised her eyebrows as if considering her alternative lifestyle. Elizabeth burst out laughing.

"I mean my boyfriend and my dog!"

James's smiling, confused face flashed through her mind. During their last call he swore he wasn't going to believe it until she was standing in front of him. Georgina, on the other hand, had no clue what was in store for her.

"A gal with a plan," the woman repeated, and started rifling through her bag.

Elizabeth watched the ground disappear below her, until the familiar landscape started to look like a map from a textbook. Her fingers tingled and her heart thudded. She was headed into uncharted territory. A new world that didn't feel new.

She was going home.

She closed her eyes and started a hundred-breath exercise to quell the fear that was making her question her decision, until she felt a swat on her arm.

"We're going to be sitting next to each other for the next ten hours, so we might as well introduce ourselves. I'm Donna." The woman thrust her hand out.

She took the woman's hand in hers.
"Nice to meet you. My name is Bess."

Chapter Forty-Seven

"Are you sure he doesn't know?" Bess asked Reid for the third time.

"He is so wrapped up in the Lost Dog Open Day that he hasn't been in for coffee in two weeks. He's in full bridezilla mode; he has no idea that you're already back."

Bess was fidgeting next to Reid on the ride from Heathrow straight to the Lost Dog open house celebration. She'd told James that she was due in on Saturday morning so that he'd have one less thing to stress about as he got ready for the brewery's first event. She'd sat in on an initial conference call with James and the Lost Dog co-founders and helped them begin brainstorming, but what James didn't know was that she'd also followed up with them to map out the details of her surprise arrival.

She pulled down the visor to check her reflection in the mirror. She looked blotchy and travel weary, but it didn't matter.

"Stop," Reid scolded. "You're a goddess, blonder and shinier than I remembered. We need to get those Fargrove freckles back."

Bess flicked the visor back up and exhaled sharply. "Why am I so nervous?"

"Because you're about to see the love of your life, your dog, your family, and your best mates for the first time in months. Oh, and you burned your ship."

"You know that quote?"

"I own a small business, Bess. I know every inspirational risk-taking quote there is." He took his eyes off the road for a moment to look at her. "Fuck that ship, you did the right thing. You belong here."

He was right. The moment she touched down she stopped worrying because she knew she was home.

"Everyone is going to be there?"

"Everyone. Rowan and Trudy. Nicky, Harriet, Des, Anna, Willard. The Fizz is playing. It's dog-friendly so all the cool pups will be there. You picked the perfect time to make the night all about your homecoming."

Bess looked at him in openmouthed horror. "Oh my God. That wasn't my intention at all! I don't want to steal the spotlight from Lost Dog."

"Relax, I'm kidding." He punched her shoulder. "If the turnout is as big as they're expecting, you're going to be fighting the crowd to grab a drink and a piece of Holworthy ass."

Signs pointed the way and parked cars flanked the road as they got closer to the Lost Dog office.

"This is great," Bess said. "So many people. They did it."

Reid maneuvered around the cars and people walking along the road to the brewery to a driveway with a chain across it.

"Pays to know the top dog," he said, leaping out to unlock the padlock, then pulled his car into the last open space in the lot.

Bess climbed out of the car and stretched, hoping that getting her blood moving would keep her from trembling with excitement. The air was rich with smells she didn't recognize, and she could hear the buzz of the crowd on the other side of the building.

"Why didn't he want to host something here?" Bess asked as she scanned the office. The large building had a modern one-story profile with a mix of wood slats, corrugated metal, and floor-to-ceiling windows. "It's amazing."

"Innit? All recycled materials. Now wait here." Reid sprinted off without another word.

Elizabeth paced in circles. Between the jet

lag and nerves she felt like she'd downed a dozen Pointer Pilsners. She heard footsteps heading her way and got ready for the first of many reunions to come.

"There she is! There's our Bess," she heard as Rowan came into view with Trudy right behind him. "Welcome home, my dear!"

He swept her into an embrace that nearly knocked her off her feet. When he finally let go Trudy stepped up to give Bess her own bone-crunching hug.

"Ouch, Trudy, I guess your arm is completely healed." Bess laughed as they rocked back and forth.

"Oh, you're back!" Trudy practically sang. "I'm not letting you go until I believe it!" It took her a few minutes to relax her grip.

They separated and stood staring at one another with huge smiles, not sure what to say or do next.

"I guess this is the beginning," Bess said with a shrug. "I'm going to figure it all out."

"Indeed you will. And we'll be right beside you," Rowan said.

Reid emerged from the shadows. "Ready for more reunions?"

"Do you guys mind if I stagger them? I'm already a little overwhelmed." She held her hand to her chest. "I can't cope with greeting everyone at once, so can you please bring Georgina to me first? I want to see her away from the crowd." She waved her hands in front of her like they were wet and bounced in place. "Why am I so *nervous*?"

"Perfectly normal," Trudy said. "Off we go, Rowan. Let her have some peace with her beloveds."

Rowan blew her a kiss as they walked away. "We'll see you in there."

Reid pointed to a patch of trees on the far corner of the property. "Wait over there. I'll bring Georgina first. Back in a tick."

A minute later she heard high-pitched barking. Georgina, but what was wrong with her?

She watched the group of people laughing and drinking as Georgina came shooting out into the yard. The dog stopped and lifted her head, then started running in a wide circle. Reid dashed after her.

Georgina zigzagged her way across the grass, alternating between scenting the air and running her nose along the ground.

"Georgie," Bess stage-whispered. "I'm here!" She dropped to her knees and whistled.

The dog lowered her body and took off like Blossom and Rosie were in the farthest corner of the field and needed to be brought to the barn stat. Georgina started making high-pitched whining noises as she got closer and didn't slow down until she plowed Bess flat on her back.

"You're huge!" Bess exclaimed as Georgina wiggled on top of her. The dog was moving so fast that she couldn't even properly pet her, she was just a blur of fur and tongue.

Reid finally reached them, panting from the jog but holding a full pint of black liquid. "She knew you were here the second I walked over to her. She smelled my hands and started freaking out."

Georgina slowed down enough to allow Bess to give her a squeeze. "I'm back! I'm back for good!" Georgina splayed out on her lap as if trying to pin her in place with her weight. She made happy *he-he-he* noises as she panted.

"This is for you, figured you need it," Reid said as he handed her the pint. "The Mastiff Milk Stout, limited edition for tonight."

She took a sip while attempting to keep Georgina from head-butting her and grimaced. "Painful."

"Acquired taste; keep at it, you'll love it by the bottom. Now what?"

"I'm going to chug this beer, then call James and freak him out."

"That's my cue to leave; I don't need to be a part of your loved-up homecoming. I know you two can't keep your hands off each other and I've seen enough of your ass."

"Will you ever let me forget that?"

Reid winked and headed back to the crowd.

She spent a few minutes sipping the beer, petting Georgina to try to get them both to calm down. It was like the dog couldn't believe that Bess was actually there and had to do dramatic half-flip head turns every few minutes to reassure herself that the lap she was sitting on was indeed her missing person's.

"I'm not going anywhere, Georgie. Don't worry," she murmured, half to the dog and half to herself.

When the dog's panting finally slowed, she pulled her phone from her pocket and dialed James with trembling hands.

Based on the noise coming from the party, she expected to have to call him several times but he picked up on the second ring. He smiled when he saw her, and her heart leapt when she realized that he was only a few hundred yards away.

"Hey! You're missing a great party, Bess. It's incredible, we're packed! I can't thank you enough for suggesting it. Here, look." He flipped the camera and panned the crowd and she looked up from her phone to see if she could see what he was showing her from her vantage point at the edge of the woods.

"Wow, looks amazing," she said when he flipped the phone back.

"Are you packing? I can't wait to see you."

"Actually, I'm not." She kept her face neutral.

"Why? What's going on?"

"I thought I should enjoy this while it's still available." She lifted the stout so that he could see it.

"What's that?"

"Why, it's a limited-edition milk stout from my favorite brewery." She smiled and took a giant sip. "The Mastiff is the name, I think?"

"*What?* You're here? Where are you?" James started running through the crowd.

"Back corner of the yard, by the trees. Come get me." She hung up and tossed the phone on the ground by the beer and started running. Georgina didn't miss a beat and fell in step beside her.

James dashed out of the crowd at full tilt and they ran across the yard until they crashed into each other, falling to the ground in one another's arms. Georgina ran around them barking like she was a referee calling them out for unnecessary roughness.

James crushed his lips to hers, and she could taste the beer he'd been sampling and smell his campfire scent. He rolled and flipped her so that she was on top of him, and neither one cared that there was a good chance that his entire customer base could see them wrapped around each other on the ground like humping teenagers. The James-fireworks filled her entire body.

Two more canine voices joined Georgina, and she stopped kissing James to say hello to Amber and Porter, who also couldn't believe their luck that Bess had magically reappeared.

"This is real, Bess? You're here for good?" James asked her when he finally stopped kissing her.

"For good," she said, resting her chin on his chest. "Now, *kish* me, please, please, please. And don't stop."

James placed a gentle hand behind her head and brought her lips to his as three happy dogs barked their approval.

She was home.

ACKNOWLEDGMENTS

Writing a book is nice work if you can get it, and it's even nicer when you're surrounded by a team that feels like friends. Forever thanks to my dream come true agent, Kevan Lyon, for supporting my dog nerdiness on the page and in real life, and for spreading the rescue and foster message like a pro. Endless gratitude to my editor, Kate Seaver, for feedback that's always bull's-eye perfect, and for letting me believe that I'm the gateway drug to her next dog. (It's going to happen!) Bridget O'Toole and Tara O'Connor, thanks for allowing this wannabe PR and marketing geek to pretend that I was contributing while the two of you were doing the actual hard work! To Craig Burke, Jeanne-Marie Hudson, and the rest of the amazing Berkley team — thank you for the warm welcome to the family.

It takes a village to build a village like Fargrove, and I was so fortunate to have incredible people helping me bring it to life. Big thanks to Meg Lomax, who enchanted me with tales of her sheep-filled youth in England and introduced me to a dog named Major; to my childhood friend turned museum badass Emily Peters for schooling me on the business side of the art world; to UK-based smallholder Rosie Hetherington for introducing me to all things sheep during a delightfully quotable video chat; to craft beer salesman extraordinaire Tom Clermont for teaching me all about casks, firkins, and what it takes to woo a pub; and to British expat and friend Brian Prowling for acting as my official slang consultant.

Then there's my standard support crew, the people who see the best and worst of me as the words come into focus. Jennifer Buckley, my beloved first reader who knows a thing or two about pub hijinks, and has the photos to prove it; Nerice Kendter and Heidi Bencsik, who cheerleaded me whether it's socks or ball gowns; and Jenni Walsh, Helen Little, and Suzanne Baltsar, my "pale mimosa" writer tribe, for helping me navigate author life.

Thanks to my parents for their unwavering support, and for telling me the stranger than fiction story of how my paternal grandparents met, which became the spark that led to Rowan's and Trudy's story.

And finally, my Fav, there are no words to express my love and gratitude other than, "It's all for you."

■ ■ ■ ■

READERS GUIDE

WHO RESCUED WHO

VICTORIA SCHADE

■ ■ ■ ■

QUESTIONS FOR DISCUSSION

1. Elizabeth uses social media as a stand-in for real relationships. How does this behavior hinder her when she arrives in Fargrove? Have you ever found yourself focusing more on "getting the shot" than participating in an important life event?

2. How did losing her mother and her subsequent relationship with her father shape Elizabeth? Do you think her life would've been different if her mother hadn't died at such a pivotal point in Elizabeth's life?

3. Elizabeth initially assumes that Rowan and Trudy's dog, Major, doesn't like her, partly because she believes that she isn't a dog person. What are some of the dog behaviors she misunderstands? How do the dogs of *Who Rescued Who* — includ-

ing Porter, Amber, and Georgina — change her view of dogs?

4. Puppyhood is challenging even for experienced pet parents, and when we meet Georgina she's a typical out of control puppy. Why do you think Elizabeth didn't give up on Georgina, even though she had no clue about what she was doing?

5. In some ways Elizabeth is forced into becoming a part of Fargrove. How do her new friends and family push Elizabeth outside of her comfort zone?

6. Elizabeth rediscovers her love of painting while in Fargrove, which helps to foster her relationship with Rowan, as well as the animals around her. Do you think their relationship would've been different if they didn't have painting in common? Do you believe that certain talents are passed down within families? Do you have a hobby that you wish you could pick up again?

7. Elizabeth experiences family love, romantic love, and friendship love in Fargrove.

Which do you think has the most impact on her?

8. Elizabeth's name is an ongoing theme in *Who Rescued Who.* Why do you think Rowan immediately started calling her Bess? How does Elizabeth's eventual acceptance of her nickname reflect the changes she's been through?

9. How does the realization of everything that happened between Elizabeth's father, Rowan, and Trudy change her perception of them? Have you ever learned a family secret that changed your family dynamic?

10. Even though we tend to think that the human end of the leash is the one doing the rescuing, the benefits usually extend to both ends. How do you think Georgina rescues Elizabeth?

ABOUT THE AUTHOR

Victoria Schade has been a dog trainer and writer for close to twenty years. She works behind the scenes on Animal Planet's *Puppy Bowl* as the lead animal wrangler and creates dog training content for a variety of pet-focused websites. She's the author of *Bonding With Your Dog, Secrets of a Dog Trainer,* and *Life on the Leash.* Victoria lives in Pennsylvania with her dogs, Millie and Olive; the occasional foster dog; and her very patient husband, Tom.